The Turing Test

The Turing Test
Verbal Behavior as the Hallmark of Intelligence

edited by Stuart M. Shieber

A Bradford Book
The MIT Press
Cambridge, Massachusetts
London, England

© 2004 Massachusetts Institute of Technology

All rights reserved. No part of this book may be reproduced in any form by any electronic or mechanical means (including photocopying, recording, or information storage or retrieval) without permission in writing from the publisher.

This book was set in Sabon by Interactive Composition Corporation and was printed and bound in the United States of America.

Library of Congress Cataloging-in-Publication Data

The Turing test : verbal behavior as the hallmark of intelligence / edited by Stuart M. Shieber.
 p. cm.
"A Bradford book."
Includes bibliographical references and index.
ISBN 0-262-69293-7 (pbk. : alk. paper)
1. Turing test. I. Shieber, Stuart M.

Q341.T874 2004
006.3—dc22

2003061234

10 9 8 7 6 5 4 3 2 1

To Cassia Wyner

"Just thinking out loud. . . . How smart's an AI, Case?"

"Depends. Some aren't much smarter than dogs. Pets. Cost a fortune anyway. The real smart ones are as smart as Turing heat is willing to let 'em get."

"Look, you're a cowboy. How come you aren't just flat-out fascinated with those things?"

"Well," he said, "for starts, they're rare. Most of them are military, the bright ones, and we can't crack the ice. That's where all the ice comes from, you know? And then there's the Turing cops, and that's bad heat." He looked at her. "I dunno, it just isn't part of the trip."

"Jockeys all the same," she said. "No imagination."

—William Gibson, *Neuromancer*

Contents

Editorial Notes

The following nonstandard textual conventions are used in this volume. Throughout the text, the American convention of moving punctuation within closing quotation marks (whether or not the punctuation is part of what is being referred to) is dropped in favor of the more logical and consistent convention of placing only the quoted material within the marks.

The close-knit set of works collected in this volume frequently cite others collected here. In such cases, chapter (and occasionally page) information is added to the references. This internal reference information is distinguished from other reference information by being placed in italics, as "(Descartes 1646, *chapter 2, 36*)". In the case of Turing's seminal *Mind* paper, where the reprinting provides information on the original pagination, page references are given to that pagination, as "(Turing 1950, 442, *chapter 4*)".

Introduction

How do you tell if something is a meter long? You compare it with an object postulated to be a meter long. If the two are indistinguishable with regard to the pertinent property, their length, then you can conclude that the tested object is the given length.

Now, how do you tell if something is intelligent? You compare it with an entity postulated to be intelligent. If the two are indistinguishable with regard to the pertinent properties, then you can conclude that the tested entity is intelligent.

A test of intelligence such as this, based on *indistinguishability*, has a certain plausibility to it, and a long history. In its modern form, such a test has come to be known as the Turing Test, after Alan Turing, the scientist who most explicitly and concretely proposed it.

In 1950, Turing published a paper entitled "Computing Machinery and Intelligence" in the journal *Mind*. In the paper, he defined a simple test as a thought experiment to crystallize the questions surrounding the possibility of an intelligent artifact. In essence, Turing proposed to test whether the artifact was indistinguishable from a person with regard to what he took to be the pertinent property, *verbal behavior*. But unlike the case of meter measurement, the identification of the pertinent properties for intelligence are subtle, and ramifies widely in the foundation of the philosophy of mind.

Although the philosophical issues that the Turing Test raises had arisen before (as seen in part I) in philosophy, science, and literature, Turing's encapsulation of them in his simple thought experiment stands out as a trenchant codification of these issues around which discussion can naturally revolve. The familiarity and immediacy of the concept can be seen in the ubiquity of the term both in technical parlance and in the popular mind. Turing is undoubtedly the only computer scientist to have a Broadway play written about him, Hugh Whitemore's *Breaking the Code* with Derek Jacobi as Turing in its New York premiere. He has been the inspiration for novels, such as Christos Papadimitriou's clever *Turing* (2003). His Test shows up in comic strips (figure 1) and collegiate humor magazines (figure 2).

This collection brings together a set of works that explore the philosophical issues surrounding the Turing Test as a test of intelligence. An exhaustive compilation of papers on the Turing Test would be impossible for reasons of both the depth and breadth

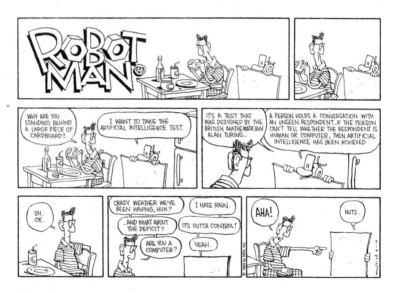

Figure 1
Robotman, Jim Meddick, 1993.

TURING TEST
ARE YOU A COMPUTER?
THE TURING TEST CAN TELL!

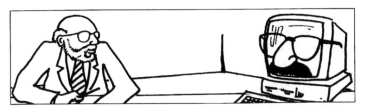

10:00 AM: Easy Questions
Turing: Hello, I am Dr. Alan Turing. I'm going to ask you a few simple questions. State your name please.
Computer: Simon III.
T: Your full name?
Simon: Max Felix John Simon III.
T: Where are you from?
Max: ...Belize.
T: Have any family?
M: No.
T: What happened to them?
M: ...Earthquake.
T: Sorry. What do you do for a living?
M: Manufacturing.
T: You mean you work in a factory, or you're a supervisor?
M: Yes.

10:30 AM: Psychology
T: Now we're going to look at some pictures. What does this look like to you?
M: It looks like an ink splotch.
T: Okay, but look deep into it, let your imagination run wild.
M: Two ink splotches.
T: Deeper, wilder.
M: Actually, four ink splotches.
T: Maybe you don't understand. Look at this picture, and then tell me what it reminds you of, like a butterfly, or a face. Try this one.
M: Butterfly.
T: Good! Now try this one.
M: Butterfly face.

11:15 AM: Tricky Questions
T: It's time to do the laundry. You need to wash a white t-shirt, a blue pinstriped button-down, a black turtleneck, and a red sweater with white polka dots. How many loads will you need to do?
M: That could all fit in one load.
T: Darks and lights in the same load?
M: Two loads would do it.

12:00 AM: Psychology Again
T: Let's play a little game. I'm going to say a word, and you say the next word that comes into your mind.
M: Sounds easy.
T: Okay, here we go. Dog.
M: Doily.
T: No, no, no. I say a word, then you say what it makes you think of.
M: Oh, I get it. Try me again.
T: Electricity.
M: Food.
T: *Food?*
M: That's what I thought of. Wouldn't it be neat if electricity were not a painful shock, but a *tasty treat?* Of course, that's not the case for humans like us.

12:45 AM: Nap Time
T: Are you a computer?
M: Nope.
T: You'd be surprised how many fall for that one.
M: Not me.

1:30 AM: Math Time
T: What's fifty-six times thirty-three?
M: One thousand eight hundred forty-eight.
T: You're pretty fast!
M: Those are my favorite numbers.
T: All right, how about five thousand and two divided by sixty-one?
M: Eighty-two.
T: Right again! Are you some sort of math whiz?
M: ...Those are more of my favorite numbers.

3:00 PM: Computer Science
T: How good are you with computers?
M: About the same as an average person, I'd say... how about you?
T: Here's an easy question. Let's say you type the following program into a computer:
10 PRINT "HELLO"
20 GOTO 10
What do you think would happen?
M:
HELLO
HELLO
HELLO
HELLO
HELLO
HELLO
HELLO
HELLO
HELLO
HELLO
HELLO
HELLO
HELLO
HELLO
HELLO
HELLO

DSJ

LAMPOON 9

Figure 2
Are you a computer? The Turing test can tell, David S. Joerg, *The Harvard Lampoon*, 1994.

of the Test's influence. In terms of depth, literally thousands of papers have been written on the possibility of machine intelligence since Turing's test was first proposed; it would be hard to imagine that any of them would not be influenced by Turing's work. In terms of breadth, the subject of the Turing Test arises not only in the context of the question of machine intelligence but in many other areas as well. Scholars have speculated about the likelihood of actually constructing a machine capable of passing the Test, argued about the use of the Test as a goal for research in the field of artificial intelligence, proposed and analyzed variations of the Test, wondered about the ethical implications of a Turing-Test-passing entity, and so forth. (The end of this section includes a discussion of some of these issues, with references to the literature.) Although these issues may be interesting in their own right, and discussion of them may be improved by being informed about the fundamental philosophical issues raised by the Turing Test, they are largely separable from the more basic concerns here.

For these reasons, this collection comprises three types of works most useful in developing a sense of the philosophical issues raised by the Turing Test. It starts with a look to philosophical precursors, early writings by Descartes and others who were the first to propose indistinguishability tests to resolve certain theological questions. In particular, Descartes first pinpointed *verbal behavior* as the crucial property for distinguishing humans from beasts, the soul-bearing from the soul-less. Second, it brings together for the first time all of Turing's own writings related to the Turing Test—the *Mind* article of course, but also little known ephemeral material. The latter answers some questions that are interesting in their own right and subjects of scholarly contention, and Turing's own status as a revolutionary mathematical thinker and a founder of modern computer science makes his personal views on the subject illuminating. Third, the book includes a select set of seminal papers culled from the philosophical literature that directly address the issue of the Turing Test as a test for intelligence, providing a broad spectrum of views that together comprise some of the most important and widely cited works on the subject. In order to sample the immediate reaction from the philosophical community, the collection incorporates essentially all of the direct responses to the *Mind* article published in that journal. The remainder of this introduction provides some background on Turing and his Test, ending with a brief exposition of the variety of issues, philosophical and otherwise, that have arisen around the general topic of the Turing Test. The following chapters present the three sets of readings, each introduced with background material that is intended to be read both as a map of the readings themselves and, taken together and sequentially, a self-contained essay on the Turing Test.

Who Was Alan Turing?

Alan Turing was born in 1912 in London and educated at King's College, Cambridge, and at Princeton where he wrote his doctoral dissertation under the eminent logician Alonzo Church. Today, we would call Turing a computer scientist, but during his career he was naturally thought of as a mathematician and logician, simply because he had not invented computer science yet. This is not hyperbole: Turing can be credited with perhaps the single most fundamental result in computer science, the existence of uncomputable functions. In the course of his solution to one of David Hilbert's famous problems, the "Entscheidungsproblem", the twenty-three-year-old Turing invented the first formal model of computation, the so-called "Turing machine", and argued that the notion "computability by a Turing machine" could serve as an apt substitute for the vague notion of computability in general. He published his seminal paper "On Computable Numbers" in 1936, arguably the first and most important paper in computer science (Turing 1936).

After completing a doctorate at Princeton in 1938 and postdoctoral work back in England, he joined the British Foreign Office as part of a government intelligence unit. His efforts led to the breaking of the German Enigma code, a central contribution to the Allied war effort, by the use of electromechanical devices for carrying out repetitive calculations, a nonprogrammable precursor of the computer.

His experiences at the Bletchley Park code-breaking unit led Turing to further work on the design and construction of early computers, including the Automatic Computing Engine at the National Physical Laboratory and the Manchester machine at the University of Manchester. As one of the first computer programmers, writing programs for the not-yet-built Manchester machine, Turing first came upon and discussed the idea of the subroutine. And in his writings on the question of whether machines could think, he laid the groundwork for the computer science subfield of "artificial intelligence" (AI), the study of the computational explication and replication of behaviors that are associated with intelligence in humans.

Through his research, Turing thus set the foundation for the major subfields of computer science: the theory of computation, the design of hardware and software, and the study of artificial intelligence. Tragically, his career came to a premature end. After his 1952 arrest under British laws against homosexuality, the authorities required him to undergo a draconian hormone treatment for his "condition". Two years later, he died of cyanide poisoning, apparently self-administered, though the nature of his death is still controversial. If his death was suicide, it seems likely that his treatment under outmoded sodomy laws contributed directly to it. In any case, Turing's premature death is certainly one of the great intellectual tragedies of the twentieth century.[1]

What Is the Turing Test?

Turing proposed the Turing Test in the context of the question "Can machines think?"[2] but not as a way of answering the question.

---

1 The authoritative biography of Turing is that of Hodges (1983), which is strongly recommended for any student of the Turing Test.

2 Turing used the terms "think" and "be intelligent" as if they were synonyms, as one can tell by a simple comparison of his article's title and first sentence. In common usage, the two often mean quite distinct things. When I say that my son is intelligent, I usually mean something beyond the fact that he is capable of thought. However, I and many authors follow Turing's practice, taking the notion of "being intelligent" under which it means "being capable of thought", rather than "being smart".

Rather, he found the original question "too meaningless to deserve discussion" and sought to replace it with something more concrete. He found his concrete form in a game-theoretic crystallization of Descartes's observation that flexibility of verbal behavior is the hallmark of humanness. He proposed an "imitation game" in which an interrogator attempts to determine which of two agents[3] is human and which a machine, based on purely verbal interaction with both. If the interrogator is not able to reliably determine which is the human, the machine has passed the test. This test has come to be known as the "Turing Test".

More specifically, Turing imagined the following setup: The two agents A and B and the interrogator C are each placed in separate rooms. C knows only that one of the agents is a human and one a machine, and is not, of course, aware of which is which. C carries on conversations with each of the agents by passing typewritten notes through a courier to each room and getting typewritten replies back. After some indeterminate but appropriately lengthy interaction, C must make a decision as to which of A and B is the machine. Now, by merely guessing blindly, C will get the answer right half the time, so any single test of this sort is not definitive, but one can imagine C going through this exercise many times, and verifying whether C can do significantly better than chance at determining which agent is the machine. If not, that is, if C can do no better than random guessing, the machine is said to have passed the Turing Test.

This, in sum, is the Turing Test. It has many attractive aspects to it as a criterion for intelligence (or a replacement). The test is *operational* or *behavioral* so as to get around (so Turing thought) the tricky definitional questions of intelligence. When asked to define "obscenity", Supreme Court Justice Potter Stewart famously demurred: "I know it when I see it." (Stewart 1964) Maybe intelligence is like that—impossible to define, but you know it when you see it. The use of *verbal interaction* is desirable because it

---

3 Again on a terminological note, the term "agent" is used here and throughout as a generic term for any entity—human or machine, simple or sophisticated—that displays behavior. The notion of agency implicit in the term should be construed broadly.

abstracts from incidental properties like visual appearance that might immediately answer the question of which entity is the machine, but not on the basis of facts pertinent to the question of intelligence. The *open-ended* nature of the interaction is crucial because it allows any possible area of human experience to be used as criterial in the decision. The *statistical* aspect of the decision is fortuitous since on any given running of a Test, even between two people, one of the two will be selected out. Failure on a single test therefore cannot be taken to be indicative of anything at all; the statistical approach moves the test in the direction of testing a disposition or capacity, rather than a singleton behavior.

Issues Surrounding the Turing Test

The commentaries on the Turing Test in this volume are included because they bear on the primary philosophical issue raised by the *Mind* paper, the relationship between the Turing Test and intelligence. The big question, or as referred to henceforth, the Big Question, is "Is passing a Turing Test criterial for intelligence?" That length is the pertinent property for determining meter-hood is uncontroversial. But exactly what the pertinent property or properties are for assessing intelligence, and whether verbal behavior in particular is the one, has become the key issue regarding the Turing Test.

The views on the Big Question have been varied. Some have argued that the Test is too difficult as a test of intelligence; intelligent agents would routinely fail. Robert French (1990, *chapter 13*), for instance, has argued that even with its restriction to verbal interaction, incidental properties, such as a lack of idiosyncratic cultural knowledge, could easily unmask a machine. Others view the test as too easy. Searle (1980, *chapter 14*), Block (1981, *chapter 15*), and Gunderson (1964, *chapter 9*) each argue that the Test misses testing for some crucial property, so that in principle at least unthinking machines could pass a Turing Test. (These various considerations can be seen as splitting the Big Question into multiple Big Questions—concerning the Turing Test as a necessary condition, as a sufficent condition, and so forth—complexities that are explored in detail in this book.) In support of a positive answer to the Big Question, some philosophers find the reasoning from passing a Turing Test to ascription of intelligence to be sound, including Dennett (1985, *chapter 16*), or at least—as Moor (1976, *chapter 17*) would have it—a convincing source of evidence. Finally, Turing's original view is reiterated by others: the Test should not be taken as criterial at all, but as a replacement for the question, and one with useful outcomes. Such a view, sidestepping the Big Question entirely, is recommended by Chomsky (*chapter 20*).

Beyond the Big Question, the Turing Test raises a wide variety of other issues. Coverage of such topics is well beyond the scope of this volume, but some of them are listed below to serve as entry into the appropriate literature.

Pragmatic Issues

In practice, could a machine pass the Turing Test? If so, when will such an event come to pass? Understanding the independence of this question and the Big Question is important. One can believe that a Turing-Test-passing machine is not intelligent, yet still believe that a machine may pass the Test at some future date. One would simply have to conclude that the performance on the Test is not proof of the intelligence of the machine.

This question is only interesting, of course, under the assumption that a machine could pass *in principle*, which many of the papers in this volume take to be controversial at best. In any case, it is clear that at current levels of technology the answer is "no". Some would argue that even assuming the ability in principle, machines will never be able to pass the Test in practice. French's paper (1990, *chapter 13*) can be read in this way. Others believe that only a few decades of continued engineering progress are required. Mitchell Kapor and Raymond Kurzweil have an outstanding bet regarding whether a machine will pass the Turing Test by 2029, for example (Kurzweil and Kapor 2002).

As it turns out, the history of research in AI is littered with predictions of the imminent passing of the Turing Test. Dreyfus (1979) has catalogued examples of this sort of hubris. One lesson learned from the past half-century of AI research is that the problems involved in generating intelligent behavior are deeper and more profound than many had ever imagined. AI researchers, even while making continued progress in many areas, more rarely make the bold predictions of walking, talking robots right around the corner. This leads directly to the issue of whether work towards passing the Turing Test is an appropriate research methodology.

Methodological Issues

Is passing the Turing Test an appropriate research goal? Research in artificial intelligence is concerned with computational explication and replication of behavioral capacities that are associated with intelligence in humans. Construction of a program capable of passing the Turing Test would seem a natural goal for the field. As the early readings in this volume attest, the duplication of human intelligence has inspired scholars for centuries. Indeed, the Turing Test did serve as a defining inspiration in the early history of AI research. Even now, some researchers take passing the Turing Test as fundamental to the field of AI research. Ginsberg (1993), for instance, defines the field as "the enterprise of constructing a physical symbol system that can reliably pass the Turing Test."

But as a goal for a concrete research program (as opposed to a philosophical thought experiment), the Turing Test is fraught with problems. First, insofar as the test is not a necessary condition for intelligence, it encumbers research efforts with extraneous burdens. In particular, as French (1990, *chapter 13*) argues, it forces the modeling of human idiosyncrasies that have nothing to do with intelligence per se. Second, the Test permits conclusions only of success or failure; there is no interesting notion of *almost* passing a Turing Test. Thus, failure in a Turing Test is not diagnostic of any particular deficiency in the test subject, and so provides no mid-course guidance for research direction towards success. Finally, it aims at a goal—the construction of an artificial human intelligence—that is not intrinsically desirable, as we already have plenty of intelligences with human abilities and disabilities and can too easily make more. Hayes and Ford (1995) make these arguments especially forcefully, concluding that the Turing Test is simply inappropriate—indeed, harmful—as a goal of research in AI. A novel argument of theirs is that the test falls prey to the evolving abilities of the judges; people these days easily unmask ELIZA-like systems that would have been convincing only twenty-five years ago. For related reasons, Whitby (1996) calls the Turing Test "AI's biggest blind alley".

Nonetheless, attempts to run Turing-like tests as competitions crop up on occasion, sometimes motivated by their entertainment value, sometimes as a purported prod to scientific research. Shieber (1994) presents a critique of a particular effort along these lines, arguing that carrying out such competitions is grossly premature at best.

Ethical and Normative Issues

Should a machine that could pass a Turing Test be subject to the rights and responsibilities accorded people? Suppose we stipulate the existence of Turing-Test-capable machines. Would it be ethical to turn them off? Should they be allowed to vote? Such science-fiction scenarios have been imagined by many. (One such scenario is the basis for the evocatively titled movie *AI: Artificial Intelligence*, for instance.) Futurists have started examining the issues in some detail (Brooks 2002; Kurzweil 1999; Moravec 1999). Science fiction authors have been exercised over the matter at least since Samuel Butler's *Erewhon*. In any case, such ethical questions, interesting and potentially important as they might be, are posterior to the Big Question of whether passing the Turing Test is criterial for thinking.

On the other hand, the corresponding ethical questions concerning *thinking* machines (ex hypothesi, as opposed to Turing-Test-passing machines) are not posterior to the Big Question, and are therefore appropriate to discuss before its resolution. But, of course, they are not questions about the Turing Test at all.

Alternative Tests

Is there a better way to design a Turing Test? Some researchers have attempted to solve problems in the design of the Turing Test through alternative formulations.

Stevan Harnad (2000), for instance, proposes a hierarchy of Turing-like tests, of which the classical Test is categorized as T2, with T3 expanding the interaction to allow full interaction with the device through auditory, visual, even tactile channels, T4 further requiring internal microfunctional indistinguishability, and T5 requiring indistinguishability at every level.

Watt (1996), arguing that ascription of mental states to others is, for certain purposes, crucial to Turing-like tests, proposes an "inverted Turing Test", in which the machine under test serves as the interrogator, trying to distinguish a human and a machine in a traditional Turing Test. "A system passes if it is itself unable to distinguish between two humans, or between a human and a machine that can pass the normal Turing test, but which can discriminate between a human and a machine that can be told apart by a normal Turing test with a human observer." (Watt 1996) Many respondents note that, regardless of its other problems, the inverted Turing Test can be emulated through a normal Turing Test (Bringsjord 1996; French 1996).

Dowe and Hajek (1998) extend the Turing Test with a nonbehavioral component, requiring that the machine be sufficiently compact, that is, the size of the program and data that it uses be small relative to its performance, so as to circumvent the type of objections to the Turing Test (e.g., those of Searle or Block) detailed in the final part of this volume. The sufficiency of such a modification is based on the close relationship between inductive inference and descriptional complexity. (Along the same lines, Hernandez-Orallo [2000] proposes to replace the Turing Test with a series of psychometric tests based on completing sequences graded according to their descriptional complexity.)

Application Issues

Is the Turing Test good for anything practical? One might think that the answer is definitively negative, given that no machine is close to passing a Turing Test nor is one likely to do so in the foreseeable future. Abstractly, however, there is still the question of whether a Turing-Test-passing machine would be of utility;

Ronald and Sipper (2001), for instance, answer this question in the negative.

Furthermore, it is exactly the inability of computers to emulate certain behaviors that people find straightforward that leads to concrete and useful applications that have arisen under the name "reverse Turing Tests". A reverse Turing Test is a Turing Test intended to be administered by a *computer* as judge. The notion was first proposed by Naor (1996), and developed by Coates et al. (2001) and von Ahn et al. (2004). Reverse Turing Tests can be used to discriminate against computer agents in access to computer services. For instance, web portal company Yahoo! requires the passing of a reverse Turing Test as a condition of signing up for a free email account. In order to sign up, an agent must type in a word that has been presented in typographically deformed form. Although people have no problem identifying the word, the optical character recognition technology that would be required of a computer agent is beyond the state of the art.

All of these issues are important in their own way and show the ability of the Turing Test to insinuate itself broadly into a tremendous range of intellectual areas. Yet all take a back seat to the key question of the relation between the Turing Test and intelligence explored further in the pages ahead.

I

Precursors

The *Bête Machine*

Can machines think? Such an idea would not even have been entertained when machines were no more sophisticated than a lever or a pulley. A medieval peasant might not have been confronted regularly with any mechanism more complicated than a trip hammer, consisting of no more than a water wheel, a pair of gears, a cog, and a lever. Imagine the peasant exercised over whether the device could think.

With the explosion of maritime exploration in the fifteenth and sixteenth centuries, the great scientific problem of the day became determination of longitude at sea. So important was the problem that as early as 1598, Philip III of Spain set up a prize to be awarded to the "discoverer of the longitude", the first person to develop an accurate method for determining longitude at sea. Many other countries followed suit, the most famous prize being that of £20,000 offered by the British Parliament in 1713–1714. Determination of longitude, it turns out, boils down to determination of relative time: How much later is it here than it is where my ship started, or at some other convenient reference point like the Greenwich Observatory. (This is why time zones correspond to longitudinal regions.) It was widely expected at the time of the prize's inauguration that it would eventually be won on the basis of advances in astronomical methods. Galileo, a member of the prize committee, was convinced that the solution would involve tables providing the Greenwich time of astronomical events that can be observed simultaneously at all longitudes, like the eclipsing of the Galilean moons of Jupiter that he himself had discovered. Such tables would serve as a way of determining Greenwich time onboard ship, with which longitude could then be computed. But a more direct alternative to determining Greenwich time is just to set a clock in Greenwich and bring it with you. This works only if the clock is sufficiently accurate that its representation of Greenwich time does not vary by more than a few seconds per day. Otherwise, the error in the computed longitude estimate renders it useless. (Actually, such an estimate would not be entirely useless, but it certainly would not qualify for prize money.)

The demands of maritime navigation led to great technological advances throughout the seventeenth century.

Attracted by the challenge, the money, the prospect of fame, the most learned men and skillful technicians in seventeenth-century Europe turned head and hands to the task. No project had ever mobilized so much talent; the list of names reads like the cast of a Hollywood spectacular on the history of science: Galileo, Pascal, Hooke, Huygens, Leibniz, Newton. And this was only the first team. (Landes 1983, 112)

The greatest horologists of the seventeenth and eighteenth centuries turned their efforts towards the longitude problem. Following in the footsteps of his father Julien Leroy, who "raised the status of French watchmaking by the perfection of his work and design" (Baillie 1929, 224), Pierre Leroy, "the most eminent horologist of France", submitted a series of innovative marine chronometers for testing by longitude prize committees. In the process, he built the first true detent escapement, and was the first to construct a balance that compensated for temperature. In Great Britain, John Harrison's H4 chronometer eventually won the award in 1765. The tremendous advancement in clockwork mechanisms starting with Christiaan Huygens' pendulum escapement and culminating in Harrison's masterpiece constituted a revolution in mechanism, which continued through the eighteenth and nineteenth centuries.

Soon, the technology found its way into fields as sublime as religion—the universe as clockwork with God as watchmaker, the basis for the "argument from design"—and as frivolous as entertainments for the rich—snuffboxes with moving singing birds, elaborate music boxes, and automata musicians.

The possibility of such mechanistic marvels leads naturally to the question of whether real animals are purely mechanistic in nature as well. The advances in horology—new escapements, the pendulum, the balance spring—and the fantastic devices they resulted in provide at least a degree of plausibility for such a view. Clockwork automata provided a foundation on which one could imagine a living machine, perhaps even a thinking one. In the midst of the seventeenth-century explosion in mechanical engineering, the issue of the mechanical nature of life and thought is found in the philosophy of Descartes; the existence of sophisticated automata made credible Descartes's doctrine of the *bête machine* (beast-machine), that animals *were* machines. His argument for the doctrine incorporated the first indistinguishability test between human and machine, the first Turing test, so to speak.

Descartes's goal was the "explanation...of the difference between our soul and that of beasts". In particular, he sought to show that humans have a "rational soul"—immaterial, immortal, and theologically potent—whereas animals have no such immortal soul. His purpose was in part theological, to provide some basis for the presumption that God's heaven would not be overrun by flies, bears, and other inconvenient fauna.[1] For our purposes, it is the nature of his argument, centering around a behavioral comparison of humans, beasts, and *machines* that is pertinent.

The structure of the argument was simple: The first premise constituted the *bête-machine* doctrine itself, that animals are machines. By "machine", Descartes had in mind clockwork automata. He says that animals "act naturally and mechanically, like a clock which tells the time better than our judgement does.... [T]hey operate like clocks." (Descartes 1646, *chapter 2, 36*). Backing up the first premise is an indistinguishability test.

---

1 This preoccupation with the distribution of souls was widespread. One of John Donne's early *Paradoxes and Problemes* entertains the question "Why hath the common opinion affoorded woemen Soules?" (Donne 1633), especially given that "we deny soules to others equall to them in all but in speech". After dismissing various options, he is left with the conjecture that "wee have given woemen soules, onely to make them capable of damnation".

If any such machines had the organs and outward shape of a monkey or of some other animal that lacks reason, we should have no way of knowing that they did not possess entirely the same nature as these animals. (Descartes 1637, *chapter 1, 27*)

Of course, this argument merely shows that animals *may be* machines, but "the Method" that Descartes follows (recall that the quote is taken from a *Discourse on the Method*), based as it is on parsimony, allows him to conclude that they are in fact machines (that is, completely material), there being no reason to assume any immaterial component or motive to their behavior.

The second premise is that humans are not machines, in the sense that they present behaviors that no machine could emulate. The grounding for this premise is a distinguishability test of a very particular (and familiar) sort, a Turing Test:

... whereas if any such machines bore a resemblance to our bodies and imitated our actions as closely as possible for all practical purposes, we should still have two very certain means of recognizing that they were not real men. (Descartes 1637, *chapter 1, 27*)

These two means are speech and wide-ranging flexibility of behavior. Descartes is careful to distinguish his notion of speech from the literal ability to utter the sounds of words. By speech, he means symbolic linguistic communication of thoughts. This definition is specifically intended to include sign languages of the deaf, for instance, even though deaf-mute conversants do not use "speech" in its acoustic sense.[2] On the other hand, the definition excludes (nonsymbolic) grunts of pain and mere (noncommunicative) stimulus responses such as the talking of Talking Barbie (tm) or a pet parrot.

The second means, flexibility of behavior, though broader in scope is clearly a secondary test for Descartes. His writing concentrates on the linguistic test and he sometimes writes as if the

---

2 In this area, Descartes is surprisingly linguistically liberal and modern. It is now widely recognized that sign languages of the deaf are full-fledged natural languages akin to, and not merely gestural transliterations of, their spoken counterparts, and complete with morphological, syntactic, semantic, and pragmatic structure, and subject even to aphasias. See, for instance, the work of Klima and Bellugi (1979).

linguistic test is the only pertinent one. "In fact, none of our external actions can show anyone who examines them that our body is not just a self-moving machine but contains a soul with thoughts, with the exception of spoken words, or other signs that have relevance to particular topics without expressing any passion." (Descartes 1646, *chapter 2, 35*)

Importantly, as Turing will later argue, the speech test is able to encompass the flexibility test. The Cartesian Géraud de Cordemoy provides an excellent summary of the Turing Test as the following "principle" involving engaging in repeated conversational trials:

That if the Bodies, which are like mine, had nothing but the facilness of pronouncing Words, I should not therefore believe that they had the advantage of being united to Souls: But then, if I finde by all the Experiments, I am capable to make, that they use speech as I do, I shall think, I have infallible reason to believe that they have a soul as I. . . .

When I shall see, that they shall give me *Ideas,* I had not before, and which shall relate to the thing, I had already in my mind: Lastly, when I shall see a great sequel between their signes and mine, I shall not be reasonable, If I believe not, that they are such as I am.

Thus I have no more cause to doubt concerning this point; for I have many a thousand like tryals, and I have not onely seen a great connexion between their *signs* and my *thoughts,* but I have also found so great an one between *their* signes and *mine,* that I can doubt no longer of their *thoughts.* (de Cordemoy 1668, 13–19)

Putting these two premises together, Descartes concludes that humans transcend animals. They possess some nonmechanical, that is, immaterial, facet that allows them speech and rational behavior; this immaterial facet is the "rational soul". His conclusion may be suspect for various reasons, some of which arise in later discussion, but the use of a linguistic test for distinguishing between human and machine is surely a clever innovation.

1

Discourse on the Method, Chapter V

René Descartes

I would gladly go on and reveal the whole chain of other truths that I deduced from these first ones. But in order to do this I would have to discuss many questions that are being debated among the learned, and I do not wish to quarrel with them. So it will be better, I think, for me not to do this, and merely to say in general what these questions are, so as to let those who are wiser decide whether it would be useful for the public to be informed more specifically about them. I have always remained firm in the resolution I had taken to assume no principle other than the one I have just used to demonstrate the existence of God and of the soul, and to accept nothing as true which did not seem to me clearer and more certain than the demonstrations of the geometers had hitherto seemed. And yet I venture to say that I have found a way to satisfy myself within a short time about all the principal difficulties usually discussed in philosophy. What is more, I have noticed certain laws which God has so established in nature, and of which he has implanted such notions in our minds, that after adequate reflection we cannot doubt that they are exactly observed in everything which exists or occurs in the world. Moreover, by considering what follows from these laws it seems to me that I have discovered many truths more useful and important than anything I had previously learned or even hoped to learn.

I endeavoured to explain the most important of these truths in a treatise which certain considerations prevent me from publishing, and I know of no better way to make them known than by summarizing its contents. My aim was to include in it everything I thought I knew about the nature of material things before I began to write it. Now a painter cannot represent all the different sides of a solid body equally well on his flat canvas, and so he chooses one of the principal ones, sets it facing the light, and shades the others so as to make them stand out only when viewed from the perspective of the chosen side. In just the same way, fearing that I could not put everything I had in mind into my discourse, I undertook merely to expound quite fully what I understood about light. Then, as the occasion arose, I added something about the sun and fixed stars, because almost all light comes from them; about the heavens, because they transmit light; about planets, comets and the earth, because they reflect light; about terrestrial bodies in particular, because they are either coloured or transparent or luminous; and finally about man, because he observes these bodies. But I did not want to bring these matters too much into the open, for I wished to be free to say what I thought about them without having either to follow or to refute the accepted opinions of the learned. So I decided to leave our world wholly for them to argue about, and to speak solely of what would happen in a new world. I therefore supposed that God now created, somewhere in imaginary spaces, enough matter to compose such a world; that he variously and randomly agitated the different parts of this matter so as to form a chaos as confused as any the poets could invent; and that he then did nothing but lend his regular concurrence to nature, leaving it to act according to the laws he established. First of all, then, I described this matter, trying to represent it so that there is absolutely nothing, I think, which is clearer and more intelligible, with the exception of what has just been said about God and the soul. In fact I expressly supposed that this matter lacked all those forms or qualities about which they dispute in the Schools, and in general that it had only those features the knowledge of which was so natural to our souls that we could not even pretend not to know them. Further, I showed what the laws of nature were, and without basing my arguments on any principle other than the infinite perfections of God, I tried to demonstrate all those laws about which we could have any doubt, and to show that they are such that, even if God created many worlds, there could not be any in which they failed to be observed. After this, I showed how, in consequence of these laws, the greater part of the matter of this chaos had to become disposed and arranged in a certain way, which made it resemble our heavens; and how, at the same time, some of its parts had to form an earth, some planets and comets, and others a sun and fixed stars. Here I dwelt upon the subject of light, explaining at some length the nature of the light that had to be present in the sun and the stars, how from there it travelled instantaneously across the immense distances of the heavens, and how it was reflected from the planets and comets to the earth. To this I added many points about the substance, position, motions and all the various qualities of these heavens and stars; and I thought I had thereby said enough to show that for anything observed in the heavens and stars of our world, something wholly similar had to appear, or at least could appear, in those of the world I was describing. From that I went on to speak of the earth in particular: how, although I had expressly supposed that God had put no gravity into the matter of which it was formed, still all its parts tended exactly towards its centre; how, there being water and air on its surface, the disposition of the heavens and heavenly bodies (chiefly the moon), had to cause an ebb and flow similar in all respects to that observed in our seas, as well as a current of both water and air from east to west like the one we observe between the tropics; how mountains, seas, springs and rivers could be formed naturally there, and how metals could appear in mines, plants grow in fields, and generally how all the bodies we call "mixed" or "composite" could come into being there. Among other things, I took pains to make everything belonging to the nature of fire very clearly understandable, because I know nothing else in the world, apart from the heavenly bodies, that produces light. Thus I made clear how it is formed and fuelled, how sometimes it possesses only heat without light, and sometimes light without heat; how it can produce different colours and various other qualities in different bodies; how it melts some bodies and hardens others; how it can consume almost all bodies, or turn them into ashes and smoke; and finally how it can, by the mere force of its action, form glass from these ashes—something I took particular pleasure in describing since it seems to me as wonderful a transmutation as any that takes place in nature.

Yet I did not wish to infer from all this that our world was created in the way I proposed, for it is much more likely that from the beginning God made it just as it had to be. But it is certain, and it is an opinion commonly accepted among theologians, that the act by which God now preserves it is just the same as that by which he created it. So, even if in the beginning God had given the world only the form of a chaos, provided that he established the laws of nature and then lent his concurrence to enable nature to operate as it normally does, we may believe without impugning the miracle of creation that by this means alone all purely material things could in the course of time have come to be just as we now see them. And their nature is much easier to conceive if we see them develop gradually in this way than if we consider them only in their completed form.

From the description of inanimate bodies and plants I went on to describe animals, and in particular men. But I did not yet have sufficient knowledge to speak of them in the same manner as I did of the other things—that is, by demonstrating effects from causes and showing from what seeds and in what manner nature must produce them. So I contented myself with supposing that God formed the body of a man exactly like our own both in the outward shape of its limbs and in the internal arrangement of its organs, using for its composition nothing but the matter that I had described. I supposed, too, that in the beginning God did not place in this body any rational soul or any other thing to serve as a vegetative or sensitive soul, but rather that he kindled in its heart one of those fires without light which I had already explained, and whose nature I understood to be no different from that of the fire which heats hay when it has been stored before it is dry, or which causes new wine to seethe when it is left to ferment from the crushed grapes. And when I looked to see what functions would occur in such a body I found precisely those which may occur in us without our thinking of them, and hence without any contribution from our soul (that is, from that part of us, distinct from the body, whose nature, as I have said previously, is simply to think). These functions are just the ones in which animals without reason may be said to resemble us. But I could find none of the functions which, depending on thought, are the only ones that belong to us as men; though I found all these later on, once I had supposed that God created a rational soul and joined it to this body in a particular way which I described.

But so that you might see how I dealt with this subject, I shall give my explanation of the movement of the heart and the arteries. [ED: *Descartes's lengthy description of the workings of the circulatory system is elided.*]

I explained all these matters in sufficient detail in the treatise I previously intended to publish. And then I showed what structure the nerves and muscles of the human body must have in order to make the animal spirits inside them strong enough to move its limbs—as when we see severed heads continue to move about and bite the earth although they are no longer alive. I also indicated what changes must occur in the brain in order to cause waking, sleep and dreams; how light, sounds, smells, tastes, heat and the other qualities of external objects can imprint various ideas on the brain through the mediation of the senses; and how hunger, thirst, and the other internal passions can also send their ideas there. And I explained which part of the brain must be taken to be the "common". sense, where these ideas are received; the memory, which preserves them; and the corporeal imagination, which can change them in various ways, form them into new ideas, and, by distributing the animal spirits to the muscles, make the parts of this body move in as many different ways as the parts of our bodies can move without being guided by the will, and in a manner which is just as appropriate to the objects of the senses and the internal passions. This will not seem at all strange to those who know how many kinds of automatons, or moving machines, the skill of man can construct with the use of very few parts, in comparison with the great multitude of bones, muscles, nerves, arteries, veins and all the other parts that are in the body of any animal. For they will regard this body as a machine which, having been made by the hands of God, is incomparably better ordered than any machine that can be devised by man, and contains in itself movements more wonderful than those in any such machine.

I made special efforts to show that if any such machines had the organs and outward shape of a monkey or of some other animal that lacks reason, we should have no means of knowing that they did not possess entirely the same nature as these animals; whereas if any such machines bore a resemblance to our bodies and imitated our actions as closely as possible for all practical purposes, we should still have two very certain means of recognizing that they were not real men. The first is that they could never use words, or put together other signs, as we do in order to declare our thoughts to others. For we can certainly conceive of a machine so constructed that it utters words, and even utters words which correspond to bodily actions causing a change in its organs (e.g. if you touch it in one spot it asks what you want of it, if you touch it in another it cries out that you are hurting it, and so on). But it is not conceivable that such a machine should produce different arrangements of words so as to give an appropriately meaningful answer to whatever is said in its presence, as the dullest of men can do. Secondly, even though such machines might do some things as well as we do them, or perhaps even better, they would inevitably fail in others, which would reveal that they were acting not through understanding but only from the disposition of their organs. For whereas reason is a universal instrument which can be used in all kinds of situations, these organs need some particular disposition for each particular action; hence it is for all practical purposes impossible for a machine to have enough different organs to make it act in all the contingencies of life in the way in which our reason makes us act.

Now in just these two ways we can also know the difference between man and beast. For it is quite remarkable that there are no men so dull-witted or stupid—and this includes even madmen—that they are incapable of arranging various words together and forming an utterance from them in order to make their thoughts understood; whereas there is no other animal, however perfect and well-endowed it may be, that can do the like. This does not happen because they lack the necessary organs, for we see that magpies and parrots can utter words as we do, and yet they cannot speak as we do: that is, they cannot show that they are thinking what they are saying. On the other hand, men born deaf and dumb, and thus deprived of speech-organs as much as the beasts or even more so, normally invent their own signs to make themselves understood by those who, being regularly in their company, have the time to learn their language. This shows not merely that the beasts have less reason than men, but that they have no reason at all. For it patently requires very little reason to be able to speak; and since as much inequality can be observed among the animals of a given species as among human beings, and some animals are more easily trained than others, it would be incredible that a superior specimen of the monkey or parrot species should not be able to speak as well as the stupidest child—or at least as well as a child with a defective brain—if their souls were not completely different in nature from ours. And we must not confuse speech with the natural movements which express passions and which can be imitated by machines as well as by animals. Nor should we think, like some of the ancients, that the beasts speak, although we do not understand their language. For if that were true, then since they have many organs that correspond to ours, they could make themselves understood by us as well as by their fellows. It is also a very remarkable fact that although many animals show more skill than we do in some of their actions, yet the same animals show none at all in many others; so what they do better does not prove that they have any intelligence, for if it did then they would have more intelligence than any of us and would excel us in everything. It proves rather that they have no intelligence at all, and that it is nature which acts in them according to the disposition of their organs. In the same way a clock, consisting only of wheels and springs, can count the hours and measure time more accurately than we can with all our wisdom.

After that, I described the rational soul, and showed that, unlike the other things of which I had spoken, it cannot be derived in any way from the potentiality of matter, but must be specially created. And I showed how it is not sufficient for it to be lodged in the human body like a helmsman in his ship, except perhaps to move its limbs, but that it must be more closely joined and united with the body in order to have, besides this power of movement, feelings and appetites like ours and so constitute a real man. Here I dwelt a little upon the subject of the soul, because it is of the greatest importance. For after the error of those who deny God, which I believe I have already adequately refuted, there is none that leads weak minds further from the straight path of virtue than that of imagining that the souls of the beasts are of the same nature as ours, and hence that after this present life we have nothing to fear or to hope for, any more than flies and ants. But when we know how much the beasts differ from us, we understand much better the arguments which prove that our soul is of a nature entirely independent of the body, and consequently that it is not bound to die with it. And since we cannot see any other causes which destroy the soul, we are naturally led to conclude that it is immortal.

If Animals Could Talk

There are inevitably three possible avenues of attack against a distinguishability test such as Descartes or Turing proposed: One can argue that (i) the Test is too hard or (ii) it is too easy or (iii) the purported facts on how the Test would come out are wrong. Descartes's opponents tended toward the third type of argument, both in arguing that Descartes had it wrong about how the animals would fare in a Test—that they *could* in principle be distinguished in speech or flexibility of behavior from machines—or that he was too magnanimous to the humans—that they couldn't be so distinguished.

In regard to the first point, we have already seen that Descartes dismisses arguments based on the mimicry of parrots and other isolated formulaic behaviors that have the mere appearance of speech or rational behavior without the substance. Michel de Montaigne, a great backer of the rational behavior of animals, provided a litany of examples of the clever abilities of various animals.

Take the swallows, when spring returns; we can see them ferreting through all the corners of our houses; from a thousand places they select one, finding it the most suitable place to make their nests: is that done without judgement or discernment? And then when they are making their nests (so beautifully and so wondrously woven together) can birds use a square rather than a circle, an obtuse angle rather than a right angle, without knowing their properties or their effects? Do they bring water and then clay without realizing that hardness can be softened by dampening? They cover the floors of their palaces with moss or down; do they do so without foreseeing that the tender limbs of their little ones will lie more softly there and be more comfortable? Do they protect themselves from the stormy winds and plant their dwellings to the eastward, without recognizing the varying qualities of those winds and considering that one is more healthy for them than another? Why does the spider make her web denser in one place and slacker in another, using this knot here and that knot there, if she cannot reflect, think, or reach conclusions?

We are perfectly able to realize how superior they are to us in most of their works and how weak our artistic skills are when it comes to imitating them. Our works are coarser, and yet we are aware of the faculties we use to construct them: our souls use all their powers when doing so. Why do we not consider that the same applies to animals? Why do we attribute to some sort of slavish natural inclination works that surpass all that we can do by nature or by art? (de Montaigne 1987b [1576], 19–20)

Descartes dismisses such examples as isolated behaviors that can at least in principle be mimicked by automata; they lack the evidence of flexibility that is the hallmark of rationality. In his letter to the Marquess of Newcastle of November 23, 1646, Descartes elaborates on the failings of this kind of argument, first by emphasizing the primacy of the linguistic test over the general behavioral one, and then by reaffirming the intuition that the particulars of animal behavior are mechanically reproducible: "I know that animals do many things better than we do, but this does not surprise me. It can even be used to prove they act naturally and mechanically, like a clock which tells the time better than our judgment does. Doubtless when the swallows come in spring, they operate like clocks." (Descartes 1646, *chapter 2*)

Modern science shows that Descartes's intuitions on this front are right. By examining how such animal "reasoning" fails, we can gain an understanding of the true nature of the behavior. Take for instance the goldtail moth in its caterpillar stage. The caterpillar displays a highly sophisticated behavior in the spring at the end of its hibernation. It climbs to the top of the shrubs on which it typically feeds in preparation for the new leaves to sprout. How, Montaigne might ask, could it know that the new leaves would be there if it could not reason about the growth pattern of the shrub, with new growth starting at the top? As further evidence of the caterpillar's brilliance, one notes its clever following of new growth from the top of the shrub downward as the new leaves open up. The explanation for the caterpillar's startling understanding of the growth pattern of these shrubs is, of course, much more mundane. Dean Wooldridge provides the answer:[1]

The tropism involved is one whereby an adequate amount of warmth automatically causes the caterpillar to leave its nest and start crawling toward the light; it can be induced at any time by an experimenter simply by applying heat. The tropism results in the caterpillar climbing as high as it can go, which is to the top of the shrub where the new growth of green leaves first emerges early in the spring. However, if other effects than this simple tropism were not operating, the caterpillar would be in difficulty as soon as it had eaten the green leaves at the top of the shrub, for its food from then on would have to be found at lower levels; reaching such levels would be in conflict with a tropism that continuously impels it upward. This problem has been handled by nature by causing the upward-climbing tropism to operate only when the caterpillar is hungry. Therefore, having eaten, the caterpillar is free to creep in any direction and will eventually make its way down and find the new leaves as they commence to open.

As with all tropisms, the behavior of the goldtail moth is completely unreasoning. For example, if caterpillars are taken as they are leaving the nest and put into a glass tube lying near a window, they will all collect in the end of the tube nearest the light and stay there. If a few young leaves from their food shrub are put at the other end of the tube, farthest from the light, the hungry, unfed caterpillars will remain held captive near the lighted end of the tube, and there they will stay until they starve. (Wooldridge 1963, 77–78)

Montaigne's argument demonstrates more our tendency to ascribe intelligence to apparently purposive behavior than the animals' possession of the intelligence ascribed.

Beyond these merely factual issues, as Keith Gunderson points out, there are methodological problems with Montaigne's argument as well. "Montaigne's reasoning is even slipperier than Descartes seems to realise. In effect Montaigne argues from the particular skills of particular animals to the general conclusion that animals are able to think, reason, and so forth, which could then be used, for example, as the basis for saying a bird can think. In other words, any one animal in effect gets credit for the skills of all other animals. The fox gets credit for the spider's weaving skills, and so forth." (Gunderson 1964a, 209 n. 2)

---

1 Dennett (1984) prefers to highlight Wooldridge's story of the digger wasp, *Sphex ichtheumoneus*, whose apparently purposive behavior is unmasked as merely reflexive via a similar experiment, and neologizes the term "sphexishness" for such behavior.

At the same time modern scientists address the basis for animal behaviors, they continue to grapple with the question of animal potential. Perhaps, contrary to Descartes's assumptions, animals can communicate in human languages. Scientists have attempted to teach chimpanzees, gorillas, parrots, and dolphins to speak English or American Sign Language or various bespoke symbol systems. The results have been at best equivocal, arguably wholly negative, and without question contentious. Washoe and her ilk have done little to undermine Descartes's indistinguishability test.

It is possible that animals are capable of speech (in Descartes's sense) but not of using human languages. Surely, we should not deny animals their rationality on the basis of our limitations in understanding them. Cyrano de Bergerac imagined a fantastic voyage to the moon (de Bergerac 1657) in which the local residents, four-legged satyrs, cage him in a zoo because they take his talk as the inarticulate gruntings of a lower animal. Similarly, perhaps earthly animals already communicate amongst themselves in their own language. Such an argument calls for humans to play Doctor Doolittle, to decipher the languages of the beasts. Again, modern science has taken up the challenge, with limited success. "To be mentioned in this connection," reports Heini Hediger,

are the great experiments of the Nobel Prize winner Karl von Frisch, who has discovered surprising facets of the language of bees, details of which today are known to every schoolchild. Also to be remembered are the discoveries of Karl von Frisch's former student, Martin Lindauer, who succeeded in understanding the "negotiations" of swarming bees concerning their next residence so well that he was able—on his bicycle— to arrive at the new location before the bees did. Another ethologist, Peter Marler, understands so thoroughly the language of the chaffinch, which consists of about twenty signals, that he can attract the bird to a simulated female, or make him flee a cat or hide from a bird of prey—all this through the reply of the appropriate calls with sensitive instruments. (Hediger 1980)

These feats are impressive and contribute greatly to our understanding of animal behavior, but they certainly do not inspire us with the generality of animal communication.

In sum, the indistinguishability test of animals and machines seems to be unassailed in the three and a half centuries since Descartes; it has been scientifically strengthened.

2

Letter to the Marquess of Newcastle

René Descartes

...I cannot share the opinion of Montaigne and others who attribute understanding or thought to animals. I am not worried that people say that human beings have absolute dominion over all the other animals; for I agree that some of them are stronger than us, and I believe that there may also be some animals which have a natural cunning capable of deceiving even the shrewdest human beings. But I consider that they imitate or surpass us only in those of our actions which are not guided by our thought. It often happens that we walk or eat without thinking at all about what we are doing; and similarly, without using our reason, we reject things which are harmful for us, and parry the blows aimed at us. Indeed, even if we expressly willed not to put our hands in front of our head when we fall, we could not prevent ourselves. I consider also that if we had no thought then we would walk, as the animals do, without having learnt to; and it is said that those who walk in their sleep sometimes swim across streams in which they would drown if they were awake. As for the movements of our passions, even though in us they are accompanied by thought because we have the faculty of thinking, it is nevertheless very clear that they do not depend on thought, because they often occur in spite of us. Consequently they can also occur in animals, even more violently than they do in human beings, without our being able to conclude from that that animals have thoughts.

In fact, none of our external actions can show anyone who examines them that our body is not just a self-moving machine but contains a soul with thoughts, with the exception of spoken words, or other signs that have relevance to particular topics without expressing any passion. I say "spoken words or other signs", because deaf-mutes use signs as we use spoken words; and I say that these signs must have reference, to exclude the speech of parrots, without excluding the speech of madmen, which has reference to particular topics even though it does not follow reason. I add also that these words or signs must not express any passion, to rule out not only cries of joy or sadness and the like, but also whatever can be taught by training to animals. If you teach a magpie to say good-day to its mistress when it sees her approach, this can only be by making the utterance of this word the expression of one of its passions. For instance it will be an expression of the hope of eating, if it has always been given a titbit when it says it. Similarly, all the things which dogs, horses and monkeys are taught to perform are only expressions of their fear, their hope or their joy; and consequently, they can be performed without any thought. Now it seems to me very striking that the use of words, so defined, is something peculiar to human beings. Montaigne and Charron may have said that there is a greater difference between one human being and another than between a human being and an animal; yet there has never been known an animal so perfect as to use a sign to make other animals understand something which bore no relation to its passions; and there is no human being so imperfect as not to do so, since even deaf-mutes invent special signs to express their thoughts. This seems to me a very strong argument to prove that the reason why animals do not speak as we do is not that they lack the organs but that they have no thoughts. It cannot be said that they speak to each other but we cannot understand them; for since dogs and some other animals express their passions to us, they would express their thoughts also if they had any.

I know that animals do many things better than we do, but this does not surprise me. It can even be used to prove that they act naturally and mechanically, like a clock which tells the time better than our judgement does. Doubtless when the swallows come in spring, they operate like clocks. The action of honeybees are of the same nature; so also is the discipline of cranes in flight, and of apes in fighting, if it is true that they keep discipline. Their instinct to bury their dead is no stranger than that of dogs and cats which scratch the earth for the purpose of burying their excrement; they hardly ever actually bury it, which shows that they act only by instinct and without thinking. The most that one can say is that though the animals do not perform any action which shows us that they think, still, since the organs of their bodies are not very different from ours, it may be conjectured that there is attached to these organs some thought such as we experience in ourselves, but of a very much less perfect kind. To this I have nothing to reply except that if they thought as we do, they would have an immortal soul like us. This is unlikely, because there is no reason to believe it of some animals without believing it of all, and many of them such as oysters and sponges are too imperfect for this to be credible. But I am afraid of boring you with this discussion, and my only desire is to show you that I am, etc.

The *Homme Machine*

What can be made of the argument against Descartes's claim of distinguishability of humans and machines? Again, the argument could be countered in three ways, and again, the prime counter-Cartesian arguments were empirical.

Ironically, some of the fodder for the empirical arguments was traceable to the *bête-machine* doctrine itself. Descartes's doctrine had inspired engineers to pursue the goal of constructing such an entity artificially. The automaton duck (figure 1) constructed by Jacques de Vaucanson is the best known example; this engineering tour de force, through its clockwork and hydromechanical design, was capable of "eating, drinking, macerating the Food, and voiding Excrements, pluming her Wings, picking her Feathers, and performing several Operations in Imitation of a living Duck." (de Vaucanson 1979 [1742])

The empirical counterargument against human/machine distinguishability was made in a kind of counterfactual way by many respondents to Descartes. If all the behaviors of animals can be mimicked mechanically, then it is but a small, though precarious, step to assume that all human behaviors might too. Vaucanson's duck was accompanied by a flute player and a shepherd playing the tambor, about which no more luminary a personage than Monsieur Fontenelle, Perpetual Secretary of the Royal Academy of Sciences, attests that the Academy "have judg'd this Machine to be extremely ingenious, and that the Author of it has found the Means of employing new and simple Contrivances ... imitating by Art all that is necessary for a Man to perform in such a Case." (de Vaucanson 1979 [1742])

Figure 1
The automaton duck of Jacques de Vaucanson, flanked by his drum and flute player automata.

The mere notion of a beast-machine makes a man-machine plausible, perhaps inevitable. But then, there would be no need for postulating a rational soul. If these behavioral criteria are the only basis for postulating soul, as Descartes would have it, then one is forced to a conclusion that humans have no souls, which was patently false on the theological ground of the day.

This precarious move was taken, and for the first time joyfully embraced, by Julien Offray de La Mettrie, in his provocatively titled book *L'Homme Machine (Machine Man)*.

> To be a machine and to feel, to think and be able to distinguish right from wrong, like blue from yellow—in a word to be born with intelligence and a sure instinct for morality and to be only an animal—are thus things which are no more contradictory than to be an ape or a parrot and to be able to give oneself pleasure.... I believe thought to be so little incompatible with organised matter that it seems to be one of its properties, like electricity, motive power, impenetrability, extension, etc." (de La Mettrie 1748, *chapter 3, 54*)

La Mettrie was a strong believer in the Cartesian doctrine of the *bête-machine;* he just thought that Descartes did not take it to its logical conclusion. Impressed by the abilities of animals, La Mettrie presumes that animals could be made to talk, and if animals can talk, then Descartes's distinguishing test between humans and machines disappears.[1]

The theological ramifications of the argument made the book quite controversial in its day. The printer, Elie Luzac, for instance, was ordered almost immediately by the local authorities "(1) to deliver all the copies of 'L'Homme Machine' that he can gather, (2) to mention the name of the [anonymous] author, (3) to express his regrets for having published the book and (4) to promise solemnly never again to press or sell again such an offense against God, the Church and Morality." (Thijssen 1977) Luzac acquiesced to the demands in short order.

Reading the work, one can understand the alarm. Not only is the thesis blasphemous, but it is stated in such grandiose, unrepentant terms as the correction of the flawed reasoning of Descartes, with every attempt to belittle ad hominem those who would disagree, that even readers with modern sensibilities can be a bit taken aback by the style of presentation. Nonetheless, many of the arguments,

---

1 Gunderson (1964a) provides an interesting discussion of the Descartes/ La Mettrie divergence and its ramifications for Turing's "thinking machine".

though rambling, may be found in modern discussions of the possibility of artificial intelligence. "We can see that there is only one substance in the universe and that man is the most perfect one. He is to the ape and the cleverest animals what Huygens's planetary clock is to one of Julien Leroy's watches. If it took more instruments, more cogs, more springs to show the movements of the planets than to show or tell the time, if it took Vaucanson more artistry to make his flautist than his duck, he would have needed even more to make a speaking machine, which can no longer be considered impossible, particularly at the hands of a new Prometheus." (de La Mettrie 1748, *chapter 3, 52*)

The early progress in building clockwork models of animal—and even human—behavior could not, however, be maintained. Ever more sophisticated mechanisms could be designed, even general-purpose computers such as Charles Babbage's "differential analyzer". But forces of friction and torsion led to intrinsic limitations on the capabilities of clockwork mechanisms, and these limitations were reached by the nineteenth century. Babbage's engine, though logically valid, was mechanically impractical. It required new technology to once again make plausible the notion of a thinking machine, made possible by the new Prometheus of the twentieth century, the computer scientist.

Until the limitations of mechanics could be transcended through the development and use of electrical devices, the moral and philosophical implications of the human-machine distinction were relegated to further exploration only in fiction. Still, here, the key distinction was verbal behavior, as Descartes had originally proposed. Samuel Butler's fictional Erewhonians note the potential for machines to outpace humans in all fields of endeavor, just as Descartes had in his reply to the Montaigne arguments. They extrapolate, however, to include verbal behavior as well. "There was a time when it must have seemed highly improbable that machines should learn to make their wants known by sound, even through the ears of man", an Erewhonian philosopher writes. "May we not conceive, then, that a day will come when those ears are no longer needed, and the hearing will be done by the delicacy of the machine's own construction?—when its language shall have been developed from the cry of animals to a speech as intricate as our own?" (Butler 1872) To forestall such a dismal future, Butler's Erewhonians destroy all of the machines before the machines can do the same to their former masters.

George Bernard Shaw's vision of the future, *Back to Methusaleh*, included the construction of simulacra of humans as the ultimate art form, the most elegant evidence of their humanity being their verbal behavior. "I have taught them to talk and read; and now they tell lies. That is so very lifelike." (Shaw 1921)

Interestingly, it is known that these works were influential on Turing himself (Hodges 1983, 73-74).[2] In fact, Turing's own philosophy is downright Erewhonian. "It seems probable" to him

that once the machine thinking method had started, it would not take long to outstrip our feeble powers. There would be no question of the machines dying, and they would be able to converse with each other to sharpen their wits. At some stage therefore, we should have to expect the machines to take control, in the way that is mentioned in Samuel Butler's "Erewhon". (Turing 1951b, *chapter 5*)

---

2 Modern popular science fiction has not, for the most part, addressed the philosophical issues surrounding machine intelligence. Writings have presupposed—as opposed to investigated—consciousness, intelligence, and motivation in their hypothesized machines. Letson (1982) discusses this point in detail. Nonetheless, the Turing name has made its way into the science fiction genre, as the epigraph to this volume shows.

3

Selections from *Machine Man*

Julien Offray de La Mettrie

For a wise man, it is not enough to study nature and the truth; he must dare to proclaim it for the benefit of the small number of those who are willing and able to think; for the others, who are the willing slaves of prejudice, are no more capable of reaching the truth than are frogs of flying.

The philosophers' systems concerning the human soul can, in my opinion, be reduced to two, the first, and the oldest, is the system of materialism, and the second is that of spiritualism.

Those metaphysicians who have implied that matter might well possess the faculty of thinking did not dishonour their reason. Why? Because they had the advantage (for in this case it is one) of expressing themselves badly. To ask whether matter, considered only in itself, can think is like asking whether matter can indicate the time. We can already see that we shall avoid the rock on which Mr Locke unfortunately foundered.

The Leibnizians with their *monads* have constructed an incomprehensible hypothesis. They have spiritualised matter rather than materialising the soul. How can we define a being whose nature is absolutely unknown to us?

Descartes and all the Cartesians, among whom the followers of Malebranche have long been included, made the same mistake. They admitted two distinct substances in man as if they had seen and counted them.

The wisest have said that the soul could not be known otherwise than by the light of faith; yet as rational beings they believed they could retain the right to examine what the Scriptures meant by the word *spirit*, which is used when speaking of the human soul. And if in their research they disagree with the theologians on this point, are the theologians any more in agreement with each other on all the other points?

Here, in a few words, is the result of all their reflections.

If there is a God, he is the creator of nature as much as of revelation; he gave us the one to explain the other, and reason to reconcile them.

To mistrust the knowledge we can gain from studying living bodies is to see nature and revelation as two mutually destructive opposites, and consequently to dare to affirm an absurdity, namely that God contradicts himself in his different works and deceives us.

If there is a revelation, it cannot belie nature. It is through nature alone that we can discover the meaning of the words of the Gospel, which can only be truly interpreted by experience. Previous commentators have only confused the truth, as we can judge from the author of the *Spectacle of Nature* "It is surprising", he says (referring to Mr Locke) "that a man who debases our soul so far as to consider it to be made of clay, dares to set up reason as the judge and sovereign arbiter of the mysteries of faith; for", he adds "what an astonishing idea of Christianity would we have if we attempted to follow reason?"

Apart from the fact that these reflections throw no light on the question of faith, they constitute such frivolous objections to the method of those who believe they can interpret the holy books that I am almost ashamed to waste time refuting them.

The excellence of reason does not depend on a grand meaningless word (immateriality) but on its force, its extent or its acuteness. Thus a "soul of clay" which discovers as if at a glance the relationships and consequences of an infinite number of ideas which are difficult to grasp would obviously be preferable to a silly, stupid soul made of the most precious elements. A true philosopher does not blush, like Pliny, at our miserable origin. What seems to be base is here the most precious object, on which nature seems to have expended the most art and effort. But since man, even if he came from an apparently even baser source, would nevertheless be the most perfect of all beings, whatever the origin of his soul, if it is pure, noble and sublime, it is a splendid soul which makes whosoever is endowed with it admirable.

Mr Pluche's second mode of reasoning seems to me to be flawed, even in his system which smacks a little of fanaticism; for if we have a conception of faith which is contrary to the clearest principles and the most incontrovertible truths, we should believe for the honour of revelation and its author, that this conception is false and that we do not yet know the meaning of the Scriptures.

Either everything—both nature itself and revelation—is illusion, or experience alone can justify faith. But could anything be more ridiculous than our author? I can imagine hearing a Peripatetician say "We must not believe Toricelli's experiment for if we did, if we abandoned nature's abhorrence of a vacuum,what an amazing philosophy we would have?"

I have shown how flawed Mr Pluche's reasoning is[1] in order to show, first, that if there is a revelation it is insufficiently proven by the authority of the Church alone, without being examined by reason, as is claimed by all those who fear reason, and second in order to shield from attack the method of those who wish to follow the path I am showing them and to interpret what is supernatural and incomprehensible in itself by the light each of us has received from nature.

Thus, experience and observation alone should guide us here. They are found in abundance in the annals of physicians who were philosophers, not in those of philosophers who were not physicians. Physicians have explored and thrown light on the labyrinth of man, they alone have revealed the springs hidden under coverings which keep so many marvels from our gaze. They alone, calmly contemplating our soul, have caught it a thousand times unawares, in its misery and its grandeur, without either despising it in one state or admiring it in the other. Once again, these are the only natural philosophers who have the right to speak on this subject. What could the others, in particular the theologians, tell us? Is it not ridiculous to hear them shamelessly pronouncing on a subject they are incapable of understanding, from which, on the contrary, they have been deflected by obscure studies that have led them into a thousand prejudices and, in a word, fanaticism, which adds to their ignorance of the mechanism of our bodies?

But although we have chosen the best guides, we shall still find many thorns and obstacles in our path.

Man is a machine constructed in such a way that it is impossible first of all to have a clear idea of it and consequently to define it. That is why all the greatest philosophers' *a priori* research, in which they tried, as it were, to use the wings of the mind, have failed. Hence it is only *a posteriori,* or by trying as it were to disentangle the soul from the body's organs, that we can, not necessarily discover with certainty the

---

1 His mistake is obviously that he begs the question.

true nature of man, but reach the greatest possible degree of probability on the subject.

Therefore let us take up the staff of experience and ignore the history of all the futile opinions of philosophers. To be blind and to believe that one can do without this staff is the height of blindness. How right a modern author is to say that it is nothing but vanity which prevents one from using secondary causes to the same effect as primary ones! We can, and even should, admire all of those great geniuses—Descartes, Malebranche, Leibniz, Wolff, etc.—in their most futile labours; but pray, what fruits have we derived from their profound meditations and all their works? So let us begin, by seeing not what people have thought, but what we should think for the sake of an untroubled life.

. . .

However discreet and reserved we may be about the conclusions we can draw from such observations and many others, concerning the sort of inconstancy of vessels and nerves, etc., nevertheless such variety cannot be the result of nature's meaningless games. They prove at least the need for a good and ample organisation, since in the whole animal world the soul becomes firmer together with the body and acquires wisdom as it gains strength.

Let us stop for a moment to consider different animals' capacity to learn. The best conceived analogy no doubt leads the mind to believe that the causes we have mentioned produce all the differences between them and us, although we must admit that our feeble understanding, limited to the crudest observations, cannot see the ties linking the cause and its effects. It is a sort of *harmony* that philosophers will never understand.

Among the animals, some learn to talk and sing; they can remember tunes and copy all the notes as precisely as musicians can. Others, while displaying more intelligence, like the monkey, cannot manage it. Why so, unless it is due to a defect in the speech organs?

But is this defect so inbuilt that it cannot be remedied? In a word, would it be absolutely impossible to teach this animal a language? I do not think so.

I would take the great ape in preference to any other, until chance leads us to discover another species more similar to ours, for there is no reason to believe that one cannot exist in as yet unknown regions. This animal bears such a strong resemblance to us that naturalists have called it the "wild man" or the "man of the woods". I would take one following the criteria of Amman's schoolchildren, that is to say I should like it to be neither too young nor too old; for those brought to Europe are usually too old. I would choose the one with the cleverest physiognomy, who best confirmed this promise in a thousand little tests. Finally, as I do not consider myself worthy of being its tutor, I would send it to the school of the excellent teacher whom I have just mentioned, or of another equally skillful one, should he exist.

You know, from Amman's book and from all those who have translated his method,[2] all the miracles he has wrought on children born deaf, whose eyes he has, as he himself explains, turned into ears, and how quickly he has taught them to hear, talk, read and write. I agree that a deaf person's eyes see better and are more intelligent than those of one who is not, because the loss of one member or sense can increase the force or the penetration of another. But the ape can see and hear, he understands what he hears and sees; he apprehends so perfectly the signs made to him, that at any other game or exercise I have no doubt that he would surpass Amman's pupils. Why then should the education of apes be impossible? Why could he not, if given sufficient care and attention, imitate, like the deaf, the sounds needed for pronunciation? I do not presume to decide whether the ape's speech organs will never be able to articulate anything whatever we do, but such an absolute impossibility would surprise me, in view of the close analogy between ape and man, and the fact that there is no animal so far known whose interior and exterior bears such a striking resemblance to man. Mr Locke, who was certainly never suspected of being credulous, had no difficulty in believing a story told by Sir William Temple in his *Memoirs* about a parrot who replied pertinently and had learnt, like us, to conduct a sort of coherent conversation. I know that some have made fun of this great metaphysician,[3] but if someone had announced to the world that generation could happen without eggs and without women, would he have found many supporters? Yet Mr Trembley has discovered generation without mating, by simple segmentation. Surely Amman would also have been considered mad if he had boasted, before experimenting successfully, that he could teach pupils like his, and in such

---

2 The author of the *Natural History of the Soul*, etc.
3 The author of the *History of the Soul.*

a short time? Yet his success has astounded the universe and, like the author of the *History of Polyps,* he has achieved instant immortality. A man who owes the miracles he performs to his own genius is, to my mind, superior to one who owes his to chance. He who has discovered the art of embellishing the finest of the kingdoms, and of providing perfections it did not have, should be placed above a lazy inventor of futile systems or a laborious author of sterile discoveries. Those of Amman are of much greater worth; he has saved men from the mere instinct to which they seemed condemned; he has given them ideas, a mind and, in a word, a soul which they would never have had. How much greater this power is?

Let us not limit nature's resources; they are infinite, particularly when assisted by great skill.

Surely the same mechanism which opens the Eustachian tube in the deaf could unblock it in monkeys? Surely a beneficial desire to imitate their masters pronunciation could free the organs of speech in animals, which can imitate so many other signs with such skill and intelligence? I defy anyone to quote a single truly conclusive experiment which proves that my plan is impossible and ridiculous; what is more, the similarity of the ape's structure and functions is such that I hardly doubt at all that if this animal were perfectly trained, we would succeed in teaching him to utter sounds and consequently to learn a language. Then he would no longer be a wild man, nor an imperfect man, but a perfect man, a little man of the town, with as much substance or muscle for thinking and taking advantage of his education as we have.

From animals to man there is no abrupt transition, as true philosophers will agree. What was man before he invented words and learnt languages? An animal of a particular species who, with much less natural instinct than the others, whose king he did not yet consider himself to be, was only distinguishable from the ape and other animals in the same way as the ape himself is; I mean by a physiognomy that indicated greater discernment. Reduced to the mere intuitive knowledge of the Leibnizians, he saw only forms and colours, without being able to distinguish any of them; old or young, a perpetual child, he stuttered out his feelings and his needs like a starved or restless dog who wants to eat or go for a walk.

Words, languages, laws, science and arts came, and thanks to them the rough diamond of our minds was finally polished. Man was trained like an animal; he became an author in the same way as he became a porter.

A mathematician learnt the most difficult proofs and calculations, as a monkey learnt to put on and take off his little hat or to ride his trained dog. Everything was done by signs, each species understood what it was able to understand, and that was how man acquired symbolic knowledge, as it is called by our German philosophers again.

As we can see, there is nothing simpler than the mechanism of our education! It all comes down to sounds, or words, which are transmitted from one person's mouth, through another's ear and into his brain, which receives at the same time through his eyes the shape of the bodies for which the words are the arbitrary signs.

But who was the first to speak? Who was the first tutor of the human race? Who invented the means to make the best use of our organism's aptitude for learning? I do not know; the names of those first welcome geniuses have been lost in the mists of time. But art is the child of nature, and nature must have long preceded it.

We must suppose that the men with the best organisms, those on whom nature had poured out its gifts, must have taught the others. They could not, for example, have heard a new sound, felt new feelings or been struck by all the different beautiful objects which form part of the enchanting spectacle of nature, without finding themselves in the same position as the famous deaf man from Chartres, whose story was first told by Fontenelle, on hearing for the first time, at the age of forty, the astonishing sound of bells.

Would it then be absurd to believe that those first mortals tried, like that deaf man or like animals and dumb people (who are another sort of animals), to express their new feelings by movements dictated by the economy of their imagination and then, as a result, by spontaneous sounds particular to each animal, this was a natural expression of their surprise, joy, emotions or needs. For doubtless those whom nature endowed with more refined feelings were also given greater facility to express them.

That is how I believe man used his feelings or his instinct to acquire his wits, and his wits to acquire knowledge. That is how, as far as I can grasp, the brain was filled with the ideas for whose reception nature had formed it. The one helped the other, and the smallest beginnings grew little by little until all of the objects in the universe were as easily perceived as a circle.

. . .

Simply admit that organised matter is endowed with a motive principle, which alone distinguishes it from unorganised matter (well, can we refuse to believe the most incontrovertible observations?), and that in animals everything is dictated by the diversity of this organisation, as I have sufficiently proved. That is enough to solve the riddle of substances and of man. We can see that there is only one substance in the universe and that man is the most perfect one. He is to the ape and the cleverest animals what Huygens's planetary clock is to one of Julien Leroy's watches. If it took more instruments, more cogs, more springs to show the movement of the planets than to show or tell the time, if it took Vaucanson more artistry to make his flautist than his duck, he would have needed even more to make a speaking machine, which can no longer be considered impossible, particularly at the hands of a new Prometheus. Thus, in the same way, nature needed more artistry and machinery to construct and maintain a machine which could continue for a whole century to tell all the beats of the heart and the mind; for if we cannot tell the time from the pulse, it is at least the barometer of heat and liveliness, from which we can judge the nature of the soul. I am not mistaken; the human body is a clock but so huge and cleverly constructed that if the cog which tells the seconds happens to stop, the one which tells the minutes goes on turning, in the same way as the cog for the quarters continues to move, and so do the others, when the first ones are rusty or out of order for some reason and stop working. For we know that, in the same way, the obstruction of a few vessels is not enough to destroy or halt the main movement in the heart, which is like the mainspring of the machine. This is because, on the contrary, the fluids, which have diminished in volume, do not have so far to go and cover the distance all the more quickly, as if carried by a new current, because the strength of the heart has increased due to the resistance it meets with at the extremities of the vessels. When the optical nerve alone is compressed and no longer lets through the images of objects, we know that this loss of sight does not prevent the use of hearing, any more than the loss of hearing, when the *portio mollis* cannot work, implies the loss of sight. Again, in the same way we know that one person can hear without being able to say that he can hear (except after his attack is over), while another, who cannot hear but whose lingual nerves are free in the brain, recounts automatically all the dreams that come into his mind. Such phenomena do not surprise enlightened physicians. They know what to expect from man's nature; and, by the way, if we compare two doctors, the best and most trustworthy is always, in my opinion, the one who knows the most about the physics or the mechanics of the human body and who, forgetting the soul and all the worries which this figment of the imagination causes in fools and ignoramuses, concentrates solely on pure naturalism.

So let the so-called Mr Charp make fun of philosophers who have considered animals to be machines. How different is my opinion! I believe that Descartes would have been an admirable man in all respects if he had been born in an age which he did not need to enlighten, and had consequently understood both the value of experiment and observation and the danger of straying from them. But it is just as fair for me to make true amends here to that great man for all those petty philosophers who make bad jokes and ape Locke and who, instead of laughing impudently in Descartes' face, would do better to realise that without him the field of philosophy would perhaps still be waste land, like the field of right thinking without Newton.

It is true that this famous philosopher made many mistakes, as nobody denies; but he understood animal nature and was the first to demonstrate perfectly that animals were mere machines. After such an important discovery which implies so much wisdom, how can we, without ingratitude, not pardon all his errors!

In my opinion they are all repaired by that great admission. For whatever he recounts about the distinction between the two substances, it is obvious that it was only a trick, a cunning device to make the theologians swallow the poison hidden behind an analogy that strikes everyone and that they alone cannot see. For it is precisely that strong analogy which forces all scholars and true judges to admit that, however much those haughty, vain beings—who are more distinguished by their pride than by the name of men—may wish to exalt themselves, they are basically only animals and vertically crawling machines. They all have that wonderful instinct, which education turns into intelligence and which is located in the brain or, failing that, when the brain is missing or ossified, in the medulla oblongata and never in the cerebellum; for I have seen it seriously injured and others[4] have found it tumefied without the soul ceasing to function.

---

4 Haller in the *Philosophical Transactions.*

To be a machine and to feel, to think and to be able to distinguish right from wrong, like blue from yellow—in a word to be born with intelligence and a sure instinct for morality and to be only an animal—are thus things which are no more contradictory than to be an ape or a parrot and to be able to give oneself pleasure. For since here we have an opportunity to say so, who would ever have guessed *a priori* that a drop of liquid ejaculated in mating would provoke such divine pleasure and that from it would be born a little creature that one day, given certain laws, would be able to enjoy the same delights? I believe thought to be so little incompatible with organised matter that it seems to be one of its properties, like electricity, motive power, impenetrability, extension, etc.

. . .

We are veritable moles in the field of nature; we hardly cover more ground than that animal and it is only our pride that places limits on things that have none. We are like a watch saying (a storyteller would make it an important character in a frivolous work): "What! Was I made by that stupid workman, I who can divide up time, who can indicate so precisely the sun's course, who can tell out loud the hours which I indicate! No, that is impossible." In the same way, ungrateful wretches that we are, we despise the common mother of all the kingdoms, to use the language of the chemists. We imagine, or rather assume, a cause higher than the one to which we owe everything and which has truly created everything in an inconceivable way. No, there is nothing vile about matter, except for crude eyes which do not understand its most brilliant productions, and nature is not a worker of limited ability. The ease and pleasure with which she produces millions of men exceed the watchmaker's toil when he creates the most complicated of watches. Her power shines out as clearly in the creation of the meanest insect as in that of the most splendid human; she does not expend greater effort on the animal than on the vegetable kingdom, or on the greatest genius than on an ear of corn. We should therefore judge what is hidden from our curious gaze and our research by what we can see, instead of imagining anything more. Observe the behaviour of the ape, the beaver, the elephant, etc. If it is clear that they could not act in that way without intelligence, why should we refuse it to those animals? And if you agree that they have a soul, you fanatics, you are doomed; however much you protest that you have said nothing about its nature and that you deny its immortality, anyone can see that that is an arbitrary statement. It is obvious to anyone that it must be either mortal or immortal, like ours, and must suffer the same fate, whatever that may be, thus you have fallen into Scylla while trying to avoid Charybdis.

Break the chains of your prejudices and take up the torch of experience, and you will honour nature in the way she deserves, instead of drawing derogatory conclusions from the ignorance in which she has left you. Simply open your eyes and ignore what you cannot understand, and you will see that a labourer whose mind and knowledge extend no further than the edges of his furrow is no different essentially from the greatest genius, as would have been proved by dissecting the brains of Descartes and Newton; you will be convinced that the imbecile or the idiot are animals in human form, in the same way as the clever ape is a little man in another form, and that, since everything depends absolutely on differences in organisation, a well-constructed animal who has learnt astronomy can predict an eclipse, as he can predict recovery or death when his genius and good eyesight have benefited from some time at the school of Hippocrates and at patients' bedsides. It is by means of this sequence of observation and truth that we can manage to link to matter the admirable property of thought, even if we cannot see how they are joined together because the subject of this attribute is essentially unknown to us.

We are not claiming that every machine, or every animal, perishes completely or takes on another form after death, for we know absolutely nothing on this subject. But to insist that an immortal machine is a paradox or a *being of reason* is as absurd a deduction as would be that of caterpillars if, on seeing the remains of their fellow caterpillars, they lamented bitterly the fate of their species which was apparently dying out. The souls of these insects (for each animal possesses its own) are too limited to understand nature's metamorphoses. Even the cleverest of them could never have imagined that it was destined to become a butterfly. We are the same. Do we know any more about our fate than about our origin? Let us therefore submit to invincible ignorance, on which our happiness depends.

Whosoever thinks in this way will be wise, just, untroubled about his fate and consequently happy. He will look forward to death without fearing it and without desiring it, cherishing life and scarcely comprehending how disgust can corrupt the heart in this delightful place; his respect for nature, thankfulness, attachment and tenderness will be in proportion to the feelings and the kindness he has received from her; he will be happy to experience her and to attend the enchanting spectacle of the universe, and will certainly never destroy her in himself or in others. What am I saying! He will be full of humanity and will love its imprint even in his enemies. Judge for yourself how he will treat others. He will pity the wicked without hating them; he will consider them as no more than misshapen men. But while pardoning defects in the construction of their minds and bodies, he will still admire just as much what beauty and virtue they possess. Those whom nature has favoured will seem to him more worthy of respect than those whom she has treated like a wicked stepmother. Thus we have seen that natural gifts, which are the root of everything that is acquired, will elicit from a materialist's mouth and heart a homage that is refused by everyone else without due reason. The materialist, convinced, whatever his vanity may object, that he is only a machine or an animal, will not ill-treat his fellows; he is too well informed as to the nature of that behaviour whose inhumanity is always proportionate to the degree of analogy that was demonstrated above. Following the law of nature given to all animals, he does not want to do to others what he would not like others to do to him.

Let us then conclude boldly that man is a machine and that there is in the whole universe only one diversely modified substance. This is not at all a hypothesis built up using questions and assumptions; it is not the work of prejudice or even of my reason alone. I would have disdained a guide that I consider to be so uncertain if my senses, carrying the torch, so to speak, had not encouraged me to follow reason by lighting its path. Experience thus spoke to me in reason's favour and so I applied them together.

But it must have been clear that I have only allowed myself the most rigorous and tightest reasoning, after a multitude of physical observations that no scholar can question. Scholars are also the only ones whom I allow to judge the consequences which I draw from these observations, for I reject here all prejudiced men who are neither anatomists nor versed in the only philosophy that is relevant here, that of the human body. What could the weak reeds of theology, metaphysics and the schools do against such a firm and solid oak, for they are childish weapons, like practice foils, which can give pleasure in fencing but can never wound an opponent. Do I need to explain that I am speaking of those empty, trivial ideas and that overused, pathetic reasoning concerning the so-called incompatibility of two substances that incessantly touch and move each other, which will be developed as long as there remains the shadow of a prejudice or superstition on earth? Here is my system, or rather the truth, unless I am very much mistaken. It is short and simple. Now if anyone wants to argue, let them!

II

Turing's Test

Computer Technology

It took the technology of the computer to make apposite again the question of whether machines could think. As Turing says, "the present interest in 'thinking machines' has been aroused by a particular kind of machine, usually called an 'electronic computer' or 'digital computer'." And it was Turing himself who almost inadvertently posed the issue in its most poignant and essential form, the form that we have come to know as the Turing Test, with its trials involving two agents, one human, one machine, and its interrogator attempting to determine which is which through separate blinded conversations.

Turing's first and best known discussion of the Turing Test is his 1950 article published in *Mind*, a scholarly journal of philosophy published continuously since 1876, and dedicated to "the expression of all that is most original and valuable in current English thought, without predilection for any special school or any special department". The presentation of the Test was introduced by analogy with an "imitation game" involving a man, a woman, and an interrogator attempting to discover which is which. This introductory game has generated its own confusion as to the exact parameters of the Test itself, an issue discussed further later. Indeed, the paper is ambiguous or equivocal on various points, which has in part led to its impressive ability to foster discussion and disagreement in a range of areas. Some of these ambiguities (such as the question of the role of gender in the Test) may be clarified by appeal to Turing's ephemeral writings, as argued below.

Other ambiguities, however, are intrinsic, such as the question of whether the Test is intended as definitional of the concept of intelligence or substitutive for it. Turing himself starts by declaring that the Test should be treated as a replacement for the question "Can machines think?", and as such, it has various salutary qualities. It eliminates certain irrelevancies such as appearance or speech quality, yet still provides access to an essentially unlimited range of behavior, allowing the machine to display arbitrary flexibility of verbal behavior. It makes no commitment to the type of machine beyond requiring it to be a digital computer of some sort, but as Turing's own results on the universality of Turing machines show, this is little if any restriction. The equivalence in computational power of Turing machines and every subsequent model of computation has lent credence to the widely acknowledged view that the notions of computability, computability by a digital computer, and computability by a Turing machine are equivalent.

But how can we know that Turing's Test is an adequate replacement for the question "Can machines think?" if we can't compare the results of the Test with the corresponding answers to the question? Turing finds himself sliding down the slippery slope from replacement to definition for just this reason. "We cannot altogether abandon the original form of the problem, for opinions will differ as to the appropriateness of the substitution and we must at least listen to what has been said in this connection." (Turing 1950, 442, *chapter 4*) He discusses, for instance, whether the Test should be thought of as a necessary or sufficient condition for attributing intelligence, finding for the latter only.

In a similar vein, he attempts to preempt various objections to the possibility of a Turing-Test-passing machine. He lists some nine objections, ranging from the frivolous "heads in the sands" objection (a thinking machine would be "too dreadful") to the technical "mathematical objection" (a machine is subject to Gödelian inconsistencies that people are not). In general, the objections rely on claims that machines are missing some intrinsic element of thinking, such as: a soul (1), transcendence of Gödelian inconsistency or Turing undecidability (3), consciousness (4), erring (5), learning (5, 6), novelty (6), continuity (7), flexibility (8), extra-sensory perception (9). (Numbers in parentheses refer to the objection number in Turing's paper.)

Modern thinking eschews certain of these arguments, especially those based on machines' lack of a soul, error, novelty, learning, continuity,[1] flexibility, and extra-sensory perception.[2] The objection based on transcendence of Gödelian inconsistency or Turing undecidability is still raised and argued with some frequency, most prominently by John Lucas (1961) and Roger Penrose (1989).[3] It is safe to say that their arguments remain controversial.

By far the most persistent philosophical argument against the suitability of the Turing Test as a test of intelligence is hidden inside of Professor Jefferson's "argument from consciousness", that it is insufficient for a machine to display certain apparently intelligent behaviors as might be elicited in a Turing Test. It must do so *for the right reason,* "because of thoughts and emotions felt, and not by the chance fall of symbols" (Turing 1950, 435, *chapter 4*). As Turing points out "this argument appears to be a denial of the validity of the test", and so it is. Jefferson presages Gunderson, Searle, Block, and the like in arguing against net results and for underlying cause. This important issue is explored in great detail in later papers.

Notes on the Reprinting

This reprinting of Turing's paper attempts to cleave tightly to the original. Page boundaries in the original are marked with an in-line

---

1 Block (1981, *chapter 15*) presents in passing a quite elegant argument against the "argument from continuity" objection. "The point is that our *concept* of intelligence allows an intelligent being to have quantized sensory devices."

2 This last objection, that machines and humans could be distinguished by the latter's superior ESP abilities, may strike modern readers as silly. In the context of 1940's science, with the apparently scientifically valid results of J. B. Rhine of Duke University showing the ability of certain people to, for instance, name the shapes on unseen cards with better-than-chance accuracy, the addressing of this issue is more understandable. The Rhine results are by now widely viewed as flawed.

3 Robertson (1999) presents a variant on this argument based not on Gödel's inconsistency theorems but on Chaitin's Algorithmic Information Theory.

[p. 433]

symbol and marginal note ⌈ thus. The text here incorporates only a few editorial corrections to the original:

Textual errors and capitalization   Spacing is modernized throughout. A few typographical errors are corrected and some capitalization standardized: On page 435,[4] "Machines concerned in the Game" is replaced by "Machines Concerned in the Game". On page 441, "at Manchester it about" is replaced by "at Manchester is about". On page 444, footnote 2, "Author's names" is replaced by "Authors' names". On page 446, "How about 'a winter's day' " is replaced by "How about 'a winter's day'?" On page 456, "Changes of the child machine" has been expanded from its abbreviated form using dittos. The phrases "Natural selection" and "Judgement of the experimenter" on that page have been transposed to parallel the ordering of the other items it is in analogy with. On page 460, "BIBLIOGRAPHY" is replaced by "Bibliography".

Footnotes   The footnotes have been renumbered consecutively.

Footnote 1 on page 443 is especially problematic, as it had no corresponding mark in the original published text. As no manuscript for Turing's paper is extant, it is impossible to determine where on that page Turing intended the footnote to go, and hence what the footnote text "This view" was intended to refer to. Reprintings of the paper differ on placement of the footnote mark. Several place the footnote after the first paragraph on the page, though it makes no sense there. Others place the footnote after the phrase "making one equal to two", where the heretical view is the purported limitation on the power of God to overrule mathematical truths; the remainder of the footnote might then be a contrasting argument (and counterargument) showing that limitations on God's power need not be heretical. The footnote is considerably more plausible when placed there, though under this reconstruction the second sentence in the note coheres poorly with the first. Unnoticed has been a third alternative, that the footnote was intended to appear after the phrase "that women have no souls?", which phrase would represent the heretical view in question. If so, the remaining text of the footnote would provide the theological basis for the hereticality of the view, with the final sentence motivating the word "possibly" in the first sentence of the footnote. The

---

4 All page references to the Turing *Mind* paper are to the original pagination.

repeated use of the word "view" in this phrase and the footnote, and the relationship between the footnote text and the view expressed in the phrase lends credence to this reconstruction. In this reprinting the second of these reconstructions is used, though the reader should note the alternative possibilities.

Internal references   Two internal references are modified. On page 450, "statement quoted on p. 21" is replaced by "statement quoted on pp. 445–446". On page 459, "point of view on pp. 24, 25" is replaced by "point of view on pp. 448–449". These two infelicities presumably resulted from the publisher's typesetting preserving the internal page references of the original manuscript. The updated page references are based on internal evidence but cannot be definitive.

No other intentional textual variations were made.

Turing used an unusual method for citations, merely placing authors' names in italics, as he notes in footnote 2. He was, unfortunately, not consistent in the practice. There is no reference to Samuel Butler's *Erewhon* to be found in the text, though it appears in the bibliography. On the other hand, no bibliographic entry is manifest for Helen Keller and J. B. Rosser, though their names appear italicized in the text. Gödel's and Russell's names appear unitalicized in the text, though there is an appropriate bibliographic entry for each; in the case of Gödel, perhaps the appearance of his name at the in-text placement of footnote 2 was deemed sufficient to mark it as a citation. The reprinted text preserves these idiosyncrasies and the original text of the bibliography verbatim, placing standardized and modernized versions of the bibliographic entries in the aggregate bibliography at the end of the volume (including correction of several errors in Turing's entries), with bracketed citations to them in the reprinted bibliography.

4

Computing Machinery and Intelligence

Alan M. Turing

1 The Imitation Game

I propose to consider the question, 'Can machines think?' This should begin with definitions of the meaning of the terms 'machine' and 'think'. The definitions might be framed so as to reflect so far as possible the normal use of the words, but this attitude is dangerous. If the meaning of the words 'machine' and 'think' are to be found by examining how they are commonly used it is difficult to escape the conclusion that the meaning and the answer to the question, 'Can machines think?' is to be sought in a statistical survey such as a Gallup poll. But this is absurd. Instead of attempting such a definition I shall replace the question by another, which is closely related to it and is expressed in relatively unambiguous words.

The new form of the problem can be described in terms of a game which we call the 'imitation game'. It is played with three people, a man (A), a woman (B), and an interrogator (C) who may be of either sex. The interrogator stays in a room apart from the other two. The object of the game for the interrogator is to determine which of the other two is the man and which is the woman. He knows them by labels X and Y, and at the end of the game he says either 'X is A and Y is B' or 'X is B and Y is A'. The interrogator is allowed to put questions to A and B thus:

C: Will X please tell me the length of his or her hair?

Now suppose X is actually A, then A must answer. It is A's ⌈ object in the [p. 434] game to try and cause C to make the wrong identification. His answer might therefore be

'My hair is shingled, and the longest strands are about nine inches long.'

In order that tones of voice may not help the interrogator the answers should be written, or better still, typewritten. The ideal arrangement is to have a teleprinter communicating between the two rooms. Alternatively the question and answers can be repeated by an intermediary. The object of the game for the third player (B) is to help the interrogator. The best strategy for her is probably to give truthful answers. She can add such things as 'I am the woman, don't listen to him!' to her answers, but it will avail nothing as the man can make similar remarks.

We now ask the question, 'What will happen when a machine takes the part of A in this game?' Will the interrogator decide wrongly as often when the game is played like this as he does when the game is played between a man and a woman? These questions replace our original, 'Can machines think?'

2   Critique of the New Problem

As well as asking, 'What is the answer to this new form of the question', one may ask, 'Is this new question a worthy one to investigate?' This latter question we investigate without further ado, thereby cutting short an infinite regress.

The new problem has the advantage of drawing a fairly sharp line between the physical and the intellectual capacities of a man. No engineer or chemist claims to be able to produce a material which is indistinguishable from the human skin. It is possible that at some time this might be done, but even supposing this invention available we should feel there was little point in trying to make a 'thinking machine' more human by dressing it up in such artificial flesh. The form in which we have set the problem reflects this fact in the condition which prevents the interrogator from seeing or touching the other competitors, or hearing their voices. Some other advantages of the proposed criterion may be shown up by specimen questions and answers. Thus:

Q   Please write me a sonnet on the subject of the Forth Bridge.

A   Count me out on this one. I never could write poetry.

Q   Add 34957 to 70764

A   (Pause about 30 seconds and then give as answer) 105621.

Q   Do you play chess?

A   Yes.

⌈Q   I have K at my K1, and no other pieces. You have only K at K6 and   [p. 435]
R at R1. It is your move. What do you play?

A   (After a pause of 15 seconds) R-R8 mate.

The question and answer method seems to be suitable for introducing almost any one of the fields of human endeavour that we wish to include. We do not wish to penalise the machine for its inability to shine in beauty competitions, nor to penalise a man for losing in a race against an aeroplane. The conditions of our game make these disabilities irrelevant. The 'witnesses' can brag, if they consider it advisable, as much as they please about their charms, strength or heroism, but the interrogator cannot demand practical demonstrations.

The game may perhaps be criticised on the ground that the odds are weighted too heavily against the machine. If the man were to try and pretend to be the machine he would clearly make a very poor showing. He would be given away at once by slowness and inaccuracy in arithmetic. May not machines carry out something which ought to be described as thinking but which is very different from what a man does? This objection is a very strong one, but at least we can say that if, nevertheless, a machine can be constructed to play the imitation game satisfactorily, we need not be troubled by this objection.

It might be urged that when playing the 'imitation game' the best strategy for the machine may possibly be something other than imitation of the behaviour of a man. This may be, but I think it is unlikely that there is any great effect of this kind. In any case there is no intention to investigate here the theory of the game, and it will be assumed that the best strategy is to try to provide answers that would naturally be given by a man.

3   The Machines Concerned in the Game

The question which we put in § 1 will not be quite definite until we have specified what we mean by the word 'machine'. It is natural that we should wish to permit every kind of engineering technique to be used in our machines. We also wish to allow the possibility than an engineer or team of engineers may construct a machine which works, but whose manner of operation cannot be satisfactorily described by its constructors because they have applied a method which is largely experimental. Finally, we wish to exclude from the machines men born in the usual manner. It is difficult to frame the definitions so as to satisfy these three conditions.

[p. 436] One might for instance insist that the team of ⌈engineers should be all of one sex, but this would not really be satisfactory, for it is probably possible to rear a complete individual from a single cell of the skin (say) of a man. To do so would be a feat of biological technique deserving of the very highest praise, but we would not be inclined to regard it as a case of 'constructing a thinking machine'. This prompts us to abandon the requirement that every kind of technique should be permitted. We are the more ready to do so in view of the fact that the present interest in 'thinking machines' has been aroused by a particular kind of machine, usually called an 'electronic computer' or 'digital computer'. Following this suggestion we only permit digital computers to take part in our game.

This restriction appears at first sight to be a very drastic one. I shall attempt to show that it is not so in reality. To do this necessitates a short account of the nature and properties of these computers.

It may also be said that this identification of machines with digital computers, like our criterion for 'thinking', will only be unsatisfactory if (contrary to my belief), it turns out that digital computers are unable to give a good showing in the game.

There are already a number of digital computers in working order, and it may be asked, 'Why not try the experiment straight away? It would be easy to satisfy the conditions of the game. A number of interrogators could be used, and statistics compiled to show how often the right identification was given.' The short answer is that we are not asking whether all digital computers would do well in the game nor whether the computers at present available would do well, but whether there are imaginable computers which would do well. But this is only the short answer. We shall see this question in a different light later.

4   Digital Computers

The idea behind digital computers may be explained by saying that these machines are intended to carry out any operations which could be done by a human computer. The human computer is supposed to be following fixed rules; he has no authority to deviate from them in any detail. We may suppose that these rules are supplied in a book, which is altered whenever he is put on to a new job. He has also an unlimited supply of paper on which he does his calculations. He may also do his multiplications and additions on a 'desk machine', but this is not important.

If we use the above explanation as a definition we shall be in ⌈ danger of [p. 437] circularity of argument. We avoid this by giving an outline of the means by which the desired effect is achieved. A digital computer can usually be regarded as consisting of three parts:

(i) Store.
(ii) Executive unit.
(iii) Control.

The store is a store of information, and corresponds to the human computer's paper, whether this is the paper on which he does his calculations or that on which his book of rules is printed. In so far as the human computer does calculations in his head a part of the store will correspond to his memory.

The executive unit is the part which carries out the various individual operations involved in a calculation. What these individual operations are will vary from machine to machine. Usually fairly lengthy operations can be done such as 'Multiply 3540675445 by 7076345687' but in some machines only very simple ones such as 'Write down 0' are possible.

We have mentioned that the 'book of rules' supplied to the computer is replaced in the machine by a part of the store. It is then called the 'table of instructions'. It is the duty of the control to see that these instructions are obeyed correctly and in the right order. The control is so constructed that this necessarily happens.

The information in the store is usually broken up into packets of moderately small size. In one machine, for instance, a packet might consist of ten decimal digits. Numbers are assigned to the parts of the store in which the various packets of information are stored, in some systematic manner. A typical instruction might say:

'Add the number stored in position 6809 to that in 4302 and put the result back into the latter storage position.'

Needless to say it would not occur in the machine expressed in English. It would more likely be coded in a form such as 6809430217. Here 17 says which of various possible operations is to be performed on the two numbers. In this case the operation is that described above, *viz.* 'Add the number....' It will be noticed that the instruction takes up 10 digits and so forms one packet of information, very conveniently. The control will normally take the instructions to be obeyed in the order of the positions in which they are stored, but occasionally an instruction such as

[p. 438] ⌈'Now obey the instruction stored in position 5606, and continue from there'

may be encountered, or again

'If position 4505 contains 0 obey next the instruction stored in 6707, otherwise continue straight on.'

Instructions of these latter types are very important because they make it possible for a sequence of operations to be repeated over and over again until some condition is fulfilled, but in doing so to obey, not fresh instructions on each repetition, but the same ones over and over again. To take a domestic analogy: suppose Mother wants Tommy to call at the cobbler's every morning on his way to school to see if her shoes are done, she can ask him afresh every morning. Alternatively she can stick up a notice once and for all in the hall which he will see when he leaves for school and which tells him to call for the shoes, and also to destroy the notice when he comes back if he has the shoes with him.

The reader must accept it as a fact that digital computers can be constructed, and indeed have been constructed, according to the principles we have described, and that they can in fact mimic the actions of a human computer very closely.

The book of rules which we have described our human computer as using is of course a convenient fiction. Actual human computers really remember what they have got to do. If one wants to make a machine mimic the behaviour of the human computer in some complex operation one has to ask him how it is done, and then translate the answer into the form of an instruction table. Constructing instruction tables is usually described as 'programming'. To 'programme a machine to carry out the operation A' means to put the appropriate instruction table into the machine so that it will do A.

An interesting variant on the idea of a digital computer is a 'digital computer with a random element'. These have instructions involving the throwing of a die or some equivalent electronic process; one such instruction might for instance be, 'Throw the die and put the resulting number into store 1000'. Sometimes such a machine is described as having free will (though I would not use this phrase myself). It is not normally possible to determine from observing a machine whether it has a random element, for a similar effect can be produced by such devices as making the choices depend on the digits of the decimal for π.

Most actual digital computers have only a finite store. There is no theoretical difficulty in the idea of a computer with an unlimited store. Of course only a finite part can have been used at any one time. Likewise only a finite amount can have been ⌈ constructed, but we can imagine   [p. 439] more and more being added as required. Such computers have special theoretical interest and will be called infinitive capacity computers.

The idea of a digital computer is an old one. Charles Babbage, Lucasian Professor of Mathematics at Cambridge from 1828 to 1839, planned such a machine, called the Analytical Engine, but it was never completed. Although Babbage had all the essential ideas, his machine was not at that time such a very attractive prospect. The speed which would have been available would be definitely faster than a human computer but something like 100 times slower than the Manchester machine, itself one of the slower of the modern machines. The storage was to be purely mechanical, using wheels and cards.

The fact that Babbage's Analytical Engine was to be entirely mechanical will help us to rid ourselves of a superstition. Importance is often attached to the fact that modern digital computers are electrical, and that the nervous system also is electrical. Since Babbage's machine was not electrical, and since all digital computers are in a sense equivalent, we see that this use of electricity cannot be of theoretical importance. Of course electricity usually comes in where fast signalling is concerned, so that it is not surprising that we find it in both these connections. In the nervous system chemical phenomena are at least as important as electrical. In certain computers the storage system is mainly acoustic. The feature of using electricity is thus seen to be only a very superficial similarity. If we wish to find such similarities we should look rather for mathematical analogies of function.

5   Universality of Digital Computers

The digital computers considered in the last section may be classified amongst the 'discrete state machines'. These are the machines which move by sudden jumps or clicks from one quite definite state to another. These states are sufficiently different for the possibility of confusion between them to be ignored. Strictly speaking there are no such machines. Everything really moves continuously. But there are many kinds of machine, which can profitably be *thought of* as being discrete state machines. For instance in considering the switches for a lighting system it is a convenient fiction that each switch must be definitely on or definitely off. There must be intermediate positions, but for most purposes we can forget about them. As an example of a discrete state machine we might consider a wheel

[p. 440]   which clicks ⌈ round through 120° once a second, but may be stopped by a lever which can be operated from outside; in addition a lamp is to light in one of the positions of the wheel. This machine could be described abstractly as follows. The internal state of the machine (which is described by the position of the wheel) may be q_1, q_2 or q_3. There is an input signal i_0 or i_1 (position of lever). The internal state at any moment is determined by the last state and input signal according to the table

Last State

		q_1	q_2	q_3
	i_0	q_2	q_3	q_1
Input				
	i_1	q_1	q_2	q_3

The output signals, the only externally visible indication of the internal state (the light), are described by the table

State	q_1	q_2	q_3
Output	o_0	o_0	o_1

This example is typical of discrete state machines. They can be described by such tables provided they have only a finite number of possible states.

It will seem that given the initial state of the machine and the input signals it is always possible to predict all future states. This is reminiscent of Laplace's view that from the complete state of the universe at one moment of time, as described by the positions and velocities of all particles, it should be possible to predict all future states. The prediction which we are considering is, however, rather nearer to practicability than that considered by Laplace. The system of the 'universe as a whole' is such that quite small errors in the initial conditions can have an overwhelming effect at a later time. The displacement of a single electron by a billionth of a centimetre at one moment might make the difference between a man being killed by an avalanche a year later, or escaping. It is an essential property of the mechanical systems which we have called 'discrete state machines' that this phenomenon does not occur. Even when we consider the actual physical machines instead of the idealised machines, reasonably accurate knowledge of the state at one moment yields reasonably accurate knowledge any number of steps later.

⌈ As we have mentioned, digital computers fall within the class of dis-   [p. 441] crete state machines. But the number of states of which such a machine is capable is usually enormously large. For instance, the number for the machine now working at Manchester is about $2^{165,000}$, *i.e.* about $10^{50,000}$. Compare this with our example of the clicking wheel described above, which had three states. It is not difficult to see why the number of states should be so immense. The computer includes a store corresponding to the paper used by a human computer. It must be possible to write into the store any one of the combinations of symbols which might have been written on the paper. For simplicity suppose that only digits from 0 to 9 are used as symbols. Variations in handwriting are ignored. Suppose the computer is allowed 100 sheets of paper each containing 50 lines each with room for 30 digits. Then the number of states is $10^{100 \times 50 \times 30}$, *i.e.* $10^{150,000}$. This is about the number of states of three Manchester machines put together. The logarithm to the base two of the number of states is usually called the 'storage capacity' of the machine. Thus the Manchester machine has a storage capacity of about 165,000 and the wheel machine of our example about 1 · 6. If two machines are put together their capacities must be added to obtain the capacity of the resultant machine. This leads to the possibility of statements such as 'The Manchester machine contains 64 magnetic tracks each with a capacity of 2560, eight electronic tubes with a capacity of 1280. Miscellaneous storage amounts to about 300 making a total of 174,380.'

Given the table corresponding to a discrete state machine it is possible to predict what it will do. There is no reason why this calculation should not be carried out by means of a digital computer. Provided it could be carried out sufficiently quickly the digital computer could mimic the behaviour of any discrete state machine. The imitation game could then be played with the machine in question (as B) and the mimicking digital computer (as A) and the interrogator would be unable to distinguish them. Of course the digital computer must have an adequate storage capacity as well as working sufficiently fast. Moreover, it must be programmed afresh for each new machine which it is desired to mimic.

This special property of digital computers, that they can mimic any discrete state machine, is described by saying that they are *universal* machines. The existence of machines with this property has the important consequence that, considerations of speed apart, it is unnecessary to design various new machines to do various computing processes. They can [p. 442] all be ⌈done with one digital computer, suitably programmed for each case. It will be seen that as a consequence of this all digital computers are in a sense equivalent.

We may now consider again the point raised at the end of § 3. It was suggested tentatively that the question, 'Can machines think?' should be replaced by 'Are there imaginable digital computers which would do well in the imitation game?' If we wish we can make this superficially more general and ask 'Are there discrete state machines which would do well?' But in view of the universality property we see that either of these questions is equivalent to this, 'Let us fix our attention on one particular digital computer C. Is it true that by modifying this computer to have an adequate storage, suitably increasing its speed of action, and providing it with an appropriate programme, C can be made to play satisfactorily the part of A in the imitation game, the part of B being taken by a man?'

6 Contrary Views on the Main Question

We may now consider the ground to have been cleared and we are ready to proceed to the debate on our question, 'Can machines think?' and the variant of it quoted at the end of the last section. We cannot altogether abandon the original form of the problem, for opinions will differ as to the appropriateness of the substitution and we must at least listen to what has to be said in this connection.

It will simplify matters for the reader if I explain first my own beliefs in the matter. Consider first the more accurate form of the question. I believe that in about fifty years time it will be possible to programme computers with a storage capacity of about 10^9 to make them play the imitation game so well that an average interrogator will not have more than 70 per cent. chance of making the right identification after five minutes of questioning. The original question, 'Can machines think?' I believe to be too meaningless to deserve discussion. Nevertheless I believe that at the end of the century the use of words and general educated opinion will have altered so much that one will be able to speak of machines thinking without expecting to be contradicted. I believe further that no useful purpose is served by concealing these beliefs. The popular view that scientists proceed inexorably from well-established fact to well-established fact, never being influenced by any unproved conjecture, is quite mistaken. Provided it is made clear which are proved facts and which are conjectures, no harm can result. Conjectures are of great importance since they suggest useful lines of research.

⌈I now proceed to consider opinions opposed to my own.   [p. 443]

(1) The Theological Objection   Thinking is a function of man's immortal soul. God has given an immortal soul to every man and woman, but not to any other animal or to machines. Hence no animal or machine can think.

I am unable to accept any part of this, but will attempt to reply in theological terms. I should find the argument more convincing if animals were classed with men, for there is a greater difference, to my mind, between the typical animate and the inanimate than there is between man and the other animals. The arbitrary character of the orthodox view becomes clearer if we consider how it might appear to a member of some other religious community. How do Christians regard the Moslem view that women have no souls? But let us leave this point aside and return to the main argument. It appears to me that the argument quoted above implies a serious restriction of the omnipotence of the Almighty. It is admitted that there are certain things that He cannot do such as making one equal to two,[1] but should we not believe that He has freedom to confer a soul on an elephant if He sees fit? We might expect that He would only exercise this power in conjunction with a mutation which provided the elephant with an appropriately improved brain to minister to the needs of this soul. An argument of exactly similar form may be made for the case of machines.

---

1 Possibly this view is heretical. St. Thomas Aquinas (*Summa Theologica* quoted by Bertrand Russell, p. 480) states that God cannot make a man to have no soul. But this may not be a real restriction on His powers, but only a result of the fact that men's souls are immortal, and therefore indestructible.

It may seem different because it is more difficult to "swallow". But this really only means that we think it would be less likely that He would consider the circumstances suitable for conferring a soul. The circumstances in question are discussed in the rest of this paper. In attempting to construct such machines we should not be irreverently usurping His power of creating souls, any more than we are in the procreation of children: rather we are, in either case, instruments of His will providing mansions for the souls that He creates.

However, this is mere speculation. I am not very impressed with theological arguments whatever they may be used to support. Such arguments have often been found unsatisfactory in the past. In the time of Galileo it was argued that the texts, "And the sun stood still … and hasted not to go down about a whole day" (Joshua x. 13) and "He laid the foun-

[p. 444] dations of the earth, ⌈ that it should not move at any time" (Psalm cv. 5) were an adequate refutation of the Copernican theory. With our present knowledge such an argument appears futile. When that knowledge was not available it made a quite different impression.

(2) **The 'Heads in the Sand' Objection**   "The consequences of machines thinking would be too dreadful. Let us hope and believe that they cannot do so."

This argument is seldom expressed quite so openly as in the form above. But it affects most of us who think about it at all. We like to believe that Man is in some subtle way superior to the rest of creation. It is best if he can be shown to be necessarily superior, for then there is no danger of him losing his commanding position. The popularity of the theological argument is clearly connected with this feeling. It is likely to be quite strong in intellectual people, since they value the power of thinking more highly than others, and are more inclined to base their belief in the superiority of Man on this power.

I do not think that this argument is sufficiently substantial to require refutation. Consolation would be more appropriate: perhaps this should be sought in the transmigration of souls.

(3) **The Mathematical Objection**   There are a number of results of mathematical logic which can be used to show that there are limitations to the powers of discrete-state machines. The best known of these results

is known as Gödel's theorem,[2] and shows that in any sufficiently powerful logical system statements can be formulated which can neither be proved nor disproved within the system, unless possibly the system itself is inconsistency. There are other, in some respects similar, results due to *Church, Kleene, Rosser,* and *Turing.* The latter result is the most convenient to consider, since it refers directly to machines, whereas the others can only be used in a comparatively indirect argument: for instance if Gödel's theorem is to be used we need in addition to have some means of describing logical systems in terms of machines, and machines in terms of logical systems. The result in question refers to a type of machine which is essentially a digital computer with an infinite capacity. It states that there are certain things that such a machine cannot do. If it is rigged up to give answers to questions as in the imitation game, there will be some questions to which it will either give a wrong answer, or fail to give an answer at all however much time is allowed for a reply. There may, of course, be many such questions, and questions which cannot be answered by one machine may be satisfactorily ⌈ answered by another. We   [p. 445] are of course supposing for the present that the questions are of the kind to which an answer 'Yes' or 'No' is appropriate, rather than questions such as 'What do you think of Picasso?' The questions that we know the machines must fail on are of this type, "Consider the machine specified as follows.... Will this machine ever answer 'Yes' to any question?" The dots are to be replaced by a description of some machine in a standard form, which could be something like that used in § 5. When the machine described bears a certain comparatively simple relation to the machine which is under interrogation, it can be shown that the answer is either wrong or not forthcoming. This is the mathematical result: it is argued that it proves a disability of machines to which the human intellect is not subject.

The short answer to this argument is that although it is established that there are limitations to the powers of any particular machine, it has only been stated, without any sort of proof, that no such limitations apply to the human intellect. But I do not think this view can be dismissed quite so lightly. Whenever one of these machines is asked the appropriate critical question, and gives a definite answer, we know that this answer

---

2 Authors' names in italics refer to the Bibliography.

must be wrong, and this gives us a certain feeling of superiority. Is this feeling illusory? It is no doubt quite genuine, but I do not think too much importance should be attached to it. We too often give wrong answers to questions ourselves to be justified in being very pleased at such evidence of fallibility on the part of the machines. Further, our superiority can only be felt on such an occasion in relation to the one machine over which we have scored our petty triumph. There would be no question of triumphing simultaneously over all machines. In short, then, there might be men cleverer than any given machine, but then again there might be other machines cleverer again, and so on.

Those who hold to the mathematical argument would, I think, mostly be willing to accept the imitation game as a basis for discussion. Those who believe in the two previous objections would probably not be interested in any criteria.

(4) **The Argument from Consciousness**   This argument is very well expressed in *Professor Jefferson's* Lister Oration for 1949, from which I quote. "Not until a machine can write a sonnet or compose a concerto because of thoughts and emotions felt, and not by the chance fall of symbols, could we agree that machine equals brain—that is, not only write it but know that it had written it. No mechanism could feel (and not merely ⌈artificially signal, an easy contrivance) pleasure at its successes, grief when its valves fuse, be warmed by flattery, be made miserable by its mistakes, be charmed by sex, be angry or depressed when it cannot get what it wants."

[p. 446]

This argument appears to be a denial of the validity of our test. According to the most extreme form of this view the only way by which one could be sure that a machine thinks is to *be* the machine and to feel oneself thinking. One could then describe these feelings to the world, but of course no one would be justified in taking any notice. Likewise according to this view the only way to know that a *man* thinks is to be that particular man. It is in fact the solipsist point of view. It may be the most logical view to hold but it makes communication of ideas difficult. A is liable to believe 'A thinks but B does not' whilst B believes 'B thinks but A does not'. Instead of arguing continually over this point it is usual to have the polite convention that everyone thinks.

I am sure that Professor Jefferson does not wish to adopt the extreme and solipsist point of view. Probably he would be quite willing to accept the imitation game as a test. The game (with the player B omitted) is frequently used in practice under the name of *viva voce* to discover whether some one really understands something or has 'learnt it parrot fashion'. Let us listen in to a part of such a *viva voce:*

Interrogator: In the first line of your sonnet which reads 'Shall I compare thee to a summer's day', would not 'a spring day' do as well or better?

Witness: It wouldn't scan.

Interrogator: How about 'a winter's day'? That would scan all right.

Witness: Yes, but nobody wants to be compared to a winter's day.

Interrogator: Would you say Mr. Pickwick reminded you of Christmas?

Witness: In a way.

Interrogator: Yet Christmas is a winter's day, and I do not think Mr. Pickwick would mind the comparison.

Witness: I don't think you're serious. By a winter's day one means a typical winter's day, rather than a special one like Christmas.

And so on. What would Professor Jefferson say if the sonnet-writing machine was able to answer like this in the *viva voce?* I do not know whether he would regard the machine as 'merely ⌈ artificially signalling' [p. 447] these answers, but if the answers were as satisfactory and sustained as in the above passage I do not think he would describe it as 'an easy contrivance'. This phrase is, I think, intended to cover such devices as the inclusion in the machine of a record of someone reading a sonnet, with appropriate switching to turn it on from time to time.

In short then, I think that most of those who support the argument from consciousness could be persuaded to abandon it rather than be forced into the solipsist position. They will then probably be willing to accept our test.

I do not wish to give the impression that I think there is no mystery about consciousness. There is, for instance, something of a paradox connected with any attempt to localise it. But I do not think these mysteries necessarily need to be solved before we can answer the question with which we are concerned in this paper.

(5) Arguments from Various Disabilities   These arguments take the form, "I grant you that you can make machines do all the things you have mentioned but you will never be able to make one to do X". Numerous features X are suggested in this connection. I offer a selection:

Be kind, resourceful, beautiful, friendly (p. 448), have initiative, have a sense of humour, tell right from wrong, make mistakes (p. 448), fall in love, enjoy strawberries and cream (p. 448), make some one fall in love with it, learn from experience (pp. 456 f.), use words properly, be the subject of its own thought (p. 449), have as much diversity of behaviour as a man, do something really new (p. 450). (Some of these disabilities are given special consideration as indicated by the page numbers.)

No support is usually offered for these statements. I believe they are mostly founded on the principle of scientific induction. A man has seen thousands of machines in his lifetime. From what he sees of them he draws a number of general conclusions. They are ugly, each is designed for a very limited purpose, when required for a minutely different purpose they are useless, the variety of behaviour of any one of them is very small, etc., etc. Naturally he concludes that these are necessary properties of machines in general. Many of these limitations are associated with the very small storage capacity of most machines. (I am assuming that the idea of storage capacity is extended in some way to cover machines other than discrete-state machines. ⌈The exact definition does not matter as no mathematical accuracy is claimed in the present discussion.) A few years ago, when very little had been heard of digital computers, it was possible to elicit much incredulity concerning them, if one mentioned their properties without describing their construction. That was presumably due to a similar application of the principle of scientific induction. These applications of the principle are of course largely unconscious. When a burnt child fears the fire and shows that he fears it by avoiding it, I should say that he was applying scientific induction. (I could of course also describe his behaviour in many other ways.) The works and customs of mankind do not seem to be very suitable material to which to apply scientific induction. A very large part of space-time must be investigated, if reliable results are to be obtained. Otherwise we may (as most English children do) decide that everybody speaks English, and that it is silly to learn French.

There are, however, special remarks to be made about many of the disabilities that have been mentioned. The inability to enjoy strawberries and cream may have struck the reader as frivolous. Possibly a machine

[p. 448]

might be made to enjoy this delicious dish, but any attempt to make one do so would be idiotic. What is important about this disability is that it contributes to some of the other disabilities, *e.g.* to the difficulty of the same kind of friendliness occurring between man and machine as between white man and white man, or between black man and black man.

The claim that "machines cannot make mistakes" seems a curious one. One is tempted to retort, "Are they any the worse for that?" But let us adopt a more sympathetic attitude, and try to see what is really meant. I think this criticism can be explained in terms of the imitation game. It is claimed that the interrogator could distinguish the machine from the man simply by setting them a number of problems in arithmetic. The machine would be unmasked because of its deadly accuracy. The reply to this is simple. The machine (programmed for playing the game) would not attempt to give the right answers to the arithmetic problems. It would deliberately introduce mistakes in a manner calculated to confuse the interrogator. A mechanical fault would probably show itself through an unsuitable decision as to what sort of a mistake to make in the arithmetic. Even this interpretation of the criticism is not sufficiently sympathetic. But we cannot afford the space to go into it much further. It seems to me that this criticism depends ⌈ on a confusion between two kinds of mistake. We [p. 449] may call them 'errors of functioning' and 'errors of conclusion'. Errors of functioning are due to some mechanical or electrical fault which causes the machine to behave otherwise than it was designed to do. In philosophical discussions one likes to ignore the possibility of such errors; one is therefore discussing 'abstract machines'. These abstract machines are mathematical fictions rather than physical objects. By definition they are incapable of errors of functioning. In this sense we can truly say that 'machines can never make mistakes'. Errors of conclusion can only arise when some meaning is attached to the output signals from the machine. The machine might, for instance, type out mathematical equations, or sentences in English. When a false proposition is typed we say that the machine has committed an error of conclusion. There is clearly no reason at all for saying that a machine cannot make this kind of mistake. It might do nothing but type out repeatedly '0 = 1'. To take a less perverse example, it might have some method for drawing conclusions by scientific induction. We must expect such a method to lead occasionally to erroneous results.

The claim that a machine cannot be the subject of its own thought can of course only be answered if it can be shown that the machine has *some* thought with *some* subject matter. Nevertheless, 'the subject matter of a machine's operations' does seem to mean something, at least to the people who deal with it. If, for instance, the machine was trying to find a solution of the equation $x^2 - 40x - 11 = 0$ one would be tempted to describe this equation as part of the machine's subject matter at that moment. In this sort of sense a machine undoubtedly can be its own subject matter. It may be used to help in making up its own programmes, or to predict the effect of alterations in its own structure. By observing the results of its own behaviour it can modify its own programmes so as to achieve some purpose more effectively. These are possibilities of the near future, rather than Utopian dreams.

The criticism that a machine cannot have much diversity of behaviour is just a way of saying that it cannot have much storage capacity. Until fairly recently a storage capacity of even a thousand digits was very rare.

The criticisms that we are considering here are often disguised forms of the argument from consciousness. Usually if one maintains that a machine *can* do one of these things, and describes the kind of method that the machine could use, one will not make ⌈ much of an impression. It is thought that the method (whatever it may be, for it must be mechanical) is really rather base. Compare the parenthesis in Jefferson's statement quoted on pp. 445–446.

[p. 450]

(6) **Lady Lovelace's Objection** Our most detailed information of Babbage's Analytical Engine comes from a memoir by *Lady Lovelace*. In it she states, "The Analytical Engine has no pretensions to *originate* anything. It can do *whatever we know how to order it* to perform" (her italics). This statement is quoted by *Hartree* (p. 70) who adds: "This does not imply that it may not be possible to construct electronic equipment which will 'think for itself', or in which, in biological terms, one could set up a conditioned reflex, which would serve as a basis for 'learning'. Whether this is possible in principle or not is a stimulating and exciting question, suggested by some of these recent developments. But it did not seem that the machines constructed or projected at the time had this property."

I am in thorough agreement with Hartree over this. It will be noticed that he does not assert that the machines in question had not got the property, but rather that the evidence available to Lady Lovelace did not encourage her to believe that they had it. It is quite possible that the machines in question had in a sense got this property. For suppose that some discrete-state machine has the property. The Analytical Engine was a universal digital computer, so that, if its storage capacity and speed were adequate, it could by suitable programming be made to mimic the machine in question. Probably this argument did not occur to the Countess or to Babbage. In any case there was no obligation on them to claim all that could be claimed.

This whole question will be considered again under the heading of learning machines.

A variant of Lady Lovelace's objection states that a machine can 'never do anything really new'. This may be parried for a moment with the saw, 'There is nothing new under the sun'. Who can be certain that 'original work' that he has done was not simply the growth of the seed planted in him by teaching, or the effect of following well-known general principles. A better variant of the objection says that a machine can never 'take us by surprise'. This statement is a more direct challenge and can be met directly. Machines take me by surprise with great frequency. This is largely because I do not do sufficient calculation to decide what to expect them to do, or rather because, although I do a calculation, I do it in a hurried, slipshod fashion, taking risks. Perhaps I say to myself, 'I suppose the voltage here ought to be the same as there: anyway let's assume it is'. ⌈Naturally I am   [p. 451] often wrong, and the result is a surprise for me for by the time the experiment is done these assumptions have been forgotten. These admissions lay me open to lectures on the subject of my vicious ways, but do not throw any doubt on my credibility when I testify to the surprises I experience.

I do not expect this reply to silence my critic. He will probably say that such surprises are due to some creative mental act on my part, and reflect no credit on the machine. This leads us back to the argument from consciousness, and far from the idea of surprise. It is a line of argument we must consider closed, but it is perhaps worth remarking that the appreciation of something as surprising requires as much of a 'creative mental act' whether the surprising event originates from a man, a book, a machine or anything else.

The view that machines cannot give rise to surprises is due, I believe, to a fallacy to which philosophers and mathematicians are particularly subject. This is the assumption that as soon as a fact is presented to a mind all consequences of that fact spring into the mind simultaneously with it. It is a very useful assumption under many circumstances, but one too easily forgets that it is false. A natural consequence of doing so is that one then assumes that there is no virtue in the mere working out of consequences from data and general principles.

(7) Argument from Continuity in the Nervous System   The nervous system is certainly not a discrete-state machine. A small error in the information about the size of a nervous impulse impinging on a neuron, may make a large difference to the size of the outgoing impulse. It may be argued that, this being so, one cannot expect to be able to mimic the behaviour of the nervous system with a discrete-state system.

It is true that a discrete-state machine must be different from a continuous machine. But if we adhere to the conditions of the imitation game, the interrogator will not be able to take any advantage of this difference. The situation can be made clearer if we consider some other simpler continuous machine. A differential analyser will do very well. (A differential analyser is a certain kind of machine not of the discrete-state type used for some kinds of calculation.) Some of these provide their answers in a typed form, and so are suitable for taking part in the game. It would not be possible for a digital computer to predict exactly what answers the differential analyser would give to a problem, but it would be quite capable of giving the right sort of answer. For instance, if asked to give the value of π (actually about $3 \cdot 1416$) it would be reasonable $\lceil$ to choose at random between the values $3 \cdot 12, 3 \cdot 13, 3 \cdot 14, 3 \cdot 15, 3 \cdot 16$ with the probabilities of $0 \cdot 05, 0 \cdot 15, 0 \cdot 55, 0 \cdot 19, 0 \cdot 06$ (say). Under these circumstances it would be very difficult for the interrogator to distinguish the differential analyser from the digital computer.

[p. 452]

(8) The Argument from Informality of Behaviour   It is not possible to produce a set of rules purporting to describe what a man should do in every conceivable set of circumstances. One might for instance have a rule that one is to stop when one sees a red traffic light, and to go if one sees a green one, but what if by some fault both appear together? One may perhaps decide that it is safest to stop. But some further difficulty may well arise from this decision later. To attempt to provide rules of conduct to cover every eventuality, even those arising from traffic lights, appears to be impossible. With all this I agree.

From this it is argued that we cannot be machines. I shall try to reproduce the argument, but I fear I shall hardly do it justice. It seems to run something like this. 'If each man had a definite set of rules of conduct by which he regulated his life he would be no better than a machine. But there are no such rules, so men cannot be machines.' The undistributed middle is glaring. I do not think the argument is ever put quite like this, but I believe this is the argument used nevertheless. There may however be a certain confusion between 'rules of conduct' and 'laws of behaviour' to cloud the issue. By 'rules of conduct' I mean precepts such as 'Stop if you see red lights', on which one can act, and of which one can be conscious. By 'laws of behaviour' I mean laws of nature as applied to a man's body such as 'if you pinch him he will squeak'. If we substitute 'laws of behaviour which regulate his life' for 'laws of conduct by which he regulates his life' in the argument quoted the undistributed middle is no longer insuperable. For we believe that it is not only true that being regulated by laws of behaviour implies being some sort of machine (though not necessarily a discrete-state machine), but that conversely being such a machine implies being regulated by such laws. However, we cannot so easily convince ourselves of the absence of complete laws of behaviour as of complete rules of conduct. The only way we know of for finding such laws is scientific observation, and we certainly know of no circumstances under which we could say, "We have searched enough. There are no such laws."

We can demonstrate more forcibly that any such statement would be unjustified. For suppose we could be sure of finding ⌈such laws if they existed. Then given a discrete-state machine it should certainly be possible to discover by observation sufficient about it to predict its future behaviour, and this within a reasonable time, say a thousand years. But this does not seem to be the case. I have set up on the Manchester computer a small programme using only 1000 units of storage, whereby the machine supplied with one sixteen figure number replies with another within two seconds. I would defy anyone to learn from these replies sufficient about the programme to be able to predict any replies to untried values. [p. 453]

(9) The Argument from Extra-Sensory Perception   I assume that the reader is familiar with the idea of extra-sensory perception, and the meaning of the four items of it, *viz.* telepathy, clairvoyance, precognition and psycho-kinesis. These disturbing phenomena seem to deny all our usual scientific ideas. How we should like to discredit them! Unfortunately the statistical evidence, at least for telepathy, is overwhelming. It is very difficult to rearrange one's ideas so as to fit these new facts in. Once one has accepted them it does not seem a very big step to believe in ghosts and bogies. The idea that our bodies move simply according to the known laws of physics, together with some others not yet discovered but somewhat similar, would be one of the first to go.

This argument is to my mind quite a strong one. One can say in reply that many scientific theories seem to remain workable in practice, in spite of clashing with E.S.P.; that in fact one can get along very nicely if one forgets about it. This is rather cold comfort, and one fears that thinking is just the kind of phenomenon where E.S.P. may be especially relevant.

A more specific argument based on E.S.P. might run as follows: "Let us play the imitation game, using as witnesses a man who is good as a telepathic receiver, and a digital computer. The interrogator can ask such questions as 'What suit does the card in my right hand belong to?' The man by telepathy or clairvoyance gives the right answer 130 times out of 400 cards. The machine can only guess at random, and perhaps gets 104 right, so the interrogator makes the right identification." There is an interesting possibility which opens here. Suppose the digital computer contains a random number generator. Then it will be natural to use this to decide what answer to give. But then the random number generator will be subject to the psycho-kinetic powers of the interrogator. Perhaps this psycho-kinesis might cause the machine to guess right more often than would be expected on a probability calculation, so that the interrogator

[p. 454] might still be unable to make the right identification. On the other hand, he might be able to guess right without any questioning, by clairvoyance. With E.S.P. anything may happen.

If telepathy is admitted it will be necessary to tighten our test up. The situation could be regarded as analogous to that which would occur if the interrogator were talking to himself and one of the competitors was listening with his ear to the wall. To put the competitors into a 'telepathy-proof room' would satisfy all requirements.

7   Learning Machines

The reader will have anticipated that I have no very convincing arguments of a positive nature to support my views. If I had I should not have taken such pains to point out the fallacies in contrary views. Such evidence as I have I shall now give.

Let us return for a moment to Lady Lovelace's objection, which stated that the machine can only do what we tell it to do. One could say that a man can 'inject' an idea into the machine, and that it will respond to a certain extent and then drop into quiescence, like a piano string struck by a hammer. Another simile would be an atomic pile of less than critical size: an injected idea is to correspond to a neutron entering the pile from without. Each such neutron will cause a certain disturbance which eventually dies away. If, however, the size of the pile is sufficiently increased, the disturbance caused by such an incoming neutron will very likely go on and on increasing until the whole pile is destroyed. Is there a corresponding phenomenon for minds, and is there one for machines? There does seem to be one for the human mind. The majority of them seem to be 'sub-critical', *i.e.* to correspond in this analogy to piles of sub-critical size. An idea presented to such a mind will on average give rise to less than one idea in reply. A smallish proportion are super-critical. An idea presented to such a mind may give rise to a whole 'theory' consisting of secondary, tertiary and more remote ideas. Animals minds seem to be very definitely sub-critical. Adhering to this analogy we ask, 'Can a machine be made to be super-critical?'

The 'skin of an onion' analogy is also helpful. In considering the functions of the mind or the brain we find certain operations which we can explain in purely mechanical terms. This we say does not correspond to the real mind: it is a sort of skin which we must strip off if we are to find the real mind. But then in what remains we find a further skin to be stripped off, and so on. ⌈Proceeding in this way do we ever come to the [p. 455] 'real' mind, or do we eventually come to the skin which has nothing in it? In the latter case the whole mind is mechanical. (It would not be a discrete-state machine however. We have discussed this.)

These last two paragraphs do not claim to be convincing arguments. They should rather be described as 'recitations tending to produce belief'.

The only really satisfactory support that can be given for the view expressed at the beginning of § 6, will be that provided by waiting for the end of the century and then doing the experiment described. But what can we say in the meantime? What steps should be taken now if the experiment is to be successful?

As I have explained, the problem is mainly one of programming. Advances in engineering will have to be made too, but it seems unlikely that these will not be adequate for the requirements. Estimates of the storage capacity of the brain vary from 10^{10} to 10^{15} binary digits. I incline to the lower values and believe that only a very small fraction is used for the higher types of thinking. Most of it is probably used for the retention of visual impressions. I should be surprised if more than 10^9 was required for satisfactory playing of the imitation game, at any rate against a blind man. (Note—The capacity of the *Encyclopaedia Britannica,* 11th edition, is 2×10^9.) A storage capacity of 10^7 would be a very practicable possibility even by present techniques. It is probably not necessary to increase the speed of operations of the machines at all. Parts of modern machines which can be regarded as analogues of nerve cells work about a thousand times faster than the latter. This should provide a 'margin of safety' which could cover losses of speed arising in many ways. Our problem then is to find out how to programme these machines to play the game. At my present rate of working I produce about a thousand digits of programme a day, so that about sixty workers, working steadily through the fifty years might accomplish the job, if nothing went into the waste-paper basket. Some more expeditious method seems desirable.

In the process of trying to imitate an adult human mind we are bound to think a good deal about the process which has brought it to the state that it is in. We may notice three components,

(a) The initial state of the mind, say at birth,
(b) The education to which it has been subjected,
(c) Other experience, not to be described as education, to which it has been subjected.

[p. 456] ⌈ Instead of trying to produce a programme to simulate the adult mind, why not rather try to produce one which simulates the child's? If this were then subjected to an appropriate course of education one would obtain the adult brain. Presumably the child-brain is something like a note-book as one buys it from the stationers. Rather little mechanism, and lots of blank sheets. (Mechanism and writing are from our point of view almost synonymous.) Our hope is that there is so little mechanism in the child-brain that something like it can be easily programmed. The amount of work in the education we can assume, as a first approximation, to be much the same as for the human child.

We have thus divided our problem into two parts. The child-programme and the education process. These two remain very closely connected. We cannot expect to find a good child-machine at the first attempt. One must experiment with teaching one such machine and see how well it learns. One can then try another and see if it is better or worse. There is an obvious connection between this process and evolution, by the identifications

Structure of the child machine = Hereditary material
Changes of the child machine = Mutations
Judgment of the experimenter = Natural selection

One may hope, however, that this process will be more expeditious than evolution. The survival of the fittest is a slow method for measuring advantages. The experimenter, by the exercise of intelligence, should be able to speed it up. Equally important is the fact that he is not restricted to random mutations. If he can trace a cause for some weakness he can probably think of the kind of mutation which will improve it.

It will not be possible to apply exactly the same teaching process to the machine as to a normal child. It will not, for instance, be provided with legs, so that it could not be asked to go out and fill the coal scuttle. Possibly it might not have eyes. But however well these deficiencies might be overcome by clever engineering, one could not send the creature to school without the other children making excessive fun of it. It must be given some tuition. We need not be too concerned about the legs, eyes, etc. The example of Miss *Helen Keller* shows that education can take place provided that communication in both directions between teacher and pupil can take place by some means or other.

⌈ We normally associate punishments and rewards with the teaching   [p. 457] process. Some simple child-machines can be constructed or programmed on this sort of principle. The machine has to be so constructed that events which shortly preceded the occurrence of a punishment-signal are unlikely to be repeated, whereas a reward-signal increased the probability of repetition of the events which led up to it. These definitions do not presuppose any feelings on the part of the machine. I have done some experiments with one such child-machine, and succeeded in teaching it a few things, but the teaching method was too unorthodox for the experiment to be considered really successful.

The use of punishments and rewards can at best be a part of the teaching process. Roughly speaking, if the teacher has no other means of communicating to the pupil, the amount of information which can reach him does not exceed the total number of rewards and punishments applied. By the time a child has learnt to repeat 'Casabianca' he would probably feel very sore indeed, if the text could only be discovered by a 'Twenty Questions' technique, every 'NO' taking the form of a blow. It is necessary therefore to have some other 'unemotional' channels of communication. If these are available it is possible to teach a machine by punishments and rewards to obey orders given in some language, *e.g.* a symbolic language. These orders are to be transmitted through the 'unemotional' channels. The use of this language will diminish greatly the number of punishments and rewards required.

Opinions may vary as to the complexity which is suitable in the child machine. One might try to make it as simple as possible consistently with the general principles. Alternatively one might have a complete system of logical inference 'built in'.[3] In the latter case the store would be largely occupied with definitions and propositions. The propositions would have various kinds of status, *e.g.* well-established facts, conjectures, mathematically proved theorems, statements given by an authority, expressions having the logical form of proposition but not belief-value. Certain propositions may be described as 'imperatives'. The machine should be so constructed that as soon as an imperative is classed as 'well-established' the appropriate action automatically takes place. To illustrate this, suppose the teacher says to the machine, 'Do your homework now'. This may cause "Teacher says 'Do your homework now'" to be included amongst the well-established facts. Another such fact might be, ⌈ "Everything that teacher says is true". Combining these may eventually lead to the imperative, 'Do your homework now', being included amongst

---

3 Or rather 'programmed in' for our child-machine will be programmed in a digital computer. But the logical system will not have to be learnt.

the well-established facts, and this, by the construction of the machine, will mean that the homework actually gets started, but the effect is very satisfactory. The processes of inference used by the machine need not be such as would satisfy the most exacting logicians. There might for instance be no hierarchy of types. But this need not mean that type fallacies will occur any more than we are bound to fall over unfenced cliffs. Suitable imperatives (expressed *within* the systems, not forming part of the rules *of* the system) such as 'Do not use a class unless it is a subclass of one which has been mentioned by teacher' can have a similar effect to 'Do not go too near the edge'.

The imperatives that can be obeyed by a machine that has no limbs are bound to be of a rather intellectual character, as in the example (doing homework) given above. Important amongst such imperatives will be ones which regulate the order in which the rules of the logical system concerned are to be applied. For at each stage when one is using a logical system, there is a very large number of alternative steps, any of which one is permitted to apply, so far as obedience to the rules of the logical system is concerned. These choices make the difference between a brilliant and a footling reasoner, not the difference between a sound and a fallacious one. Propositions leading to imperatives of this kind might be "When Socrates is mentioned, use the syllogism in Barbara" or "If one method has been proved to be quicker than another, do not use the slower method". Some of these may be 'given by authority', but others may be produced by the machine itself, *e.g.* by scientific induction.

The idea of a learning machine may appear paradoxical to some readers. How can the rules of operation of the machine change? They should describe completely how the machine will react whatever its history might be, whatever changes it might undergo. The rules are thus quite time-invariant. This is quite true. The explanation of the paradox is that the rules which get changed in the learning process are of a rather less pretentious kind, claiming only an ephemeral validity. The reader may draw a parallel with the Constitution of the United States.

An important feature of a learning machine is that its teacher will often be very largely ignorant of quite what is going on inside, although he may still be able to some extent to predict his pupil's behaviour. This should apply most strongly to the ⌈ later education of a machine arising [p. 459] from a child-machine of well-tried design (or programme). This is in clear contrast with normal procedure when using a machine to do computations: one's object is then to have a clear mental picture of the state of the machine at each moment in the computation. This object can only be achieved with a struggle. The view that 'the machine can only do what we know how to order it to do',[4] appears strange in face of this. Most of the programmes which we can put into the machine will result in its doing something that we cannot make sense of at all, or which we regard as completely random behaviour. Intelligent behaviour presumably consists in a departure from the completely disciplined behaviour involved in computation, but a rather slight one, which does not give rise to random behaviour, or to pointless repetitive loops. Another important result of preparing our machine for its part in the imitation game by a process of teaching and learning is that 'human fallibility' is likely to be omitted in a rather natural way, *i.e.* without special 'coaching'. (The reader should reconcile this with the point of view on pp. 448–449.) Processes that are learnt do not produce a hundred per cent. certainty of result; if they did they could not be unlearnt.

It is probably wise to include a random element in a learning machine (see p. 438). A random element is rather useful when we are searching for a solution of some problem. Suppose for instance we wanted to find a number between 50 and 200 which was equal to the square of the sum of its digits, we might start at 51 then try 52 and go on until we got a number that worked. Alternatively we might choose numbers at random until we got a good one. This method has the advantage that it is unnecessary to keep track of the values that have been tried, but the disadvantage that one may try the same one twice, but this is not very important if there are several solutions. The systematic method has the disadvantage that there may be an enormous block without any solutions in the region which has to be investigated first. Now the learning process may be regarded as a search for a form of behaviour which will satisfy the teacher (or some other criterion). Since there is probably a very large number of satisfactory solutions the random method seems to be better than the systematic. It should be noticed that it is used in the analogous process of evolution. But there the systematic method is not possible. How could one keep track

---

4 Compare Lady Lovelace's statement (p. 450), which does not contain the word 'only'.

⌈ of the different genetical combinations that had been tried, so as to avoid [p. 460] trying them again? We may hope that machines will eventually compete with men in all purely intellectual fields. But which are the best ones to start with? Even this is a difficult decision. Many people think that a very abstract activity, like the playing of chess, would be best. It can also be maintained that it is best to provide the machine with the best sense organs that money can buy, and then teach it to understand and speak English. This process could follow the normal teaching of a child. Things would be pointed out and named, etc. Again I do not know what the right answer is, but I think both approaches should be tried.

We can only see a short distance ahead, but we can see plenty there that needs to be done.

Bibliography

Samuel Butler, Erewhon, London, 1865. Chapters 23, 24, 25, *The Book of the Machines.* [ED: *Butler 1872*]

Alonzo Church, "An Unsolvable Problem of Elementary Number Theory", *American J. of Math.*, 58 (1936), 345–363. [ED: *Church 1936*]

K. Gödel, "Über formal unentscheidbare Sätze der Principia Mathematica und verwandter Systeme, I", *Monatshefte für Math. und Phys.*, (1931), 173–189. [ED: *Gödel 1931*]

D. R. Hartree, *Calculating Instruments and Machines*, New York, 1949. [ED: *Hartree 1950*]

S. C. Kleene, "General Recursive Functions of Natural Numbers" *American J. of Math.*, 57 (1935), 153–173 and 219–244. [ED: *Kleene 1935a,b*]

G. Jefferson, "The Mind of Mechanical Man". Lister Oration for 1949. *British Medical Journal*, vol. i (1949), 1105–1121. [ED: *Jefferson 1949*]

Countess of Lovelace, 'Translator's notes to an article on Babbage's Analytical Engine', *Scientific Memoirs* (ed. by R. Taylor), vol. 3 (1842), 691–731. [ED: *Lovelace 1842*]

Bertrand Russell, *History of Western Philosophy*, London, 1940. [ED: *Russell 1940*]

A. M. Turing, "On Computable Numbers, with an Application to the Entscheidungsproblem", *Proc. London Math. Soc.* (2), 42 (1937), 230–265. [ED: *Turing 1936*]

Victoria University of Manchester.

The Ephemera

After publication of the *Mind* article, Turing was requested to speak on the topic of machine cognition on several occasions. Several of these speeches and interviews have extant transcriptions in the Turing Archives (Newman, Turing, Jefferson, and Braithwaite 1952; Turing 1951a,b, *chapters 5–7*), providing a unique opportunity to gauge Turing's views on the topic in a more immediate and informal way than his published papers. Two questions, in particular, regarding the interpretation of the Test as described in the *Mind* article have exercised readers from early on. These are the question of Turing's predictions on passing the Test, and the question of gender in the Test. These little-known ephemera shed light on both of these questions.[1]

When Will the Test Be Passed?

It is popular to pull up the following quote as evidence of Turing's overoptimistic prediction of when a machine might actually pass a Turing Test.

It will simplify matters for the reader if I explain first my own beliefs in the matter.... I believe that in about fifty years' time it will be possible to programme computers, with a storage capacity of about 10^9, to make them play the imitation game so well that an average interrogator

---

1 The first publications of these papers was in 1999 (Copeland 1999). Copeland (2000) has independently noted the importance of these materials for the question discussed here.

will not have more than 70 per cent. chance of making the right identification after five minutes of questioning. (Turing 1950, *chapter 4*)

Many authors have taken this to be a prediction by Turing that
computers would pass the Turing Test some time before the turn of
the millennium,[2] and certainly, his estimate of a gigabyte memory
capacity is easily within current computer capabilities.

The first thing to note about the prediction is that it is not a prediction about the Test per se: Turing expects 70 percent prediction
accuracy, not the more difficult 50 percent expected by chance,
and this after only a limited conversation of five minutes. He is
therefore predicting passage of a test much simpler than the Test.

Not only does the prediction not presuppose a full Turing Test,
but it could well be argued that it had already come to pass with the
advent of Joseph Weizenbaum's ELIZA some thirty-five years early
(Weizenbaum 1976). Weizenbaum developed a simple computer
program that attempted to imitate the parroting conversational
style of a Rogerian psychotherapist. (See figure 1 for a sample interaction.) Although the methods used were quite simple—repeating
the user's question after adjusting some pronouns, throwing in
a stock phrase every now and then—the result was, in its own
way, extremely convincing. Block (1981, *chapter 15*) rehearses the
now familiar story of Weizenbaum's secretary asking him to leave
the room while she talks with the program. It seems likely that
an unsuspecting person might have mistaken ELIZA for a person
70 percent of the time after only a five minute interaction. Nonetheless, ELIZA and similar programs based on that technology are not
on the path to passing the Turing Test.

Returning to the question of Turing's own opinion on the prediction question, the ephemeral material speaks directly to the matter,
much more so than his published quote.

---

2 See for instance, the remark by Purtill (1971, *chapter 10*): "Turing's
prediction that a computer which could play the imitation game would
be built within fifty years from the date of his paper (that is in 2000) was
obviously a wild exaggeration." Similarly, Sampson (1973, *chapter 11*)
states that Turing "predicted that by A.D. 2000 some computer will pass
the test."

Men are all alike.

In what way

They're always bugging us about something or other.

Can you think of a specific example

Well, my boyfriend made me come here.

Your boyfriend made you come here

He says I'm depressed much of the time.

I am sorry to hear you are depressed

It's true. I am unhappy.

Do you think coming here will help you not to be unhappy

I need some help, that much seems certain.

What would it mean to you if you got some help

Perhaps I could get along with my mother.

Tell me more about your family

My mother takes care of me.

Who else in your family takes care of you

My father.

Your father

Figure 1
Sample interaction with ELIZA acting as a psychotherapist, its responses in slanted type (from Weizenbaum (1976))

In "Can Digital Computers Think?", a talk broadcast on the BBC Third Programme in May 1951, Turing seems quite agnostic as to the empirical question of whether the Test would be passed at all.

[It] seems that the wisest ground on which to criticise the description of digital computers as "mechanical brains" or "electronic brains" is that, although they might be programmed to behave like brains, we do not at present know how this should be done. With this outlook I am in full agreement. It leaves open the question as to whether we will or will not eventually succeed in finding such a programme. I, personally, am inclined to believe that such a programme will be found. I think it is probable for instance that at the end of the century it will be possible to program a machine to answer questions in such away that it will be extremely difficult to guess whether the answers are being given by a man or by the machine. ... This only represents my opinion; there is plenty of room for others. (Turing 1951a, *chapter 6*)

There are plenty of hedges in this statement: "inclined to believe", "difficult to guess" (but not impossible), "only my opinion".

More explicitly, a 1952 BBC interview (Newman, Turing, Jefferson, and Braithwaite 1952, *chapter 7*) reproduced here includes the only extant explicit prediction by Turing of when he believes the actual Turing Test is likely to be passed. This discussion among three University of Manchester faculty members (M. H. A. Newman, Professor of Mathematics; Turing, who was then a Reader in Mathematics; and Sir Geoffrey Jefferson, Professor of Neuro-Surgery) and R. B. Braithwaite, Fellow of King's College, Cambridge, was broadcast January 14 and 23, 1952. Following Newman's questioning, Turing makes the following prediction:

Newman: I should like to be there when your match between a man and a machine takes place, and perhaps to try my hand at making up some of the questions. But that will be a long time from now, if the machine is to stand any chance with no questions barred?

Turing: Oh yes, at least 100 years, I should say.

Turing was thus not sanguine about the short term possibility of a thinking machine—not in his life time, or most of ours.

Sex and the Turing Test

Much has been made by several authors of the gender issues in Turing's test. The method that Turing uses to introduce the Test practically guarantees confusion. His personal history—especially his homosexuality—has contributed to speculation about whether Turing was making some special point about gender or sexuality with his test.

In the *Mind* article, Turing first introduces the Test by discussing a preliminary game in which an interrogator (C) of indeterminate sex engages in separate conversations (by means of "teleprinters") with two people whom he knows as X and Y. These two people are a man (A) and a woman (B), who both are trying to convince the interrogator that they are female. C is asked to report which of the two people is A and which is B, that is, he is to assert at the end of the game "X is A and Y is B" or "X is B and Y is A", thereby showing that C has determined which is the true woman and which the pretender. With this preliminary game as background, the actual game is introduced. "We now ask the question, 'What will happen when a machine takes the part of A in this game?' Will the interrogator decide wrongly as often when the game is played like this as he does when the game is played between a man and a woman?" The confusion arises among Turing interpreters from the several ways of understanding "when the game is played like this"; the problem follows from the semantic indeterminacy of the phrase "like this".

As Nunberg (1984) has noted, the phrase "the same x", and related phrases, admit of interpretations that differ based on what properties of the object being picked out are relevant to the discourse at hand. For example, in the sentence "Enzo drives the same car that I used to drive", the phrase "the same car" might mean the same individual (I may have sold it to Enzo) or the same model year (55 Thunderbirds, say), or the same model (Thunderbirds), or the same make (Fords), and so on. There is no fact of the matter as to what "the same x" means independent of its use in a given context. This indeterminacy holds of other phrases that incorporate a notion of identity, for instance, "identify" meaning "to know to be the same as", and, presumably, "like this" meaning "in the same way".

Turing's use of the phrase "like this" thus invites confusion depending on which properties of the imitation game the readers think are relevant for individuating instances of the game for purposes of the analogy Turing makes. On one reading of the phrase, Turing might have meant that the machine A should still pretend to be a woman, and the interrogator should still be informed (erroneously in this instance) that X and Y are a man and a woman and that he should decide which is which. Let us call this the gendered variant. On another, he might have meant the nongendered variant, that not only does the machine replace the man, but the male/female distinction in the game is replaced wholesale by the machine/human distinction. Thus, A should "pretend" to be human, the interrogator is informed that X and Y are a machine and a human and that he should decide which is which. Or he might mean that the interrogator is informed that X and Y are a machine and a woman, and A should imitate not a human in general but a woman in particular. Or any of a host of other possibilities.

Some think the sex issue is a red herring. Davidson (1990), for instance, refers to the "sexist aspect of the Test" as "obviously adventitious, and just as obviously, it can be eliminated by making the choice one between a person and a machine."

But many authors have become exercised over the gendered variant of the Turing Test. For instance, Peter Naur (1986, 183) remarks

This uncertainty seems to me quite important in relation to the more general question of why Turing proposes his particular form of the imitation game, where the interrogator faces two other players, A and B, and has to discover their sexes, instead of a simpler form, in which the interrogator C faces just one other player and has to discover whether this player is human or not. One may suspect that Turing's motivation for his choice of the forms of the game was that he would consider the simpler form too difficult for the machine.

Hayes and Ford (1995) views the test as "a woman and a machine each trying to convince the judge that they are a woman, and the judge's task is still to decide which is the woman and which, therefore, is not. But this judge is not thinking about the differences between women and machines, but between women and men."

Similarly, David Gelernter interprets Turing's proposed test as this complex, gendered variant, which he aptly terms "slightly odd": The test "specifically requires that the interrogator distinguish a genuine woman from a computer that is pretending to be a man. The interrogator's success is judged relative to his success in an earlier round in which he was trying to tell the woman from a man claiming to be a woman. Nowadays these particulars are almost universally set aside, and the Turing Test boiled down to a one-round, person-versus-computer imitation game." (Gelernter 1994, 150)

The most extended version of this view is laid out by Judith Genova (1994, 313–314) in her paper "Turing's Sexual Guessing Game". "[T]he test of the machine's ability to think turns not on whether it can convince the human interrogator that it too is human and not machine, but whether it can fool player C into believing that it is one kind of human rather than another, i.e., male, not female." Genova builds on this view through deconstruction to find a range of novel feminist interpretations of Turing's paper.

It is incontrovertible that the gender view of the Turing Test is fascinating in its own right, especially in the context of Turing's sexual history, independently of whether it was the view that Turing himself had in mind. Nonetheless, ascribing this view to Turing raises the stakes of the argument; it is thus useful to investigate what Turing might have thought himself on the issue.[3]

Although Turing's use of the context-dependent phrase "like this" cannot be interpreted definitively in and of itself, there can still be evidence of one sort or another indicating what Turing had in mind.

There is weak internal evidence in the *Mind* paper itself that the nongendered variant was what Turing had in mind. For instance, he later states "It might be urged that when playing the 'imitation game' the best strategy for the machine may possibly be something other than imitation of the behaviour of a man." (Turing 1950, 435, *chapter 4*) The presupposition here is that imitating a man would be the more obvious tactic, but this is a reasonable tactic only for the nongendered variant. (The gendered variant calls for imitating a woman of course.) Apparently, Turing is using the word 'man' here in a generic sense.[4] More importantly, but at the

---

3 See the papers by Piccinini (2000) and Moor (2001) for further presentations of arguments for the nongendered variant, some drawing on these additional Turing materials. Traiger (2000) provides an extended argument for the contrary view that Turing specifically intended the gendered over the nongendered variant.

4 Other uses by Turing (1950, *chapter 4*) of the generic "man" include: "The new problem has the advantage of drawing a fairly sharp line between the physical and the intellectual capacities of a man." (434) "We do not wish to penalise the machine for its inability to shine in beauty competitions, nor to penalise a man for losing in a race against an aeroplane." (435) "Finally, we wish to exclude from the machines men born in the usual manner." (435) "[I]t is probably possible to rear a complete individual from a single cell of the skin (say) of a man." (436) "The displacement of a single electron by a billionth of a centimetre at one moment might make the difference between a man being killed by an avalanche a year later, or escaping." (440)

same time more abstractly, the "Turing syllogism" (page 136) makes sense only in the nongendered variant.

Here again, the ephemeral Turing clarifies the issue. In his BBC talk, Turing (1951a, *chapter 6, 114*) describes the test as "something like a viva-voce examination, but with the questions and answers all typewritten in order that we need not consider such irrelevant matters as the faithfullness with which the human voice can be imitated", and where we are to "guess whether the answers are being given by a man or by the machine". No reference to gender complicates this description of his previously published Test.

In his BBC interview, Turing describes the Test thus:

The idea of the test is that the machine has to pretend to be a man, by answering questions put to it, and it will only pass if the pretence is reasonably convincing.... We had better suppose that each jury has to judge quite a number of times, and that sometimes they really are dealing with a man and not a machine. That will prevent them saying "It must be a machine" every time without proper consideration. (Newman, Turing, Jefferson, and Braithwaite 1952, *chapter 7, 118*)

This excerpt makes clear first that the interrogator's task is to verify the machine/human distinction, rather than the male/female one, and further, that Turing uses the term "man" in its generic sense. The test that Turing described in this interview is exactly that "simpler form" that Naur incorrectly thought Turing avoided and that Gelernter and Genova believed was a post-Turing construction.

5

Intelligent Machinery, A Heretical Theory

Alan M. Turing

"You cannot make a machine to think for you." This is a commonplace that is usually accepted without question. It will be the purpose of this paper to question it.

Most machinery developed for commercial purposes is intended to carry out some very specific job, and to carry it out with certainty and considerable speed. Very often it does the same series of operations over and over again without any variety. This fact about the actual machinery available is a powerful argument to many in favour of the slogan quoted above. To a mathematical logician this argument is not available, for it has been shown that there are machines theoretically possible which will do something very close to thinking. They will, for instance, test the validity of a formal proof in the system of Principia Mathematica, or even tell of a formula of that system whether it is provable or disprovable. In the case that the formula is neither provable nor disprovable such a machine certainly does not behave in a very satisfactory manner, for it continues to work indefinitely without producing any result at all, but this cannot be regarded as very different from the reaction of the mathematicians, who have for instance worked for hundreds of years on the question as to whether Fermat's last theorem is true or not. For the case of machines of this kind a more subtle argument is necessary. By Gödel's famous theorem, or some similar argument, one can show that however the machine is constructed there are bound to be cases where the machine fails to give an answer, but a mathematician would be able to. On the other hand, the machine has certain advantages over the mathematician. Whatever it does can be relied upon, assuming no mechanical "breakdown", whereas the mathematician makes a certain proportion of mistakes. I believe that this danger of the mathematician making mistakes is an unavoidable corollary of his power of sometimes hitting upon an entirely new method. This seems to be confirmed by the well known fact that the most reliable people will not usually hit upon really new methods.

My contention is that machines can be constructed which will simulate the behaviour of the human mind very closely. They will make mistakes at times, and at times they may make new and very interesting statements, and on the whole the output of them will be worth attention to the same sort of extent as the output of a human mind. The content of this statement lies in the greater frequency expected for the true statements, and it cannot, I think, be given an exact statement. It would not, for instance, be sufficient to say simply that the machine will make any true statement sooner or later, for an example of such a machine would be one which makes all possible statements sooner or later. We know how to construct these, and as they would (probably) produce true and false statements about equally frequently, their verdicts would be quite worthless. It would be the actual reaction of the machine to circumstances that would prove my contention, if indeed it can be proved at all.

Let us go rather more carefully into the nature of this "proof". It is clearly possible to produce a machine which would give a very good account of itself for any range of tests, if the machine were made sufficiently elaborate. However, this again would hardly be considered an adequate proof. Such a machine would give itself away by making the same sort of mistake over and over again, and being quite unable to correct itself, or to be corrected by argument from outside. If the machine were able in some way to "learn by experience" it would be much more impressive. If this were the case there seems to be no real reason why one should not start from a comparatively simple machine, and, by subjecting it to a suitable range of "experience" transform it into one which was more elaborate, and was able to deal with a far greater range of contingencies. This process could probably be hastened by a suitable selection of the experiences to which it was subjected. This might be called "education". But here we have to be careful. It would be quite easy to arrange the experiences in such a way that they automatically caused the structure of the machine to build up into a previously intended form, and this would obviously be a gross form of cheating, almost on a par with having a man inside the machine. Here again the criterion as to what would be considered reasonable in the way of "education" cannot be put into mathematical terms, but I suggest that the following would be adequate in practice. Let us suppose that it is intended that the machine shall understand English, and that owing to its having no hands or feet, and not needing to eat, nor desiring to smoke, it will occupy its time mostly in playing games such as Chess and GO, and possibly Bridge. The machine is provided with a type-writer keyboard on which any remarks to it are typed, and it also types out any remarks that it wishes to make. I suggest that the education of the machine should be entrusted to some highly competent schoolmaster who is interested in the project but who is forbidden any detailed knowledge of the inner workings of the machine. The mechanic who has constructed the machine, however, is permitted to keep the machine in running order, and if he suspects that the machine has been operating incorrectly may put it back to one of its previous positions and ask the schoolmaster to repeat his lessons from that point on, but he may not take any part in the teaching. Since this procedure would only serve to test the *bona fides* of the mechanic, I need hardly say that it would not be adopted at the ex-perimental stages. As I see it, this education process would in practice be an essential to the production of a reasonably intelligent machine within a reasonably short space of time. The human analogy alone suggests this.

I may now give some indication of the way in which such a machine might be expected to function. The machine would incorporate a memory. This does not need very much explanation. It would simply be a list of all the statements that had been made to it or by it, and all the moves it had made and the cards it had played in its games. This would be listed in chronological order. Besides this straightforward memory there would be a number of "indexes of experiences". To explain this idea I will suggest the form which one such index might possibly take. It might be an alphabetical index of the words that had been used giving the "times" at which they had been used, so that they could be looked up in the memory. Another such index might contain patterns of men on parts of a GO board that had occurred. At comparatively late stages of education the memory might be extended to include important parts of the configuration of the machine at each moment, or in other words it would begin to remember what its thoughts had been. This would give rise to fruitful new forms of indexing. New forms of index might be introduced on account of special features observed in the indexes already used. The indexes would be used in this sort of way. Whenever a choice has to be made as to what to do next, features of the present situation are looked up in the indexes available, and the previous choice in the similar situations, and the outcome, good or bad, is discovered. The new choice is made accordingly. This raises a number of problems. If some of the indications are favourable and some are unfavourable what is one to do? The answer to this will probably differ from machine to machine and will also vary with its degree of education. At first probably some quite crude rule will suffice, e.g. to do whichever has the greatest number of votes in its favour. At a very late stage of education the whole question of procedure in such cases will probably have been investigated by the machine itself, by means of some kind of index, and this may result in some highly sophisticated, and, one hopes, highly satisfactory, form of rule. It seems probable however that the comparatively crude forms of rule will themselves be reasonably satisfactory, so that progress can on the whole be made in spite of the crudeness of the choice of rules. This seems to be verified by the fact that engineering problems are sometimes solved by the crudest rule of thumb procedure which deals only with the most superficial aspects of the problem, e.g. whether a function increases or decreases with one of its variables. Another problem raised by this picture of the way behaviour is determined is the idea of "favourable outcome". Without some such idea, corresponding to the "pleasure principle" of the psychologists, it is very difficult to see how to proceed. Certainly it would be most natural to introduce some such thing into the machine. I suggest that there should be two keys which can be manipulated by the schoolmaster, and which represent the ideas of pleasure and pain. At later stages in education the machine would recognise certain other conditions as desirable owing to their having been constantly associated in the past with pleasure, and likewise certain others as undesirable. Certain expressions of anger on the part of the schoolmaster might, for instance, be recognised as so ominous that they could never be overlooked, so that the schoolmaster would find that it became unnecessary to "apply the cane" any more.

To make further suggestions along these lines would perhaps be unfruitful at this stage, as they are likely to consist of nothing more than an analysis of actual methods of education applied to human children. There is, however, one feature that I would like to suggest should be incorporated in the machines, and that is a "random element". Each machine should be supplied with a tape bearing a random series of figures, e.g. 0

and 1 in equal quantities, and this series of figures should be used in the choices made by the machine. This would result in the behaviour of the machine not being by any means completely determined by the experiences to which it was subjected, and would have some valuable uses when one was experimenting with it. By faking the choices made one would be able to control the development of the machine to some extent. One might, for instance, insist on the choice made being a particular one at, say, 10 particular places, and this would mean that about one machine in 1024 or more would develop to as high a degree as the one which had been faked. This cannot very well be given an accurate statement because of the subjective nature of the idea of "degree of development" to say nothing of the fact that the machine that had been faked might have been also fortunate in its unfaked choices.

Let us now assume, for the sake of argument, that these machines are a genuine possibility, and look at the consequences of constructing them. To do so would of course meet with great opposition, unless we have advanced greatly in religious toleration from the days of Galileo. There would be great opposition from the intellectuals who were afraid of being put out of a job. It is probable though that the intellectuals would be mistaken about this. There would be plenty to do, trying to understand what the machines were trying to say, i.e. in trying to keep one's intelligence up to the standard set by the machines, for it seems probable that once the machine thinking method had started, it would not take long to outstrip our feeble powers. There would be no question of the machines dying, and they would be able to converse with each other to sharpen their wits. At some stage therefore we should have to expect the machines to take control, in the way that is mentioned in Samuel Butler's "Erewhon".

6

Can Digital Computers Think?

Alan M. Turing

Digital computers have often been described as mechanical brains. Most scientists probably regard this description as a mere newspaper stunt, but some do not. One mathematician has expressed the opposite point of view to me rather forcefully in the words "It is commonly said that these machines are not brains, but you and I know that they are." In this talk I shall try to explain the ideas behind the various possible points of view, though not altogether impartially. I shall give most attention to the view which I hold myself, that it is not altogether unreasonable to describe digital computers as brains. A different point of view has already been put by Professor Hartree.

First we may consider the naive point of view of the man in the street. He hears amazing accounts of what these machines can do: most of them apparently involve intellectual feats of which he would be quite incapable. He can only explain it by supposing that the machine is a sort of brain, though he may prefer simply to disbelieve what he has heard.

The majority of scientists are contemptuous of this almost superstitious attitude. They know something of the principles on which the machines are constructed and of the way in which they are used. Their outlook was well summed up by Lady Lovelace over a hundred years ago, speaking of Babbage's Analytical Engine. She said, as Hartree has already quoted, "The Analytical Engine has no pretensions whatever to *originate* anything. It can do whatever *we know how to order it to perform*." This very well describes the way in which digital computers are actually used at the present time, and in which they will probably mainly be used for many years to come. For any one calculation the whole procedure that the machine is to go through is planned out in advance by a mathematician.

The less doubt there is about what is going to happen the better the mathematician is pleased. It is like planning a military operation. Under these circumstances it is fair to say that the machine doesn't originate anything.

There is however a third point of view, which I hold myself. I agree with Lady Lovelace's dictum as far as it goes, but I believe that its validity depends on considering how digital computers *are* used rather than how they *could be* used. In fact I believe that they could be used in such a manner that they could appropriately be described as brains. I should also say that "If any machine can appropriately be described as a brain, then any digital computer can be so described."

This last statement needs some explanation. It may appear rather startling, but with some reservations it appears to be an inescapable fact. It can be shown to follow from a characteristic property of digital computers, which I will call their *universality*. A digital computer is a *universal* machine in the sense that it can be made to replace any machine of a certain very wide class. It will not replace a bulldozer or a steam-engine or a telescope, but it will replace any rival design of calculating machine, that is to say any machine into which one can feed data and which will later print out results. In order to arrange for our computer to imitate a given machine it is only necessary to programme the computer to calculate what the machine in question would do under given circumstances, and in particular what answers it would print out. The computer can then be made to print out the same answers.

If now some particular machine can be described as a brain we have only to programme our digital computer to imitate it and it will also be a brain. If it is accepted that real brains, as found in animals, and in particular in men, are a sort of machine it will follow that our digital computer suitably programmed, will behave like a brain.

This argument involves several assumptions which can quite reasonably be challenged. I have already explained that the machine to be imitated must be more like a calculator than a bulldozer. This is merely a reflection of the fact that we are speaking of mechanical analogues of brains, rather than of feet or jaws. It was also necessary that this machine should be of the sort whose behaviour is in principle predictable by calculation. We certainly do not know how any such calculation should be done, and it was even argued by Sir Arthur Eddington that on account of the indeterminacy principle in quantum mechanics no such prediction is even theoretically possible.

Another assumption was that the storage capacity of the computer used should be sufficient to carry out the prediction of the behaviour of the machine to be imitated. It should also have sufficient speed. Our present computers probably have not got the necessary storage capacity, though they may well have the speed. This means in effect that if we wish to imitate anything so complicated as the human brain we need a very much larger machine than any of the computers at present available. We probably need something at least a hundred times as large as the Manchester Computer. Alternatively of course a machine of equal size or smaller would do if sufficient progress were made in the technique of storing information.

It should be noticed that there is no need for there to be any increase in the complexity of the computers used. If we try to imitate ever more complicated machines or brains we must use larger and larger computers to do it. We do not need to use successively more complicated ones. This may appear paradoxical, but the explanation is not difficult. The imitation of a machine by a computer requires not only that we should have made the computer, but that we should have programmed it appropriately. The more complicated the machine to be imitated the more complicated must the programme be.

This may perhaps be made clearer by an analogy. Suppose two men both wanted to write their autobiographies, and that one had had an eventful life, but very little had happened to the other. There would be two difficulties troubling the man with the more eventful life more seriously than the other. He would have to spend more on paper and he would have to take more trouble over thinking what to say. The supply of paper would not be likely to be a serious difficulty, unless for instance he were on a desert island, and in any case it could only be a technical or a financial problem. The other difficulty would be more fundamental and would become more serious still if he were not writing his life but a work on something he knew nothing about, let us say about family life on Mars. Our problem of programming a computer to behave like a brain is something like trying to write this treatise on a desert island. We cannot get the storage capacity we need: in other words we cannot get enough paper to write the treatise on, and in any case we don't know what we should write down if we had it. This is a poor state of affairs, but, to continue the analogy, it is something to know how to write, and to appreciate the fact that most knowledge can be embodied in books.

In view of this it seems that the wisest ground on which to criticise the description of digital computers as "mechanical brains" or "electronic brains" is that, although they might be programmed to behave like brains, we do not at present know how this should be done. With this outlook I am in full agreement. It leaves open the question as to whether we will or will not eventually succeed in finding such a programme. I, personally, am inclined to believe that such a programme will be found. I think it is probable for instance that at the end of the century it will be possible to programme a machine to answer questions in such a way that it will be extremely difficult to guess whether the answers are being given by a man or by the machine. I am imagining something like a viva-voce examination, but with the questions and answers all typewritten in order that we need not consider such irrelevant matters as the faithfulness with which the human voice can be imitated. This only represents my opinion: there is plenty of room for others.

There are still some difficulties. To behave like a brain seems to involve free will, but the behaviour of a digital computer, when it has been pro-grammed, is completely determined. These two facts must somehow be reconciled, but to do so seems to involve us in an age-old controversy, that of "free will and determinism". There are two ways out. It may be that the feeling of free will which we all have is an illusion. Or it may be that we really have got free will, but that there is no way of telling from our behaviour that this is so. In the latter case, however well a ma-chine imitates a man's behaviour it is to be regarded as a mere sham. I do not know how we can ever decide between these alternatives but whichever is the correct one it is certain that a machine which is to imi-tate a brain must appear to behave as if it had free will, and it may well be asked how this is to be achieved. One possibility is to make its behaviour depend on something like a roulette wheel or a supply of radium. The behaviour of these may perhaps be predictable, but if so, we do not know how to do the prediction.

It is, however, not really even necessary to do this. It is not difficult to design machines whose behaviour appears quite random to anyone who does not know the details of their construction. Naturally enough the inclusion of this random element, whichever technique is used, does not solve our main problem, how to programme a machine to imitate the brain, or as we might say more briefly, if less accurately, to think. But it gives us some indication of what the process will be like. We must not always expect to know what the computer is going to do. We should be pleased when the machine surprises us, in rather the same way as one is pleased when a pupil does something which he had not been explicitly taught to do.

Let us now reconsider Lady Lovelace's dictum. "The machine can do whatever *we know how to order it to perform*." The sense of the rest of the passage is such that one is tempted to say that the machine can *only* do what we know how to order it to perform. But I think this would not be true. Certainly the machine can only do what we *do* order it to perform, anything else would be a mechanical fault. But there is no need to suppose that, when we give it its orders we know what we are doing, what the consequences of these orders are going to be. One does not need to be able to understand how these orders lead to the machine's subsequent behaviour, any more than one needs to understand the mechanism of germination when one puts a seed in the ground. The plant comes up whether one understands or not. If we give the machine a programme which results in its doing something interesting which we had not anticipated I should be inclined to say that the machine *had* originated something, rather than to claim that its behaviour was implicit in the programme, and therefore that the originality lies entirely with us.

I will not attempt to say much about how this process of "programming a machine to think" is to be done. The fact is that we know very little about it, and very little research has yet been done. There are plentiful ideas, but we do not yet know which of them are of importance. As in the detective stories, at the beginning of the investigation any trifle may be of importance to the investigator. When the problem has been solved, only the essential facts need to be told to the jury. But at present we have nothing worth putting before a jury. I will only say this, that I believe the process should bear a close relation to that of teaching.

I have tried to explain what are the main rational arguments for and against the theory that machines could be made to think, but something should also be said about the irrational arguments. Many people are extremely opposed to the idea of a machine that thinks, but I do not believe that it is for any of the reasons that I have given, or any other rational reason, but simply because they do not like the idea. One can see many features which make it unpleasant. If a machine can think, it might think more intelligently than we do, and then where should we be? Even if we could keep the machines in a subservient position, for instance by turning off the power at strategic moments, we should, as a species, feel greatly humbled. A similar danger and humiliation threatens us from the possibility that we might be superseded by the pig or the rat. This is a theoretical possibility which is hardly controversial, but we have lived with pigs and rats for so long without their intelligence much increasing, that we no longer trouble ourselves about this possibility. We feel that if it is to happen at all it will not be for several million years to come. But this new danger is much closer. If it comes at all it will almost certainly be within the next millennium. It is remote but not astronomically remote, and is certainly something which can give us anxiety.

It is customary, in a talk or article on this subject, to offer a grain of comfort, in the form of a statement that some particularly human characteristic could never be imitated by a machine. It might for instance be said that no machine could write good English, or that it could not be influenced by sex-appeal or smoke a pipe. I cannot offer any such comfort, for I believe that no such bounds can be set. But I certainly hope and believe that no great efforts will be put into making machines with the most distinctively human, but non-intellectual characteristics such as the shape of the human body; it appears to me to be quite futile to make such attempts and their results would have something like the unpleasant quality of artificial flowers. Attempts to produce a thinking machine seem to me to be in a different category. The whole thinking process is still rather mysterious to us, but I believe that the attempt to make a thinking machine will help us greatly in finding out how we think ourselves.

7

Can Automatic Calculating Machines Be Said to Think?

M. H. A. Newman, Alan M. Turing, Sir Geoffrey Jefferson, and R. B. Braithwaite

Braithwaite: We're here today to discuss whether calculating machines can be said to think in any proper sense of the word. Thinking is ordinarily regarded as so much a speciality of man, and perhaps of other higher animals, that the question may seem too absurd to be discussed. But, of course, it all depends on what is to be included in thinking. The word is used to cover a multitude of different activities. What would you, Jefferson, as a physiologist, say were the most important elements involved in thinking?

Jefferson: I don't think that we need waste too much time on a definition of thinking since it will be hard to get beyond phrases in common usage, such as having ideas in the mind, cogitating, meditating, deliberating, solving problems or imagining. Philologists say that the word "Man" is derived from a Sanskrit word that means "to think", probably in the sense of judging between one idea and another. I agree that we could no longer use the word "thinking" in a sense that restricted it to man. No one would deny that many animals think, though in a very limited way. They lack insight. For example, a dog learns that it is wrong to get on cushions or chairs with muddy paws, but he only learns it as a venture that doesn't pay. He has no conception of the real reason, that he damages fabrics by doing that.

The average person would perhaps be content to define thinking in very general terms such as revolving ideas in the mind, of having notions in one's head, of having one's mind occupied by a problem, and so on. But it is only right to add that our minds are occupied much of the time with trivialities. One might say in the end that thinking was the general result of having a sufficiently complex nervous system. Very simple ones do not provide the creature with any problems that are not answered by simple reflex mechanisms. Thinking then becomes all the things that go on in one's brain, things that often end in an action but don't necessarily do so. I should say that it was the sum total of what the brain of man or animal does. Turing, what do you think about it? Have you a mechanical definition?

Turing: I don't want to give a definition of thinking, but if I had to I should probably be unable to say anything more about it than that it was a sort of buzzing that went on inside my head. But I don't really see that we need to agree on a definition at all. The important thing is to try to draw a line between the properties of a brain, or of a man, that we want to discuss, and those that we don't. To take an extreme case, we are not interested in the fact that the brain has the consistency of cold porridge. We don't want to say "This machine's quite hard, so it isn't a brain, and so it can't think." I would like to suggest a particular kind of *test* that one might apply to a machine. You might call it a test to see whether the machine thinks, but it would be better to avoid begging the question, and say that the machines that pass are (let's say) "Grade A" machines. The idea of the test is that the machine has to try and pretend to be a man, by answering questions put to it, and it will only pass if the pretence is reasonably convincing. A considerable proportion of a jury, who should not be expert about machines, must be taken in by the pretence. They aren't allowed to see the machine itself—that would make it too easy. So the machine is kept in a far away room and the jury are allowed to ask it questions, which are transmitted through to it: it sends back a typewritten answer.

Braithwaite: Would the questions have to be sums, or could I ask it what it had had for breakfast?

Turing: Oh yes, anything. And the questions don't really have to be questions, any more than questions in a law court are really questions. You know the sort of thing. "I put it to you that you are only pretending to be a man" would be quite in order. Likewise the machine would be permitted all sorts of tricks so as to appear more man-like, such as waiting a bit before giving the answer, or making spelling mistakes, but it can't make smudges on the paper, any more than one can send smudges by telegraph. We had better suppose that each jury has to judge quite a number of times, and that sometimes they really are dealing with a man and not a machine. That will prevent them saying "It must be a machine" every time without proper consideration.

Well, that's my test. Of course I am not saying at present either that machines really could pass the test, or that they couldn't. My suggestion is just that this is the question we should discuss. It's not the same as "Do machines think", but it seems near enough for our present purpose, and raises much the same difficulties.

Newman: I should like to be there when your match between a man and a machine takes place, and perhaps to try my hand at making up some of the questions. But that will be a long time from now, if the machine is to stand any chance with no questions barred?

Turing: Oh yes, at least 100 years, I should say.

Jefferson: Newman, how well would existing machines stand up to this test? What kind of things can they do now?

Newman: Of course, their strongest line is mathematical computing, which they were designed to do, but they would also do well at some questions that don't look numerical, but can easily be made so, like solving a chess problem or looking you up a train in the time-table.

Braithwaite: Could they do that?

Newman: Yes. Both these jobs can be done by trying all the possibilities, one after another. The whole of the information in an ordinary time-table would have to be written in as part of the programme, and the simplest possible routine would be one that found the trains from London to Manchester by testing every train in the timetable to see if it calls at both places, and printing out those that do. Of course, this is a dull, plodding method, and you could improve on it by using a more complicated routine, but if I have understood Turing's test properly, you are not allowed to go behind the scenes and criticise the method, but must abide by the scoring on correct answers, found reasonably quickly.

Jefferson: Yes, but all the same a man who has to look up trains frequently gets better at it, as he learns his way about the time-table. Suppose I give a machine the same problem again, can it learn to do better without going through the whole rigmarole of trying everything over every time?

I'd like to have your answer to that because it's such an important point. Can machines learn to do better with practice?

Newman: Yes, it could. Perhaps the chess problem provides a better illustration of this. First I should mention that *all* the information required in any job—the numbers, times of trains, positions of pieces, or whatever it is, and also the instructions saying what is to be done with them—all this material is stored in the same way. (In the Manchester machine it is stored as a pattern on something resembling a television screen.) As the work goes on the pattern is changed. Usually it is the part of the pattern that contains the data that changes, while the instructions stay fixed. But it is just as simple to arrange that the instructions themselves shall be changed now and then. Well, now a programme could be composed that would cause the machine to do this: a 2-move chess problem is recorded into the machine in some suitable coding, and whenever the machine is started, a white move is chosen at random (there is a device for making random choices in our machine). All the consequences of this move are now analysed, and if it does *not* lead to forced mate in two moves, the machine prints, say, "P–Q3, wrong move", and stops. But the analysis shows that when the right move is chosen the machine not only prints, say, "B–Q5, solution", but it changes the instruction calling for a random choice to one that says "Try B–Q5". The result is that whenever the machine is started again it will immediately print out the right solution—and this without the man who made up the routine knowing beforehand what it was. Such a routine could certainly be made now, and I think this can fairly be called learning.

Jefferson: Yes, I suppose it is. Human beings learn by repeating the same exercises until they have perfected them. Of course it goes further, and at the same time we learn generally to shift the knowledge gained about one thing to another set of problems, seeing relevances and relationships. Learning means remembering. How long can a machine store information for?

Newman: Oh, at least as long as a man's lifetime, if it is refreshed occasionally.

Jefferson: Another difference would be that in the learning process there is much more frequent intervention by teachers, parental or otherwise, guiding the arts of learning. You mathematicians put the programme once into the machine and leave it to it. You wouldn't get any distance at all with human beings if that is what you did. In fact, the only time you do that in the learning period is at examinations.

Turing: It's quite true that when a child is being taught, his parents and teachers are repeatedly intervening to stop him doing this or encourage him to do that. But this will not be any the less so when one is trying to teach a machine. I have made some experiments in teaching a machine to do some simple operation, and a very great deal of such intervention was needed before I could get any results at all. In other words the machine learnt so slowly that it needed a great deal of teaching.

Jefferson: But who was learning, you or the machine?

Turing: Well, I suppose we both were. One will have to find out how to make machines that will learn more quickly if there is to be any real success. One hopes too that there will be a sort of snowball effect. The more things the machine has learnt the easier it ought to be for it to learn others. In learning to do any particular thing it will probably also be learning to learn more efficiently. I am inclined to believe that when one has taught it to do certain things one will find that some other things which one had planned to teach it are happening without any special teaching being required. This certainly happens with an intelligent human mind, and if it doesn't happen when one is teaching a machine there is something lacking in the machine. What do you think about learning possibilities, Braithwaite?

Braithwaite: No-one has mentioned what seems to me the great difficulty about learning, since we've only discussed learning to solve a particular problem. But the most important part of human learning is learning from experience—not learning from one particular kind of experience, but being able to learn from experience in general. A machine can easily be constructed with a feed-back device so that the programming of the machine is controlled by the relation of its output to some feature in its external environment—so that the working of the machine in relation to the environment is self-corrective. But this requires that it should be some particular feature of the environment to which the machine has to adjust itself. The peculiarity of men and animals is that they have the power of adjusting themselves to almost all the features. The feature to which adjustment is made on a particular occasion is the one the man is attending to and he attends to what he is *interested in*. His interests are determined, by and large, by his appetites, desires, drives, instincts—all the things that together make up his "springs of action". If we want to construct a machine which will vary its attention to things in its environment so that it will sometimes adjust itself to one and sometimes to another, it would seem to be necessary to equip the machine with something corresponding to a set of appetites. If the machine is built to be treated only as a domestic pet, and is spoon-fed with particular problems, it will not be able to learn in the varying way in which human beings learn. This arises from the necessity of adapting behaviour suitably to environment if human appetites are to be satisfied.

Jefferson: Turing, you spoke with great confidence about what you are going to be able to do. You make it sound as if it would be fairly easy to modify construction so that the machine reacted more like a man. But I recollect that from the time of Descartes and Borelli on people have said that it would be only a matter of a few years, perhaps 3 or 4 or maybe 50, and a replica of man would have been artificially created. We shall be wrong, I am sure, if we give the impression that these things would be easy to do.

Newman: I agree that we are getting rather far away from computing machines as they exist at present. These machines have rather restricted appetites, and they can't blush when they're embarrassed, but its quite hard enough, and I think a very interesting problem, to discover how near these actually existing machines can get to thinking. Even if we stick to the reasoning side of thinking, it is a long way from solving chess problems to the invention of new mathematical concepts or making a generalisation that takes in ideas that were current before, but had never been brought together as instances of a single general notion.

Braithwaite: For example?

Newman: The different kinds of number. There are the integers. 0, 1, −2, and so on; there are the real numbers used in comparing lengths, for example the circumference of a circle and its diameter; and the complex numbers involving $\sqrt{-1}$; and so on. It is not at all obvious that these are instances of one thing, "number". The Greek mathematicians used entirely different words for the integers and the real numbers, and had no single idea to cover both. It is really only recently that the general notion of kinds of number has been abstracted from these instances and accurately defined. To make this sort of generalisation you need to have the power of recognising similarities, seeing analogies between things that had not been put together before. It is not just a matter of testing things for a specified property and classifying them accordingly. The concept itself has to be framed, something has to be created, say the idea of a number-field. Can we even guess at the way a machine could make such an invention from a programme composed by a man who had not the concept in his own mind?

Turing: It seems to me, Newman, that what you said about "trying out possibilities" as a method applies to quite an extent, even when a machine is required to do something as advanced as finding a useful new concept. I wouldn't like to have to define the meaning of the word "concept", nor to give rules for rating their usefulness, but whatever they are they've got outward and visible forms, which are words and combinations of words. A machine could make up such combinations of words more or less at random, and then give them marks for various merits.

Newman: Wouldn't that take a prohibitively long time?

Turing: It would certainly be shockingly slow, but it could start on easy things, such as lumping together rain, hail, snow and sleet, under the word "precipitation". Perhaps it might do more difficult things later on if it was learning all the time how to improve its methods.

Braithwaite: I don't think there's much difficulty about seeing analogies that can be formally analysed and explicitly stated. It is then only a question of designing the machine so that it can recognise similarities of mathematical structure. The difficulty arises if the analogy is a vague one about which little more can be said than that one has a feeling that there is some sort of similarity between two cases but one hasn't any idea as to the respect in which the two cases are similar. A machine can't recognise similarities when there is nothing in its programme to say what are the similarities it is expected to recognise.

Turing: I think you could make a machine spot an analogy, in fact it's quite a good instance of how a machine could be made to do some of those things that one usually regards as essentially a human monopoly. Suppose that someone was trying to explain the double negative to me, for instance, that when something isn't not green it must be green, and he couldn't quite get it across. He might say "Well, it's like crossing the road. You cross it, and then you cross it again, and you're back where you started." This remark might just clinch it. This is one of the things one would like to work with machines, and I think it would be likely to happen with them. I imagine that the way analogy works in our brains is something like this. When two or more sets of ideas have the same pattern of logical connections, the brain may very likely economise parts by using some of them twice over, to remember the logical connections both in the one case and in the other. One must suppose that some part of my brain was used twice over in this way, once for the idea of double negation and once for crossing the road, there and back. I am really supposed to know about both these things but can't get what it is the man is driving at, so long as he is talking about all those dreary nots and not-nots. Somehow it doesn't get through to the right part of the brain. But as soon as he says his piece about crossing the road it gets through to the right part, but by a different route. If there is some such purely mechanical explanation of how this argument by analogy goes on in the brain, one could make a digital computer do the same.

Jefferson: Well, there isn't a mechanical explanation in terms of cells and connecting fibres in the brain.

Braithwaite: But could a machine really do this? How would it do it?

Turing: I've certainly left a great deal to the imagination. If I had given a longer explanation I might have made it seem more certain that what I was describing was feasible, but you would probably feel rather uneasy about it all, and you'd probably exclaim impatiently. "Well, yes. I see that a machine could do all that, but I wouldn't call it thinking." As soon as one can see the cause and effect working themselves out in the brain, one regards it as not being thinking, but a sort of unimaginative donkey-work. From this point of view one might be tempted to define thinking as consisting of "those mental processes that we don't understand". If this is right then to make a thinking machine is to make one which does interesting things without our really understanding quite how it is done.

Jefferson: If you mean that we don't know the wiring in men, as it were, that is quite true.

Turing: No, that isn't at all what I mean. We know the wiring of our machine, but it already happens there in a limited sort of way. Sometimes a computing machine does do something rather weird that we hadn't expected. In principle one could have predicted it, but in practice it's usually too much trouble. Obviously if one were to predict everything a computer was going to do one might just as well do without it.

Newman: It is quite true that people are disappointed when they discover what the big computing machines actually do, which is just to add and multiply, and use the results to decide what further additions and multiplications to do. *"That's* not thinking", is the natural comment, but this is rather begging the question. If you go into one of the ancient churches in Ravenna you see some most beautiful pictures round the walls, but if you peer at them through binoculars you might say, "Why, they aren't really pictures at all, but just a lot of little coloured stones with cement in between." The machine's processes are mosaics of very simple standard parts, but the designs can be of great complexity, and it is not obvious where the limit is to the patterns of thought they could imitate.

Braithwaite: But how many stones are there in your mosaic? Jefferson, is there a sufficient multiplicity of the cells in the brain for them to behave like a computing machine?

Jefferson: Yes, there are thousands, tens of thousands more cells in the brain than there are in a computing machine, because the present machine contains—how many did you say?

Turing: Half a million digits. I think we can assume that is the equivalent of half a million nerve cells.

Braithwaite: If the brain works like a computing machine then the present computing machine cannot do all the things the brain does. Agreed; but if a computing machine were made that could do all the things the brain does, wouldn't it require more digits than there is room for in the brain?

Jefferson: Well. I don't know. Suppose that it is right to equate digits in a machine with nerve cells in a brain. There are various estimates, somewhere between ten thousand million and fifteen thousand million cells are supposed to be there. Nobody knows for certain, you see. It is a colossal number. You would need 20,000 or more of your machines to equate digits with nerve cells. But it is not, surely, just a question of size. There would be too much logic in your huge machine. It wouldn't be really like a human output of thought. To make it more like, a lot of the machine parts would have to be designed quite differently to give greater flexibility and more diverse possibilities of use. It's a very tall order indeed.

Turing: It really is the size that matters in this case. It is the amount of information that can be stored up. If you think of something very complicated that you want one of these machines to do, you may find the particular machine you have got won't do, but if any machine can do it at all, then it can be done by your first computer, simply increased in its storage capacity.

Jefferson: If we are really to get near to anything that can be truly called "thinking" the effects of external stimuli cannot be missed out; the intervention of all sorts of extraneous factors, like the worries of having to make one's living, or pay one's taxes, or get food that one likes. These are not in any sense minor factors, they are very important indeed, and worries concerned with them may greatly interfere with good thinking, especially with creative thinking. You see a machine has no environment, and man is in constant relation to his environment, which, as it were punches him whilst he punches back. There is a vast background of memories in a man's brain that each new idea or experience has to fit in with. I wonder if you could tell me how far a calculating machine meets that situation. Most people agree that man's first reaction to a new idea (such as the one we are discussing today) is one of rejection, often immediate and horrified denial of it. I don't see how a machine could as it were say "Now Professor Newman or Mr. Turing, I don't like this programme at all that you've just put into me, in fact I'm not going to have anything to do with it."

Newman: One difficulty about answering that is one that Turing has already mentioned. If someone says, "Could a machine do this, e.g. could it say 'I don't like the programme you have just put into me'", and a lirogramme for doing that very thing is duly produced, it is apt to have an artificial and ad hoc air, and appear to be more of a trick than a serious answer to the question. It is like those passages in the Bible, which worried me as a small boy, that say that such and such was done "that the prophecy might be fulfilled which says" so and so. This always seemed to me a most unfair way of making sure that the prophecy came true. If I answer your question, Jefferson, by making a routine which simply caused the machine to say just the words "Newman and Turing, I don't like your programme", you would certainly feel this was a rather childish trick, and not the answer to what you really wanted to know. But yet it's hard to pin down what you want.

Jefferson: I want the machine to reject the problem because it offends it in some way. That leads me to enquire what the ingredients are of ideas that we reject because we instinctively don't care for them. I don't know why I like some pictures and some music and am bored by other sorts. But I'm not going to carry that line on because we are all different, our dislikes are based on our personal histories and probably too on small differences of construction in all of us. I mean by heredity. Your machines have no genes, no pedigrees. Mendelian inheritance means nothing to wireless valves. But I don't want to score debating points! We ought to make it clear that not even Turing thinks that all that he has to do is to put a skin on the machine and that it is alive! We've been trying for a more limited objective whether the sort of thing that machines do can be considered as thinking. But is not your machine more certain than any human being of getting its problem right at once, and infallibly?

Newman: Oh!

Turing: Computing machines aren't really infallible at all. Making up checks on their accuracy is quite an important part of the art of using them. Besides making mistakes they sometimes haven't done quite the calculation one had expected, and one gets something that might be called a "misunderstanding".

Jefferson: At any rate, they are not influenced by the emotions. You have only to upset a person enough and he becomes confused, he can't think of the answers and may make a fool of himself. It is high emotional content of mental processes in the human being that makes him quite different from a machine. It seems to me to come from the great complexity of his nervous system with its 10^{10} cells and also from his endocrine system which imports all sorts of emotions and instincts, such as those to do with sex. Man is essentially a chemical machine, he is much affected by hunger and fatigue, by being "out of sorts" as we say, also by innate judgements, and by sexual urges. This chemical side is tremendously important, not the least so because the brain does exercise a remote control over the most important chemical processes that go on in our bodies. Your machines don't have to bother with that, with being tired or cold or happy or satisfied. They show no delight at having done something never done before. No, they are "mentally" simple things. I mean that however complicated their structure is (and I know it *is* very complicated), compared with man they are very simple and perform their tasks with an absence of distracting thoughts which is quite *inhuman*.

Braithwaite: I'm not sure that I agree. I believe that it will be necessary to provide the machine with something corresponding to appetites, or other "springs of action", in order that it will pay enough attention to relevant features in its environment to be able to learn from experience. Many psychologists have held that the emotions in men are by-products of their appetites and that they serve a biological function in calling higher levels of mental activity into play when the lower levels are incapable of coping with an external situation. For example, one does not feel afraid when there is no danger, or a danger which can be avoided more or less automatically: fear is a symptom showing that the danger has to be met by conscious thought. Perhaps it will be impossible to build a machine capable of learning in general from experience without incorporating in it an emotional apparatus, the function of which will be to switch over to a different part of the machine when the external environment differs too much from what would satisfy the machine's appetites by more than a certain amount. I don't want to suggest that it will be necessary for the machine to be able to throw a fit of tantrums. But in humans tantrums frequently fulfil a definite function—that of escaping from responsibility; and to protect a machine against a too hostile environment it may be essential to allow it, as it were, to go to bed with a neurosis, or psychogenic illness—just as, in a simpler way, it is provided with a fuse to blow, if the electric power working it threatens its continued existence.

Turing: Well, I don't envisage teaching the machine to throw temperamental scenes. I think some such effects are likely to occur as a sort of by-product of genuine teaching, and that one will be more interested in curbing such displays than in encouraging them. Such effects would probably be distinctly different from the corresponding human ones, but recognisable as variations on them. This means that if the machine was being put through one of my imitation tests, it would have to do quite a bit of acting, but if one was comparing it with a man in a less strict sort of way the resemblance might be quite impressive.

Newman: I still feel that too much of our argument is about what hypothetical future machines will do. It is all very well to say that a machine could easily be made to do this or that, but, to take only one practical point, what about the time it would take to do it? It would only take an hour or two to make up a routine to make our Manchester machine analyse all possible variations of the game of chess right out, and find the best move that way—*if* you didn't mind its taking thousands of millions of years to run through the routine. Solving a problem on the machine doesn't mean finding a way to do it between now and eternity, but within a reasonable time. This is not just a technical detail that will be taken care of by future improvements. It's most unlikely that the engineers can ever give us a factor of more than a thousand or two times our present speeds. To assume that runs that would take thousands of millions of years on our present machines will be done in a flash on machines of the future, is to move into the realms of science fiction.

Turing: To my mind this time factor is the one question which will involve all the real technical difficulty. If one didn't know already that these things can be done by brains within a reasonable time one might think it hopeless to try with a machine. The fact that a brain can do it seems to suggest that the difficulties may not really be so bad as they now seem.

Braithwaite: I agree that we ought not to extend our discussion to cover whether calculating machines could be made which would do everything that a man can do. The point is, surely, whether they can do all that it is proper to call thinking. Appreciation of a picture contains elements of thinking, but it also contains elements of feeling; and we're not concerned with whether a machine can be made that will feel. Similarly with moral questions: we're only concerned with them so far as they are also intellectual ones. We haven't got to give the machine a sense of duty or anything corresponding to a will: still less need it be given temptations which it would then have to have an apparatus for resisting. All that it has got to do in order to think is to be able to solve, or to make a good attempt at solving, all the intellectual problems with which it might be confronted by the environment in which it finds itself. This environment, of course, must include Turing asking it awkward questions as well as natural events such as being rained upon, or being shaken up by an earthquake.

Newman: But I thought it was you who said that a machine wouldn't be able to learn to adjust to its environment if it hadn't been provided with a set of appetites and all that went with them.

Braithwaite: Yes, certainly. But the problems raised by a machine having appetites are not properly our concern today. It may be the case that it wouldn't be able to learn from experience without them; but we're only required to consider whether it would be able to learn at all—since I agree that being able to learn is an essential part of thinking. So oughtn't we to get back to something centred on thinking? Can a machine make up new concepts, for example?

Newman: There are really two questions that can be asked about machines and thinking, first, what do we require before we agree that the machine does *everything* that we call thinking? This is really what we have been talking about for most of the time; but there is also another interesting and important question: Where does the doubtful territory begin? What is the *nearest* thing to straight computing that the present machines perhaps can't do?

Braithwaite: And what would your own answer be?

Newman: I think perhaps to solve mathematical problems for which no method is known, in the way that men do; to find new methods. This is a much more modest aim than inventing new mathematical concepts. What happens when you try to solve a new problem in the ordinary way is that you think about it for a few seconds, or a few years, trying out all the analogies you can think of with problems that have been solved, and then you have an idea. You try it out in detail. If it is no good you must wait for another idea. This is a little like the chess-problem routine, where one move after another is tried, but with one very important difference, that if I am even a moderately good mathematician the ideas that I get are not just random ones, but are pre-selected so that there is an appreciable chance that after a few trials one of them will be successful. Henry Moore says about the studies he does for his sculpture, "When the work is more than an exercise, inexplicable jumps occur. This is where the imagination comes in." If a machine could really be got to imitate this sudden pounce on an idea, I believe that everyone would agree that it had begun to think, even though it didn't have appetites or worry about the income tax. And suppose that we also stuck to what we know about the physiology of human thinking, how much would that amount to, Jefferson?

Jefferson: We know a great deal about the end-product, thinking itself. Are not the contents of our libraries and museums the total up to date? Experimental psychology has taught us a lot about the way that we use memory and association of ideas, how we fill in gaps in knowledge and improvise from a few given facts. But exactly how we do it in terms of nerve cell actions we don't know. We are particularly ignorant of the very point that you mentioned just now, Newman, the actual physiology of the pounce on an idea, of the sudden inspiration. Thinking is clearly a motor activity of the brain's cells, a suggestion supported by the common experience that so many people think better with a pen in their hand than viva voce or by reverie and reflection. But you can't so far produce ideas in a man's mind by stimulating his exposed brain here or there electrically. It would have been really exciting if one could have done that—if one could have perhaps excited original thoughts by local stimulation. It can't be done. Nor does the electro-encephalograph show us how the process of thinking is carried out. It can't tell you what a man is thinking about. We can trace the course, say, of a page of print or of a stream of words into the brain, but we eventually lose them. If we could follow them to their storage places we still couldn't see how they are reassembled later as ideas. You have the great advantage of knowing how your machine was made. We only know that we have in the human nervous system a concern compact in size and in its way perfect for its job. We know a great deal about its microscopical structure and its connections. If fact, we know everything except how those myriads of cells allow us to think. But, Newman, before we say "not only does this machine think but also here in this machine we have an exact counterpart of the wiring and circuits of human nervous systems", I ought to ask whether machines have been built or could be built which are as it were anatomically different, and yet produce the same work.

Newman: The logical plan of all of them is rather similar, but certainly their anatomy, and I suppose you could say their physiology, varies a lot.

Jefferson: Yes, that's what I imagined—we cannot then assume that any one of these electronic machines is a replica of part of a man's brain even though the result of its actions has to be conceded as thought. The real value of the machine to you is its end results, its performance, rather than that its plan reveals to us a model of our brains and nerves. Its usefulness lies in the fact that electricity travels along wires 2 or 3 million times faster than nerve impulses pass along nerves. You can set it to do things that man would need thousands of lives to complete. But that old slow coach, man, is the one with the ideas—or so I think. It would be fun some day, Turing, to listen to a discussion, say on the Fourth Programme, between two machines on why human beings think that they think!

III

Philosophical Reaction and the *Mind* Responsa

Immediate Responses

The centrality of Turing's test in the philosophy of mind is undisputed. The nature of thought is the key question of the field and the reduction of thought to mechanism is currently the key approach to that question. Turing, in proposing his Test, had packaged in one easily graspable form many of the central problems of philosophy of mind that had exercised people for centuries: the mind-body problem, how mental states relate to the world, the problem of the existence of other minds.

There is a certain irony in the centrality of the Turing Test in philosophy. As we have seen, Turing himself was of, at best, mixed mind as to the role of the Test, of what it is a test *of*. Is it a test of thinking, or intelligence, or intelligent behavior, or none of these? According to Turing, passing of the Test was not intended as *definitional* of intelligence; the Test was intended to *replace* the question of machine intelligence, not to answer it. He thought the latter question too imprecise and woolly to be a respectable topic of inquiry, "too meaningless to deserve discussion". Block (1990) notes the direct analogy with Turing's earlier work on the Turing machine. Computability by a Turing machine was intended to serve as a precise replacement for the vaguer notion of mechanical computability. In the same way, Turing hoped that passing of the Turing Test could serve as a precise replacement for the vaguer notion of mechanical thought. But as Moor points out,

if Turing intends that the question of the success of the machine at the imitation game replace the question about machines thinking, then it is difficult to understand how we are to judge the propriety and adequacy of the replacement if the question being replaced is too meaningless to

Premise 1:   Humans are intelligent.

Premise 2:   The conversational verbal behavior of humans reveals that (human) intelligence.

Premise 3:   If an agent has behavior of a type that can reveal intelligence and that is indistinguishable from that of an intelligent agent, the former agent is itself intelligent.

Premise 4:   Any agent that passes the Turing Test has conversational verbal behavior indistinguishable from that of humans.

Conclusion: Therefore, any agent that passes the Turing Test is intelligent.

Figure 1
The Turing syllogism

deserve discussion. Our potential interest in the imitation game is aroused not by the fact that a computer might learn to play yet another game, but that in some way this test reveals a connection between possible computer activities and our ordinary concept of human thinking. (Moor 1976, *chapter 17*)

Thus, philosophers have been inexorably led to the question of the relationship between a machine's passing of the Test and its thinking capacity, the Big Question.

Turing's view notwithstanding, it is possible to reason from a machine's passing of the Test to its intelligence according to a kind of syllogism, presented in figure 7.1, which is implicitly assumed by all philosophers investigating the ramifications of the Turing Test beyond the limited confines that Turing himself proposed it within. Turing himself never explicitly supports this syllogism. Indeed, he finds the conclusion of the syllogism to be meaningless. The nearest he comes to approving of it is an implication that passing the Test "ought to be described as thinking", in his discussion of the fact that the Test is not a necessary condition, of which more below.

The Turing Test Not a Necessary Condition
If the syllogism works at all, it works in only one direction; the converse of the conclusion—that is, "Any intelligent agent can pass the Turing Test"—need not follow from the premises. The

test is in a certain sense too hard. A machine that "ought to be described as thinking" might fail the Turing Test for all kinds of incidental reasons. Perhaps it gives itself away by typing its answers too quickly or accurately, for instance.[1]

The Turing syllogism is thus an argument for the Turing Test being a sufficient, but not necessary, condition of intelligence. Even Turing admitted that the Test would not serve as a necessary condition. Turing found the objection to be "very strong, but at least we can say that if, nevertheless, a machine can be constructed to play the imitation game satisfactorily, we need not be troubled by this objection." (Turing 1950, 435, *chapter 4*) However, the problem with sufficient conditions is that nothing prevents them from being so excessively burdensome as to be useless. If we make it a sufficient condition to being a lifeguard that the candidate be able to swim 100 kilometers carrying a 300 kilogram weight, we are sure to hire only qualified lifeguards, but we are equally sure to hire too few.

For this reason, Turing himself attempted to eliminate from the Test certain incidental properties of machines that seemed irrelevant for determining intelligent behavior. For example, possessing skin should not be indicative one way or another of possessing intelligence (says Turing), so the Test does not allow the interrogator to view the participants while conversing. Rather, the interlocution proceeds by means of typewritten messages. Despite these attempts by Turing to eliminate incidental properties, Robert French (1990, *chapter 13*) argues that the Turing Test is, like the super-lifeguard test, so difficult that it is essentially useless as a test of intelligent behavior. Rather, he says, it is inherently a test of culturally-oriented, human intelligence, and as such may be irrelevant to the question of whether machines can exhibit intelligent behavior.

---

1 In the science-fiction movie *Blade Runner* (Scott 1982), the character Deckard and other "blade runners" are specially trained police whose job is to identify human-like machine "replicants". They use a "Voight-Kampff" test, a kind of über-Turing-Test, a dialogue with the subject in which the tell-tale sign is not the verbal behavior at all, but subtle coincident movements of the iris detectable only by special equipment. We can take this to be the paradigmatic example of an incidental distinction.

The Turing Test Not a Sufficient Condition

On the other hand, it might be argued that the Test is not even a sufficient condition for determining intelligent behavior. This is tantamount to denying the syllogism in one (or more) of its premises.

Premise 1 is relatively uncontroversial (although its falsehood is raised as a possibility by Purtill [1971, *chapter 10*] and denied explicitly by Sampson [1973, *chapter 11*]).

Premise 2 is essentially Descartes's observation. Denial of it amounts to a form of solipsism.

Premise 4 constitutes the very definition of the notion of "passing the Turing Test", and is thus true by fiat.

Premise 3 is by far the most popular of the premises to deny. In order to show that the Test is not a sufficient condition, that it is somehow too easy, it can be demonstrated that an artifact that is patently unintelligent is capable of passing the Test (though perhaps not likely to do so). This is surprisingly easy. Imagine a machine that responds to the interrogator's queries by emitting a random sequence of keystrokes. (The idea is conventionally implemented using monkeys and typewriters.) There is some (admittedly astronomically small) probability that these keystrokes will fortuitously spell out perfectly plausible responses to the queries, and the interrogator would therefore be fooled into confusing the random keystroke generator with a human. If one holds the incontrovertible stance that the random typing responses were not true intelligent behavior—how could they be, as they were not produced by an intelligent being?—then the *mere possibility* of such an occurrence, by itself, demonstrates that passing the Turing Test is not a sufficient condition for intelligent behavior, at least in the strongest sense of the term "sufficient".

Attempts to drive a wedge between the two concepts "agent that could pass the Turing Test" and "agent exhibiting intelligent behavior" much more sophisticated than this have been provided in the philosophical literature. (See the chapter The Wedge and The Spark on page 147 below.) Keith Gunderson's "toe-stepping machine" (1964b, *chapter 9*), Ned Block's "Aunt Bertha" (1981, *chapter 15*), and John Searle's "Chinese Room" (1980, *chapter 14*) are crisp, if controversial, examples.

In the face of such examples, three responses are possible. First, one might find fault with the examples, as many of the critics of Searle do. (See, for example, Hofstadter [1981], Dennett [1987a].)

Second, one might back off from such a strong notion of sufficient condition, as Moor (1976, *chapter 17*) does. Rather than viewing passing the Turing Test as a *guarantee* of intelligent behavior, we might embrace a slightly weaker notion of passing the Turing Test as *evidence* of intelligent behavior. We thereby move our view of the Test from a criterion to an indication of intelligence; because of the difficulty of the task, however, the evidence can be of almost arbitrary strength (Shieber 2004).

Finally, one might deny the distinction in the first place, as Turing himself seems to have wanted to do. Determining the relationship between the two concepts assumes that they have independent status. But the original point of the Turing Test, contra its usage as a philosophical thought experiment, was not to serve in the determination of the property of behaving intelligently, but to serve as a replacement for the notion of intelligence and intelligent behavior, which are such ill-defined notions that no arguments concerning them can have any import. This gambit, taken by Chomsky (*chapter 20*), is internally consistent, and certainly solves Turing's problem, but it may do little to further an understanding of the philosophical issues Turing raises. And perhaps that is all for the best.

The papers in this final part of the collection cover the range of replies to and views of the Turing Test from the philosophical community. They fall into two classes, with some overlap: first, essentially the entire responsa from 1950 on to the article published in *Mind*, comprising the papers by Pinsky, Gunderson, Purtill, Sampson, Millar, and French; second, a selection of the most important papers from throughout the philosophical literature covering the full range of view on the Big Question. These include the papers by Gunderson, French, Block, Searle, Dennett, and a new, previously unpublished paper by Chomsky.

No two respondents to Turing's proposals share the same interpretation of the Turing Test. In part, this is what makes the Test such a fascinating thought experiment. But all would agree that it provides a lens with which to focus discussion on the central issue in philosophy of mind, the characterization of thought itself.

Can Machines Have Neuroses?

Letters in the Turing Archives at King's College, Cambridge University demonstrate the interest in the ideas presented in the *Mind* article even at the time:

I am most pleased to have it [offprint of Turing, 1950], as I enjoyed it very much when it first came out. And, you may be amused to hear, so did Bertrand Russell who was here at the time. (Crawshay-Williams 1951)

Not everyone took the paper so seriously, however. The first reply to the paper, that of Leonard Pinsky (1951, *chapter 8*), satirizes the test, proposing to replace it with a test of whether the machine can *misuse* its thinking powers: "This, I suggest, is the experiment crucial."

Therapeutic positivism (Farrell 1946) is the Wittgensteinian doctrine that philosophical problems can be resolved by pointing out to the questioner that his or her problem is based on a confusion of language use in context. Pinsky's reply to Turing, the earliest in the *Mind* responsa, is a glib parody, a story of the thinking computer confronted with the philosophical problems that its mere existence raises. No mechanic, engineer, or pychologist can repair the poor machine. Fortunately, the therapeutic positivist can, by that field's normal methods, and in so doing, provides "the experiment crucial" of the machine's thinking, resolving the philosophical problem at the same time.

It is hard to know what to make of this fairy tale, and probably not sensible to make too much of it. But as the first in the long history of Turing responses, it may serve to prevent our taking these issues too seriously.

8

Do Machines Think about Machines Thinking

Leonard Pinsky

In a recent article, Mr. A. M. Turing (1950, *chapter 4*) proposed an alternative formulation of the question, "Can machines think". The new formulation was based upon what Mr. Turing called the "imitation game". The object of the game is for an interrogator, by proposing questions to the participants in the game, to determine which of the participants is a human being and which a machine. If the interrogator cannot distinguish the machine from the human player in a high percentage of the attempts, presumably machines do think.

I would like to suggest another technique which, I believe, will not only eliminate some of the problems in Mr. Turing's game, and definitively answer the question, but will provide an additional task for a group of contemporary philosophers.

Before proposing my experiment, a few comments are in order. According to Aristotle, the property which properly distinguishes man from the rest of the universe is possession and use of the faculty of reason. If one may read between the lines of certain writings on the part of some philosophers who have been termed *Therapeutic Positivists* (Farrell 1946), Aristotle's distinction requires modification; man is unique by virtue of the ability to *mis*use the faculty of reason. All philosophical activity prior to approximately 1933 (Black 1949) was, according to the Therapeutic Positivist (hereafter referred to as T.P.) due to the misuse of reason. To be more explicit, philosophers reasoned incorrectly about the use of ordinary language; this resulted in the assertion of "metaphysical" sentences. Descartes, according to the T.P., was recommending a verbal change when he asserted the reality of three substances. Spinoza, with his insistence that there is but one real substance, was only recommending an alternative notation. The fact that both Descartes and Spinoza thought that they were talking of something which was not linguistic, and were hardly interested in philology, is irrelevant, for the T.P. has the insight which reveals what they were *really* doing. The role of the T.P. is to verbally exercise the perplexed (e.g., Spinoza and Descartes) by showing them puzzle after paradox resulting from their assertions, until they eventually recognise that they were merely suggesting linguistic changes. This revelation thereupon causes them to desist from masking these linguistic recommendations as statements about the universe.

Now, for the experiment: Let us take one of Mr. Turing's highly complex electronic or digital computers and, for a Christmas gift, send it a subscription to *Mind*, retroactive to October, 1950.[1] This means that the first article which will become part of its "store", and so part of its experience, will be Mr. Turing's article, on the problem, "Can Machines Think". The machine finds the article stimulating, probably, and a thought (the term is used loosely with no intention to prejudge the issue) runs through its wiring—it is thinking about the possibility of machines thinking! Since this is the very sort of thing which led philosophy astray for so many centuries, it will not surprise us when we discover that the machine suffers a nervous breakdown. (According to Norbert Wiener (1948), machines have breakdowns under pressure which cannot be distinguished from the nervous breakdowns of human beings.) Its efficiency is greatly decreased, the answers the machine gives are paradoxical, and the engineer is worried. Presumably, the engineer can fix the machine by ordinary means. In this instance, however, the machine fails to respond to the customary electronic therapy; the engineer is forced to call in assistance. Since the machine can be regarded as a nervous organism, the nerve specialist comes to the engineer's aid. After a thorough inspection and consultation with other specialists, the conclusion is reached that the machine's difficulty is psychosomatic. The clinical psychologist is called. After a reasonable length of time, it is evident that the Rogerian non-directive technique is of no avail, and the psychoanalyst insists that he be allowed to try his hand. The psychoanalyst finds no syndrome for which he can account in his system. The machine has no oedipus complex, for it had no parents. Since it had no childhood, plunging into its past does no good.

---

1 The suggestion that the machine be given *Mind* as a gift is due to Professor R. Popkin.

The machine has failed to respond to any of the traditional forms of psychotherapy.

Where do we turn now? To none other than the Therapeutic Positivist, or T.P. The T.P. sits down near the machine, asks it a few questions and discovers that it is perplexed about the problem "Can machines think". The job of the T.P. is to show the machine that it has been making "metamechanical" statements. In other words, in discussing this problem with itself, it has really only been recommending changes in its calculus, in the binary code. This revelation should make it clear to the machine that it was only tussling with a pseudo-problem, and it will thereupon desist from making "metamechanical" utterances. If the T.P. can perform this therapy upon the machine, we have, a fortiori, shown that the machine does think, since it has been able to misuse its thinking powers! This, I suggest, is the experiment crucial. We may leave it to the engineer to work out the technical elaborations.

Bibliography

Black, Max. 1949. *Language and philosophy*. Ithaca, NY: Cornell Press.

Farrell, Brian A. 1946. An appraisal of therapeutic positivism. *Mind* LV:217–218.

Turing, Alan M. 1950. Computing machinery and intelligence. *Mind* LIX(236): 433–460. *Reprinted in chapter 4.*

Wiener, Norbert. 1948. *Cybernetics: Or control and communication in the animal and the machine*. Cambridge, MA: MIT Press.

The Wedge and the Spark

The beauty of the Turing Test is that as a test of a machine it requires no screwdrivers. There is no need to analyze the internal workings of the machine, investigate *how* the machine does what it does. One merely subjects the machine *in toto* to the Test and see if it can pass.

With regard to the Big Question, however, the flaw in the Turing Test as a test for intelligence is that it allows no screwdrivers. Perhaps intelligence is not a property determinable externally in the way the Turing Test requires. Keith Gunderson first attacked the Turing Test in just this way, in a reply to Turing in *Mind* in 1964.

People may be let out of a building by either an electric-eye or a doorman. The end result is the same. But though a doorman may be rude or polite, the electric-eye neither practices nor neglects etiquette. Turing brandishes net results. But I think the foregoing at least indicates certain difficulties with any account of thinking or decision as to whether a certain thing is capable of thought which is based primarily on net results. (Gunderson 1964b, *chapter 9*)

Gunderson's is an instance of a class of arguments based on the presumed existence of some crucial property that people have but machines do not (or at least the Turing Test does not demonstrate the existence of). Gunderson starts off the chain of such arguments by noting the general possibility, that is, by arguing that there exist notions that are not reducible to net results because they require some crucial property. This style of argument is a direct assault on premise 3 in the Turing syllogism (page 136).

Let us examine the general form of such arguments. We have some test T (the Turing Test, for example) purported to be criterial for some property P, (intelligence, say). Step one in the argument is to describe a machine that can pass T but that obviously lacks P. This is sufficient to eliminate T as a sufficient condition for P (to negatively answer the Big Question, in the case of the Turing Test). Such a device drives a wedge between the notion "passing T" and "possessing P". We will call the device "the Wedge". Step two, the diagnostic step, is to pinpoint some substance or further property that is the reason that the Wedge fails to possess P. We might call this phlogistic substance "the Spark", as it serves as the Promethean spark of life, the "spark of being" that Shelley's Dr. Frankenstein "infuses" into a "lifeless being".

Gunderson pioneers this argument style with his device the "toe-stepping machine", a box of rocks that serves as the Wedge between the property P of imitating and the test T of being dropped on someone's toe. Just because the toe-stepper is indistinguishable from a person stepping on one's toe does not mean that it can imitate. The second step, pinpointing the Spark, is not pursued; the efficacy of the style of argument is what is at issue.

This style of argument, constructing the Wedge with or without identification of the Spark, is the standard attack on the Big Question. Block's "Aunt Bertha machine" is a Wedge, though he refuses to identify the Spark beyond a reference to "richness of information processing" (Block 1981, *chapter 15, 248*). Searle's "Chinese room" is the quintessential Wedge; with the Spark of intentionality. Davidson (1990) presents a Wedge to show that the Spark is semantics.

In the case of the Turing Test, Gunderson does address the Spark. He thinks that what the Test is missing is generality. "It is because thinking cannot be identified with what can be shown by any one example or type of example, that Turing's approach to the question 'Can a machine think?' via the imitation game is less than convincing." (Gunderson 1964b, *chapter 9, 159*) Gunderson denies the property of verbal behavior that led Descartes to make it primary as his criterion for the soul and that Turing described as being "suitable for introducing almost any one of the fields of human endeavour that we wish to include." (Turing 1950, 435, *chapter 4*) He believes that the Turing Test is *literally* too easy, its passing a mere parlor trick.

Over the years since Turing's original article, researchers in artificial intelligence, and especially in computational linguistics and natural-language processing, have gained increasingly greater appreciation for the profound difficulties in even the simplest natural-language-processing tasks. In 1964, the same year in which Gunderson's article appeared, Yehoshua Bar Hillel first noted the importance of arbitrary world knowledge in even apparently simple natural-language-processing tasks as might be required for machine translation or dialogue.

[T]here exist extremely simple sentences in English—and the same holds, I am sure, for any other natural language—which, within certain linguistic contexts, would be uniquely (up to plain synonymy) and unambiguously translated into any other language by anyone with a sufficient knowledge of the two languages involved, though I know of no program that would enable a machine to come up with this unique rendering unless by a completely arbitrary and *ad hoc* procedure whose futility would show itself in the next example.
A sentence of this kind is the following:
The box was in the pen.
The linguistic context from which this sentence is taken is, say, the following:
Little John was looking for his toy box. Finally, he found it. The box was in the pen. John was very happy.
Assume, for simplicity's sake, that *pen* in English has only the following two meanings (1) a certain writing utensil, (2) an enclosure where small children can play. I now claim that no existing or imaginable program will enable an electronic computer to determine that the word *pen* in the given sentence within the given context has the second of the above meanings, whereas every reader with a sufficient knowledge of English will do this "automatically." (Bar Hillel 1964, 174–175)

The reason for Bar Hillel's pessimism is that the discriminating factor in this case is the reader's "*knowledge* that the relative sizes of pens, in the sense of writing implements, toy boxes, and pens, in the sense of playpens, are such that when someone writes under ordinary circumstances and in something like the given context, 'The box was in the pen,' he almost certainly refers to a playpen and most certainly not to a writing pen." (Bar Hillel 1964, 176)

Since then, and increasingly, there has been wide acknowledgment in the AI community that natural-language-processing tasks of many sorts, even apparently simple ones like determining the referent of a pronoun,[1] require knowledge and reasoning of essentially arbitrary complexity.

The notion that the full-blown Turing Test is therefore too easy in a literal, technical sense is these days a bit difficult to swallow, but the general point about the structure of argument necessary to dismiss the Turing Test as a necessary condition still holds, and is pursued further by Gunderson and others in later works.

---

1 For convincing evidence of this, see Terry Winograd's classic pronoun resolution examples (Winograd 1972), which are presented again by Dennett (1985, *chapter 16*).

9

The Imitation Game

Keith Gunderson

I

Disturbed by what he took to be the ambiguous, if not meaningless, character of the question "Can machines think?" the late A. M. Turing in his article "Computing Machinery and Intelligence" (Turing 1950, *chapter 4*) sought to replace that question in the following way. He said:

The new form of the problem can be described in terms of a game which we call the "imitation game." It is played with three people, a man (A), a woman (B), and an interrogator (C) who may be of either sex. The interrogator stays in a room apart from the other two. The object of the game for the interrogator is to determine which of the other two is the man and which is the woman. He knows them by labels X and Y, and at the end of the game he says either "X is A and Y is B" or "X is B and Y is A". The interrogator is allowed to put questions to A and B thus:
C: Will X please tell me the length of his or her hair?
   Now suppose X is actually A, then A must answer. It is A's object in the game to try and cause C to make the wrong identification. His answer might therefore be
My hair is shingled, and the longest strands are about nine inches long.
   In order that tones of voice may not help the interrogator the answers should be written, or better still, typewritten. The ideal arrangement is to have a teleprinter communicating between the two rooms. Alternatively the questions and answers can be repeated by an intermediary. The object of the game for the third player (B) is to help the interrogator. The best strategy for her is probably to give truthful answers, ... but it will avail nothing as the man can make similar remarks. We now ask the question, "What will happen when a machine takes the part of A in this game?" Will the interrogator decide wrongly as often when the game is played like this as he does when the game is played between a man and a woman? These questions replace our original, "Can machines think?"

And Turing's answers to these latter questions are more or less summed up in the following passage:

> I believe that in about fifty years time it will be possible to programme computers with a storage capacity of about 10^9 to make them play the imitation game so well that an average interrogator will not have more than 70 per cent. chance of making the right identification after five minutes of questioning.

And though he goes on to reiterate that he suspects that the original question "Can machines think?" is meaningless, and that it should be disposed of and replaced by a more precise formulation of the problems involved (a formulation such as a set of questions about the imitation game and machine-capacities), what finally emerges is that Turing does answer the "meaningless" question after all, and that his answer is in the affirmative and follows from his conclusions concerning the capabilities of machines which might be successfully substituted for people in the imitation game context.

It should be pointed out that Turing's beliefs about the possible capabilities and capacities of machines are not limited to such activities as playing the imitation game as successfully as human beings. He does not, for example, deny that it might be possible to develop a machine which would relish the taste of strawberries and cream, though he thinks it would be "idiotic" to attempt to make one, and confines himself on the whole in his positive account to considerations of machine-capacities which could be illustrated in terms of playing the imitation game.

So we shall be primarily concerned with asking whether or not a machine which could play the imitation game as well as Turing thought it might would thus be a machine which we would have good reasons for saying was capable of thought and what would be involved in saying this.

Some philosophers[1] and others[2] have not been satisfied with Turing's treatment of the question "Can a machine think?" But the imitation game itself, which indeed seems to constitute the hub of his positive treatment, has been little more than alluded to or remarked on in passing. I shall

---

1 See Michael Scriven's articles: "The Mechanical Concept of Mind" (Scriven 1953) and "The Compleat Robot: A Prolegomena to Androidology" (Scriven 1961). Also, a remark by Paul Ziff in "The Feelings of Robots" (Ziff 1959, pages 66–67).

2 For example, C. E. Shannon and J. McCarthy in their preface to *Automata Studies* (Shannon and McCarthy 1956).

try to develop in a somewhat more detailed way certain objections to it. Objections which, I believe, Turing altogether fails to anticipate. My remarks shall thus in the main be critically orientated, which is not meant to suggest that I believe there are no plausible lines of defence open to a supporter of Turing. I shall, to the contrary, close with a brief attempt to indicate what some of these might be and some general challenges which I think Turing has raised for the philosopher of mind. But these latter I shall not elaborate upon.

II

Let us consider the following question: "Can rocks imitate?" One might say that it is a question "too meaningless to deserve discussion". Yet it seems possible to reformulate the problem in relatively unambiguous words as follows:

The new form of the problem can be described in terms of a game which we call the "toe-stepping game". It is played with three people, a man (A), a woman (B), and an interrogator (C) who may be of either sex. The interrogator stays in a room apart from the other two. The door is closed, but there is a small opening in the wall next to the floor through which he can place most of his foot. When he does so, one of the other two may step on his toe. The object of the game for the interrogator is to determine, by the way in which his toe is stepped on, which of the other two is the man and which is the woman. He knows them by labels X and Y, and at the end of the game he says either "X is A and Y is B" or "X is B and Y is A". Now the interrogator—rather the person whose toe gets stepped on—may indicate before he puts his foot through the opening, whether X or Y is to step on it. Better yet, there might be a narrow division in the opening, one side for X and one for Y (one for A and one for B).

Now suppose C puts his foot through A's side of the opening (which may be labeled X or Y on C's side of the wall). It is A's object in the game to try and cause C to make the wrong identification. His step on the toe might therefore be quick and jabbing like some high-heeled woman.

The object of the game for the third player (B) is to help the person whose toe gets stepped on. The best strategy for her is probably to try to step on it in the most womanly way possible. She can add such things as a light twist of a high heel to her stepping, but it will avail nothing as the man can step in similar ways, since he will also have at his disposal various shoes with which to vary his toe-stepping.

We now ask the question: "What will happen when a rock box (a box filled with rocks of varying weights, sizes, and shapes) is constructed with an electric eye which operates across the opening in the wall so that it releases a rock which descends upon C's toe whenever C puts his foot through A's side of the opening, and thus comes to take the part of A in this game?" (The situation can be made more convincing by constructing the rock-box so that there is a mechanism pulling up the released rock shortly after its descent, thus avoiding tell-tale noises such as a rock rolling on the floor, etc.) Will then the interrogator—the person whose toe gets stepped on—decide wrongly as often as when the game is played between a man and a woman? These questions replace our original, "Can rocks imitate?"

I believe that in less than fifty years' time it will be possible to set up elaborately constructed rock-boxes, with large rock-storage capacities, so that they will play the toe-stepping game so well that the average person who would get his toe stepped on would not have more than 70 per cent. chance of making the right identification after about five minutes of toe-stepping.

The above seems to show the following: what follows from the toe-stepping game situation surely is not that rocks are able to imitate (I assume no one would want to take that path of argument) but only that they are able to be rigged in such a way that they could be substituted for a human being in a toe-stepping game without changing any essential characteristics of that game. And this is claimed in spite of the fact that if a human being were to play the toe-stepping game as envisaged above, we would no doubt be correct in saying that that person was imitating, etc. To be sure, a digital computer is a more august mechanism than a rock-box, but Turing has not provided us with any arguments for believing that its role in the imitation game, as distinct from the net results it yields, is any closer a match for a human being executing such a role, than is the rock-box's execution of its role in the toe-stepping game a match for a human being's execution of a similar role. The parody comparison can be pushed too far. But I think it lays bare the reason why there is no contradiction involved in saying, "Yes, a machine can play the imitation game, but it can't think." It is for the same reason that there is no contradiction in saying "Of course a rock-box of such-and-such a sort can be set up, but rocks surely can't imitate." For thinking (or imitating) cannot be fully described simply by pointing to net results such as those illustrated above. For if this were not the case it would be correct to say that a piece of chalk could think or compose because it was freakishly blown about by a tornado in such a way that it scratched a rondo on a blackboard, and that a phonograph could sing, and that an electric-eye could see people coming.

People may be let out of a building by either an electric-eye or a doorman. The end result is the same. But though a doorman may be rude or polite, the electric-eye neither practises nor neglects etiquette. Turing brandishes net results. But I think the foregoing at least indicates certain difficulties with any account of thinking or decision as to whether a certain thing is capable of thought which is based primarily on net results. And, of course, one could always ask whether the net results were really the same. But I do not wish to follow that line of argument here. It is my main concern simply to indicate where Turing's account, which is cast largely in terms of net results, fails because of this. It is not an effective counter to reply: "But part of the net results in question includes intelligent people being deceived!" For what would this add to the general argument? No doubt people could be deceived by rock-boxes! It is said that hi-fidelity phonographs have been perfected to the point where blindfolded music critics are unable to distinguish their "playing" from that of, let us say, the Budapest String Quartet. But the phonograph would never be said to have performed with unusual brilliance on Saturday, nor would it ever deserve an encore.

III

Now perhaps comparable net results achieved by machines and human beings is all that is needed to establish an analogy between them, but it is far from what is needed to establish that one sort of subject (machines) can do the same thing that another sort of subject (human beings or other animals) can do. Part of what things do is how they do it. To ask whether a machine can think is in part to ask whether machines can do things in certain ways.

The above is relevant to what might be called the problem of distinguishing and evaluating the net results achieved by a machine as it is touched on by Scriven (1961) in his discussion of what he calls "the performatory problem" and "the personality problem". In "The Compleat Robot: A Prolegomena to Androidology" he writes:

The performatory problem here is whether a computer can produce results which, when translated, provide what would count as an original solution or proof *if it came from a man*. The personality problem is whether we are entitled to call such a result a solution or proof, despite the fact that it did *not* come from a man.

And continues:

The logical trap is this: no *one* performatory achievement will be enough to persuade us to apply the human-achievement vocabulary, but if we refuse to use this vocabulary in each case separately, on this ground, we will, perhaps wrongly, have committed ourselves to avoiding it even when all the achievements are simultaneously attained.

My concern is not, however, with what is to count as an original solution or proof. Scriven, in the above, is commenting on the claims: "Machines only do what we tell them to do. They are incapable of genuinely original thought." He says that two "importantly different points are run together". The above is his attempt to separate these points. But it seems that there are at least three, and not just two, points which are run together in the just-mentioned claims. The third point, the one not covered by Scriven's distinction between the performatory and personality problems, is simply the problem, mentioned above, of discerning when one subject (a machine) has *done the same thing* as another subject (a human being). And here "doing the same thing" does not simply mean "achieved similar end result". (Which is not to suggest that the phrase can never be used in that way in connection with thinking.) This is of interest in respect to Scriven's discussion, since it might be the case that all the achievements were simultaneously attained by a machine, as Scriven suggests, and that we had decided on various grounds that they should count as original proofs and solutions and thus surmounted the personality problem, but yet felt unwilling to grant that the machines were capable of "genuinely original thought". Our grounds for this latter decision might be highly parallel to our grounds for not wanting to say that rocks could imitate (even though rock-boxes had reached a high level of development). Of course our grounds might not be as sound as these. I am simply imagining the case where they are, which is also a case where all the achievements are attained in such a way that they count as original solutions or proofs. In this case we would see that answers to questions about originality and performance and the logical trap mentioned by Scriven would be wholly separate from whatever answers might be given to the question whether or not the machines involved thought, and would thus be unsuitable as answers to the question whether or not they were capable of "genuinely original thought". In other words, questions as to originality and questions as to thinking are not the same, but this dissimilarity is left unacknowledged in Scriven's account.

IV

But let us return to the imitation game itself. It is to be granted that if human beings were to participate in such a game, we would almost surely regard them as deliberating, deciding, wondering—in short, "thinking things over"—as they passed their messages back and forth. And if someone were to ask us for an example of Johnson's intellectual prowess or mental capabilities, we might well point to this game which he often played, and how he enjoyed trying to outwit Peterson and Hanson who also participated in it. But we would only regard it as one of the many examples we might give of Peterson's mental capacities. We would ordinarily not feel hard pressed to produce countless other examples of Peterson deliberating, figuring, wondering, reflecting, or what in short we can call thinking. We might, for example, relate how he works over his sonnets or how he argues with Hanson. Now, I do not want to deny that it is beyond the scope of a machine to do these latter things. I am not, in fact, here concerned with giving an answer to the question, "Can machines think?" What I instead want to emphasize is that what we would say about Peterson in countless other situations is bound to influence what we say about him in the imitation game. A rock rolls down a hill and there is, strictly speaking, no behaviour or action on the part of the rock. But if a man rolls down a hill we might well ask if he was pushed or did it intentionally, whether he's enjoying himself, playing a game, pretending to be tumbleweed, or what. We cannot think of a man as simply or purely rolling down a hill—unless he is dead. *A fortiori,* we cannot understand him being a participant in the imitation game apart from his dispositions, habits, etc., which are exhibited in contexts other than the imitation game. Thus we cannot hope to find any decisive answer to the question as to how we should characterize a machine which can play (well) the imitation game, by asking what we would say about a man who could play (well) the imitation game. Thinking, whatever positive characterization or account is correct, is not something which any one example will explain or decide. But the part of Turing's case which I've been concerned with rests largely on one example.

V

The following might help to clarify the above. Imagine the dialogue below:

Vacuum Cleaner Salesman: Now here's an example of what the all-purpose Swish 600 can do. (*He then applies the nozzle to the carpet and it sucks up a bit of dust.*)

Housewife: What else can it do?

Vacuum Cleaner Salesman: What do you mean "What else can it do?" It just sucked up that bit of dust, didn't you see?

Housewife: Yes, I saw it suck up a bit of dust, but I thought it was all-purpose. Doesn't it suck up larger and heavier bits of straw or paper or mud? And can't it get in the tight corners? Doesn't it have other nozzles? What about cat hair on the couch?

Vacuum Cleaner Salesman: It sucks up bits of dust. That's what vacuum cleaners are for.

Housewife: Oh, that's what it does. I thought it was simply an example of what it does.

Vacuum Cleaner Salesman: It is an example of what it does. What it does is to suck up bits of dust.

We ask: Who's right about examples? We answer: It's not perfectly clear that anyone is lying or unjustifiably using the word "example". And there's no obvious linguistic rule or regularity to point to which tells us that if *S* can only do *x*, then *S*'s doing *x* cannot be an example of what *S* can do since being an example presupposes or entails or whatnot that other kinds of examples are forthcoming (sucking up mud, cat hair, etc.). Yet, in spite of this, the housewife has a point. One simply has a right to expect more from an all-purpose Swish 600 than what has been demonstrated. Here clearly the main trouble is with "all-purpose" rather than with "example", though there may still be something misleading about saying, "Here's an example ... ", and it would surely mislead to say, "Here's *just* an example ... " followed by "... of what the all-purpose Swish 600 can do". The philosophical relevance of all this to our own discussion can be put in the following rather domestic way: "thinking" is a term which shares certain features with "all-purpose" as it occurs in the phrase "all-purpose Swish 600". It is not used to designate or refer to one capability, capacity, disposition, talent, habit, or feature of a given subject any more than "all-purpose" in the above example is used to mark out one particular operation of a vacuum cleaner. Thinking, whatever positive account one might give of it, is not, for example, like swimming or tennis playing. The question as to whether Peterson can swim or play tennis can be settled by a few token examples of Peterson swimming or playing tennis. (And it might be noted it is hardly imaginable that the question as to whether Peterson could think or not would be raised. For in general it is not at all interesting to ask that question of contemporary human beings, though it might be interesting for contemporary human beings to raise it in connection with different anthropoids viewed at various stages of their evolution.) But if we suppose the question were raised in connection with Peterson the only appropriate sort of answer to it would be one like, "Good heavens, what makes you think he can't?" (as if anticipating news of some horrible brain injury inflicted on Peterson). And our shock would not be at his perhaps having lost a particular talent. It would not be like the case of a Wimbledon champion losing his tennis talent because of an amputated arm.

It is no more unusual for a human being to be capable of thought than it is for a human being to be composed of cells. Similarly, "He can think" is no more an answer to questions concerning Peterson's mental capacities or intelligence, than "He's composed of cells" is an answer to the usual type of question about Peterson's appearance. And to say that Peterson can think is not to say there are a few token examples of thinking which are at our fingertips, any more than to say that the Swish 600 is all-purpose is to have in mind a particular manoeuvre or two of which the device is capable. It is because thinking cannot be identified with what can be shown by any one example or type of example, that Turing's approach to the question "Can machines think?" via the imitation game is less than convincing. In effect he provides us below with a dialogue very much like the one above:

Turing: You know, machines can think.

Philosopher: Good heavens. Really. How do you know?

Turing: Well, they can play what's called the imitation game. *(This is followed by a description of same.)*

Philosopher: Interesting. What else can they do? They must be capable of a great deal if they can really think.

Turing: What do you mean, "What else can they do?" They play the imitation game. That's thinking, isn't it? *(Etc.)*

But Turing, like the vacuum cleaner salesman, has trouble making his sale. Nonetheless, I will indicate shortly why certain of our criticisms of his approach might have to be modified.

VI

But one last critical remark before pointing to certain shortcomings of the foregoing. As indicated before, Turing's argument benefits from his emphasizing the fact that a machine is being substituted for a human being in a certain situation, and does as well as a human being would do in that situation. No one, however, would want to deny that machines are able to do a number of things as well as or more competently than human beings, though surely no one would want to say that every one of such examples provided further arguments in support of the claim that machines can think. For in many such cases one might instead of emphasizing that a machine can do what a human being can do, emphasize that one hardly needs to be a human being to do such things. For example: "I don't even have to think at my job; I just seal the jars as they move along the belt", or, "I just pour out soft drinks one after the other like some machine". The latter could hardly be construed as suggesting "My, aren't soft-drink vending machines clever", but rather suggests, "Isn't my job stupid; it involves little or no mental effort at all". Furthermore, as Professor Ryle has suggested to me, a well-trained bank cashier can add, subtract, multiply, and divide without having to think about what he is doing and while thinking about something else, and can't many of us run through the alphabet or a popular song without thinking? This is not meant to be a specific criticism of Turing as much as it is meant as a reminder that being able to do what human beings can do hardly implies the presence of intellectual or mental skills real or simulated, since so many things which human beings do involve little if any thinking. Those without jobs constitute a somewhat different segment of the population from those without wits.

VII

But the following considerations seem to temper some of the foregoing criticisms. A defender of Turing might emphasize that a machine that is able to play the imitation game is also able to do much more: it can compute, perhaps be programmed to play chess, etc., and consequently displays capacities far beyond the "one example" which has been emphasized in our criticisms. I shall not go into the details which I think an adequate reply to this challenge must take into account. But in general I believe it would be possible to formulate a reply along the lines that would show that even playing chess, calculating, and the performance of other (most likely mathematical) operations provides us with at best a rather narrow range of examples and still fails to satisfy our intuitive concept of thinking. The parallel case in respect to the Housewife and Vacuum Cleaner Salesman would be where the Housewife still refused to accept the vacuum cleaner as all-purpose even though it had been shown to be capable of picking up scraps somewhat heavier than dust. Nonetheless, even if our reply were satisfactory, the more general question would remain unanswered: what range of examples would satisfy the implicit criteria we use in our ordinary characterization of subjects as "those capable of thought"?

A corollary: If we are to keep the question "Can machines think?" interesting, we cannot withhold a positive answer simply on the grounds that it (a machine) does not duplicate human activity in every respect. The question "Can a machine think if it can do everything a human being can do?" is not an interesting question, though it is somewhat interesting to ask whether there would not be a logical contradiction in supposing such to be, in fact, a machine. But as long as we have in mind subjects which obviously are machines, we must be willing to stop short of demanding their activities to fully mirror human ones before we say they can think, if they can. But how far short? Again the above question as to the variety and extent of examples required is raised.

Furthermore, it might be asserted that with the increasing role of machines in society the word "think" itself might take on new meanings, and that it is not unreasonable to suppose it changing in meaning in such a way that fifty years hence a machine which could play the imitation game would in ordinary parlance be called a machine which could think. There is, however, a difference between asking whether a machine can think given current meanings of "machine" and "think" and asking whether a machine can think given changes in the meanings of "machine" and "think". My own attention has throughout this paper been centred on the first question. Yet there is a temporal obscurity in the question "Can machines think?" For if the question is construed as ranging over possible futures, it may be difficult to discuss such futures without reference to changing word meanings. But this raises an entire family of issues which there is not space to discuss here. To some extent Turing's own views are based on certain beliefs he has about how we will in the future talk about machines. But these are never discussed in any detail, and he does not address himself to the knotty problems of meaning which interlace with them.

VIII

A final point: the stance is often taken that thinking is the crowning capacity or achievement of the human race, and that if one denies that machines can think, one in effect assigns them to some lower level of achievement than that attained by human beings. But one might well contend that machines can't think, for they do much better than that. We could forever deny that a machine could think through a mathematical problem, and still claim that in many respects the achievement of machines was on a higher level than that attained by thinking beings, since machines can almost instantaneously and infallibly produce accurate and sometimes original answers to many complex and difficult mathematical problems with which they are presented. They do not need to "think out" the answers. In the end the steam drill outlasted John Henry as a digger of railway tunnels, but that didn't prove the machine had muscles; it proved that muscles were not needed for digging railway tunnels.

Bibliography

Scriven, Michael. 1953. The mechanical concept of mind. *Mind* LXII(246): 230–240.

———. 1961. The compleat robot: A prolegomena to androidology. In *Dimensions of mind*, ed. Sidney Hook. New York, NY: New York University Press.

Shannon, Claude E., and John McCarthy, eds. 1956. *Automata studies*. Princeton, NJ: Princeton University Press.

Turing, Alan M. 1950. Computing machinery and intelligence. *Mind* LIX(236): 433–460. *Reprinted in chapter 4.*

Ziff, Paul. 1959. The feelings of robots. *Analysis* 66–67.

Early Harbingers of Later Issues

Richard Purtill (1971, *chapter 10*) presents a series of thought experiments also aiming at, but not quite forming, the Wedge. He asks us to imagine a machine that is patently unthinking but that can pass the Turing Test (or at least a variant of it). Indeed, Purtill's device is a primitive version of what will become Block's Aunt Bertha machine. Unlike the anti-operationalists, however, Purtill misses the opportunity to argue that the Test is not a sufficient condition for intelligence, failing to use the thought experiment to drive the wedge between the Turing Test and intelligent behavior. That move is left to Searle, Block, and the like. Instead, Purtill vacillates on the Big Question, reiterating versions of "Lady Lovelace's objection", finally dismissing the Test as academic for purely pragmatic reasons.

In fact, he seems to admit grudgingly that the Test is an appropriate metric of thinking, though he comes to the surprising conclusion that were a machine to pass the test, it would be better to abandon premise 1 of the Turing syllogism: it "would seem to show that human beings do not in fact think rather than that computers do think." Sampson's reply to Purtill (Sampson 1973, *chapter 11*), in addition to clarifying some confusions, makes the point that redefining the word "think" is not one of the open options. The question raised by Turing's paper is exactly whether machines can think *by the definition of the word under which we say that people can.*

Following from Purtill's essay, Millar (1973, *chapter 12*) presents a series of "vices", early presentations of themes that will arise repeatedly later. The most prominent are: that the binary nature of the Test provides no aid in setting research direction or measuring progress (the methodological vice of page 10); that it fails to acknowledge the graded nature of human intelligence as we understand it; and finally, that the test fails as a necessary condition. This latter objection is studied in greater detail by French in chapter 13.

10

Beating the Imitation Game

Richard Purtill

Some years ago, A. M. Turing wrote a shortish paper about thinking and computers (Turing 1950, *chapter 4*) in which he proposed a sort of operational test of whether a computer might be carrying on an activity at least comparable to human thinking. The paper has been reprinted in several places and has provoked several interesting replies and discussions (Gunderson 1964b, *chapter 9*) . In this paper, I want to raise a number of fundamental objections to Turing's paper and to those who have taken his "imitation game" seriously. In my criticism I speak mainly as a philosopher, but also as a person who has done a certain amount of computer programming (Purtill 1969).

Turing begins, you will recall, by saying that the question of computers and thought in its usual forms, e.g. "can computers think?", is too vague to be tackled successfully and proposes that we substitute for it the more easily manageable question "Can a digital computer play the imitation game?" This game is a development of a game involving only human players in which a questioner tries to determine which of two concealed respondents is actually a woman, which a man imitating a woman. The woman is trying to help the questioner guess correctly and answer the questions truthfully, while the man is trying to make the questioner guess wrongly and is allowed to lie freely. The players communicate by teletype, typed notes or some similar device to avoid physical clues.

Before going on to the man-computer imitation game, let us pause for a moment to examine this original game. Turing suggests as a possible question "How long is your hair" and later on comments that the woman player can say things like "I'm the woman, don't believe him", but that this will be of little use since the imitating player can do the same. But fairly obviously that sort of question is no help to the questioner, and that sort of comment by the woman is unlikely to help the questioner either. A quick-witted questioner might ask things like "What's your dress size?" "How long would you cook a five pound pork roast?" "How much do you pay for nylons?" "Where is the ladies' room in this building?" His object, in other words, would be to try to discover which of the players had certain sorts of *information*. However, if the adversary player, the imitator, were equally quickwitted, and knew about as much about women as the questioner (a married man might have an advantage over a bachelor) he might manage to deceive the questioner. Attitudes and opinions might seem more promising ground, but again the adversary might use his knowledge of women to give plausible answers. In fact, his best strategy might be to think of some woman he knew well and answer as he thought she might. At any rate there seems to be no sure-fire strategy for the questioner.

When the game is played with two human beings and a computer the situation is not as much like the original imitation game as it might appear. To give some initial plausibility to the situation, imagine that the questioner is restricted to a list of twenty stock questions. He has a limited time period and after asking as many of these questions as he likes and examining the answers he must make a guess as to which of his two respondents is a human being, which a computer. How often would an able questioner guess wrongly?

The question has some interest, and in fact it might be fun to program the game and try it on a group of students. But if we think about programming the game a fundamental difficulty comes to light. Where would the computer's answers come from. Would they be simply written out by the programmer and stored in the machine? But then, of course, the questioner would be right whichever respondent he chose as the human being. A set of answers will either have been given by the human respondent, who typed his answers himself, or gave them to a secretary, or else they were given by the programmer, also a human being, who transmitted them to the questioner via the computer. The question then becomes really "Which set of human-originated answers were transmitted via computer, which were not?"

It might be amusing to try to guess the answer to this question, and it might not even be unduly difficult. For example, if I were the questioner,

I might try asking the same question a dozen or so times. If the programmer were unimaginative, I would get the same answer each time, a dead give-away. If he were a bit cleverer he might have "backup" answers for questions asked more than once, but unless he had foreseen my strategy he might not have enough. Still, a clever programmer might have a series of increasingly exasperated "I've already told you … !!!" answers stored to counter just such a strategy.

But it now becomes clear what the difficulty is about this version of the game. It is really a battle of wits between questioner and programmer: the computer is non-essential. There might just as well be a series of numbered mailboxes containing prewritten answers to the stock questions, and some simple mechanism for delivery. Even if the questioner consistently lost, no one would be inclined to say that the mailboxes were thinking. Whatever thinking activity is going on is plainly in the brain of the programmer, not in the mechanism by which his answers are transmitted.

Let us now move one step closer to Turing's imagined game. The questions remain a stock selection, but in some way the computer evolves the answers itself. Let us imagine one faintly plausible way in which this might happen. Let us give our imagined computer some mechanism for generating random grammatical sentences. We then have the computer play a great number of "one question imitation games" as follows: a human questioner asks one question and the machine offers a random sentence as a response. The human questioner then punches a white button if the reply is one which might be given by a human to that question or a black button if the sentence offered is irrelevant or otherwise defective. The computer stores all sentences which get a white button response. After the machine has stored a number of "white-buttoned" answers for each stock question it plays a second series of games in which it offers a random selection from its "white-buttoned" answers in response to stock questions. It then discards all answers which are not "successful" most of the time. This second series of games might even be real imitation games: the white button could be labelled "A human being gave this reply", the black button "A machine gave this reply". The machine then goes on to play extended imitation games using its stock of tested answers.

Of course, this device for getting machine-generated answers is impractically cumbersome and time-consuming, but it eliminates the human programmer to a very large extent, and will do as a thought-experiment. It is also vulnerable to my repetition-of-one-question strategy, but in principle an extension of this technique could deal with that strategy. For the sake of simplicity let us say that we allow a rule against repeated questions in the imitation game.

However, a difficulty very similar to one we have already encountered robs this new version of the game of much significance. For again, nothing in it depends especially on the use of a computer. Suppose we generate our random sentences by means of a series of mechanically operated wheels. Pressing the white button causes the sentence to be photographed on a slide, developed and stored in a projector for the next stage. The black button is a dummy. In the second stage of the game the sentences are projected on a screen, some simple mechanical randomizer selecting the slide to be shown. This time the white button is a dummy and the black button discards the slide. In the full imitation game a simple mechanical hookup selects a slide file to correspond to the question asked and a randomizer selects a slide. Even if questioners were regularly deceived by this setup, practically no one would be inclined to think that anything in our collection of hardware was thinking.

I say that practically no one would be inclined to say this, but I suppose that some extreme mechanists and behaviourists would say that human thinking was simply an enormously complicated collection of such simple quasi-mechanical processes. An adequate reply to this position would amount to an adequate reply to the whole mechanist and behaviourist position, for which I lack space here. Even if a mechanist-behaviourist account of this sort could be demonstrated to be true it would seem to show that human beings do not in fact think rather than that computers do think.

When we arrive at the full-scale version of Turing's imitation game which has apparently somewhat the same rules as the original man-woman version in which *any* questions may be asked it is hard to know what to say. There is no way, nor would any competent computer programmer suggest that there is, to program a computer to make *any* meaningful response to all of the myriad of questions which can be asked in English, much less responses which would deceive a human questioner into thinking that he was being responded to by a fellow human. Suppose that I approached any computer expert and offered him a fabulous prize if he designed a computer which could give a relevant response to some question or other which I would put to it after it had been designed. No information about the question would be given, of course, until the day I came to ask it of the completed machine. Show me a computer expert who would take me up on that offer, and I'll show you a man who has lost touch with reality.

Of course, computer men have their dreams, as all of us do. There are promising hints, and faint glimmerings and high hopes. But if anyone at present has any real notion of the principles on which a machine which could carry out my hypothetical assignment would be built, I'll eat my computer library.

Thus it seems that Turing's "imitation game" is just an interesting piece of science fiction. Possibly there may some day be computers which can offer appropriate response to anything which can be said to them. Possibly someday there may be spaceships which travel at speeds near the speed of light. Interesting stories can be told about both but nothing in present-day knowledge makes that sort of computer much more likely than that sort of spaceship. At any rate Turing's prediction that a computer which could play the imitation game would be built within fifty years from the date of his paper (that is in 2000) was obviously a wild exaggeration.

In fact, the effectiveness of Turing's paper lies to a rather large extent in its science-fiction aspect. Those little bits of dialogue between the questioner and the respondent who may be a computer are extremely effective: "Write me a sonnet on the subject of the Forth Bridge", "Sorry, I've never been much good at poetry." If a machine could actually make responses that apposite to whatever random question came into the mind of the questioner it might indeed make us wonder whether that machine was capable of thought.

For after all, what sort of test would we apply to see if intelligent thought were present in some being, say a Martian or a man recovering from a brain operation? Would we not try to establish communication and judge the presence of thought by appropriateness of response?

It may seem to some critics of Turing that I have "sold the pass" by admitting even the logical possibility of a machine giving responses which might cause us to consider it a thinking being. But it does not seem to me that this is a question which can without absurdity be settled *a priori*. If a machine could be constructed which would behave as the computers in some science-fiction stories do, I would be prepared to grant that this computer was capable of thought. It might then of course be appropriate to call this entity something other than a machine, but it would be a mere evasion to deny on this ground that a computer was capable of thought.

On the other hand, I do not want to be hailed as an ally by those supporters of Turing who, once logical possibility is granted, brush aside the immense improbability involved as a mere matter of waiting for technological development. Let me get away entirely from the "imitation game" and state my most basic objection in this way: any output of any computer presently existing or foreseeable on the basis of present technology can be explained as the result of a program inserted into the machine by a human programmer or the interaction of such a program and inputs of various kinds (e.g. data). Except for mechanical malfunctions the output is totally determined by the program and the input. In some programs a random element is inserted into the program, but even in such cases the range of possible outputs, the relative frequency of various outputs, etc., is determined by the program and the nature of the randomizing device. Any computer output can be explained along these lines.

As opposed to this, hardly any behaviour of thinking beings can be shown to be completely determined by "programming" (i.e. teaching or conditioning) plus external "inputs" (i.e. experience of various kinds). There are, indeed, those who claim that human behaviour is thus determined and can be explained purely "mechanically". But that of course is a much wider and older question, and has nothing specifically to do with computers and thought. As I said above, if the behaviourists were proved right it would so alter our conception of ourselves as to rather make us say that men did not think than that computers did. (This claim would, I think, be untenable, but that is another, and far knottier question.) To sum up then; if a computer could play the complete, "any question" imitation game it might indeed cause us to consider that perhaps that computer was capable of thought. But that any computer might be able to play such a game in the foreseeable future is so immensely improbable as to make the whole question academic.

Bibliography

Gunderson, Keith. 1964. The imitation game. *Mind* 73(290):234–245. *Reprinted in chapter 9.*

Purtill, Richard L. 1969. Doing logic by computer. *Notre Dame Journal of Formal Logic* X(2).

Turing, Alan M. 1950. Computing machinery and intelligence. *Mind* LIX(236): 433–460. *Reprinted in chapter 4.*

11

In Defence of Turing

Geoffrey Sampson

Turing (1950, *chapter 4*) proposed his "imitation game" as a criterion for deciding whether a computer can think, and he predicted that by A.D. 2000 some computer will pass the test. Purtill (1971, *chapter 10*) advances three arguments against Turing, which I shall now refute.

(1) At present, the nearest a computer could come to meeting Turing's criterion would be to play various restricted versions of the imitation game suggested by Purtill. It is not reasonable, Purtill claims, to take these restricted games as criteria for thinking. But then Turing did not suggest that the restricted games were criteria, only the unrestricted game.

As for Purtill's comment that current computer systems are far from being able to play the unrestricted game: one reason for this is a purely practical one. To make meaningful comments on any subject raised by an interrogator would presumably require vast storage to accommodate an encyclopaedic set of facts about the world; but there is no theoretical interest in expanding a computer's storage to accommodate enormous quantities of data. There is also, admittedly, at least one theoretical difficulty which Turing, writing in 1950, would not have appreciated. To respond meaningfully to an undetermined input involves the ability to recognise whether a string of letters is an English sentence (assuming that English is the language the computer is claimed to "understand"), and to parse the sentence if it is one. Chomsky and his followers have shown that this is a much thornier problem than was previously supposed, and one that cannot at present be reduced to an algorithm. But that is not to say that the problem will never be solved.

(2) Any computer, now or in the future, will be such that its behaviour is always fully determined by the program and data it has been given. (Purtill mentions the possibilities, already brought up by Turing, of mechanical

breakdown or a randomising device, but claims they are irrelevant to his argument: I agree.) It cannot be shown that human behaviour, on the other hand, is determined by teaching or "conditioning" together with experience, and such a position would be held only by "extreme behaviourists".

First, there is a confusion here in Purtill's analogy between human experience and computer input. In discussing the workings of a computer, the distinction between "program" and "data" is meaningless. The distinction exists only in the mind of the practising programmer, who is concerned to distinguish the elements of input provided by his client, which will typically vary from one occasion when a computer is used to the next, from the elements that the programmer himself has composed, which will typically remain constant for numerous computer "runs". Purtill, who takes the distinction between program and data to be basic, wants an analogous distinction in the case of humans: he equates teaching and/or "conditioning" with the computer's program, and (other) human experience with its data. This has an important effect on Purtill's argument: having singled out teaching/conditioning experiences for special consideration among a human's full range of inputs, he then labels "behaviourist" the view that human behaviour can be reduced to computer-like mechanisms. But the behaviourism v. rationalism issue is irrelevant to Purtill's thesis. What Purtill should have said is that any computer's behaviour is determined jointly by its input and its internal state (an important omission in Purtill's account); and now the question is whether a human's behaviour is fully determined by his state at birth (or rather, perhaps, conception) together with his total experience. This is the determinism v. free will issue, which is neutral vis-à-vis behaviourism v. rationalism. (The thesis of "extreme behaviourism" is, to put it crudely, that in discussing the determination of human behaviour one needs to say a lot about experience but very little about initial state.)

The argument that computers cannot think because human thought is subject to free will whereas all computer activity is determined, is a more subtle argument than any Purtill discusses. It is beyond my scope: I shall content myself by pointing out that Russell (1929) denied that determinism and free will were incompatible.

Secondly, the fact that computer behaviour is known to be determined while *human* behaviour is not can easily be explained:

(i) Computers are designed by humans; humans are not designed by humans.

(ii) Computers are equipped with mechanisms expressly intended to permit the cause of their behaviour to be studied (e.g. the "dumping" facility which gives a computer operator a complete statement of the machine's internal state at any given moment); humans are not so equipped.

(iii) Humans are known to be very much more complex, in terms both of range of possible internal states and range of possible experiences/inputs at a given moment, than any contemporary computer.

Any one of these three points would alone be sufficient to explain the difference in what we know about the behaviour of the respective organisms.

(3) Although "some extreme mechanists and behaviourists" would claim that human thinking is simply a more complicated version of the sort of mechanical activity which a computer can perform, for Purtill the consequence of this view would be that men do not think, rather than that machines do. Purtill adds that he does not believe this consequence to be tenable, "but that is another, and far knottier question". But this will not do. Thinking is by definition a thing humans (at least) do. There is no difficulty in contradicting someone who suggests that perhaps humans do not think. Philosophers may legitimately analyse the notion of thought in terms of other notions, and may legitimately ask whether organisms other than humans should be said to think. But anyone who suggests that humans perhaps do not think is simply using a special word $think_2$, not synonymous with the familiar word, $think_1$. Furthermore, this new verb will have the odd property that it apparently cannot be truly predicated of any subject. In any case, $think_2$ is beside the point: what makes Turing's article interesting is that it suggests that computers can $think_1$.

Bibliography

Purtill, Richard L. 1971. Beating the imitation game. *Mind* LXXX(318):290–294. *Reprinted in chapter 10.*

Russell, Bertrand. 1929. *Our knowledge of the external world.* W.W. Norton.

Turing, Alan M. 1950. Computing machinery and intelligence. *Mind* LIX(236): 433–460. *Reprinted in chapter 4.*

12

On the Point of the Imitation Game

P. H. Millar

Turing's suggestion for an operational test to determine whether computing machinery is performing in a way which we might be justified in calling "intelligent" (Turing 1950, *chapter 4*) has both virtues and vices. The following are principal:

(i) it constitutes an operational definition which, given a computer terminal system, can be used as a criterion

(ii) it involves direct comparison with a standard or reference point. We can only attack it by saying either that the human competitor is not a proper standard of intelligence, or by saying that the constraints imposed by the game situation necessarily obscure the display of intelligence (presumably by either competitor)

(iii) it provides a means of measuring one's success in the task of creating an artificial intelligence, but does not readily admit of any analysis which reveals necessary steps along the path to success. It characterises the goal without giving information as to the *direction* in which it is to be sought.

Of these, (i) is a virtue to which few alternative proposals can lay claim, (ii) is a virtue to some and a vice to others, and (iii) is a vice or at least a shortcoming which has provoked some impatience even on the part of those actively engaged in artificial intelligence work (Meltzer 1971).

The respect in which (ii) highlights a virtue is clear. It has always been possible to talk of non-human objects being intelligent or thinking, so long as we were talking *metaphorically*. The question Turing faced was that of recommending a usage which was to be literal; the machine was "really" thinking. It is an eminently sensible step to choose as the standard for calibrating this new use, that to which the term was previously confined in its literal sense.

When reading attacks on Turing's suggestion, we may profit from bearing (ii) in mind. Does the writer contest the use of a human being as a standard, or does he claim that the comparison situation is inadequate, and in which respects. Richard L. Purtill (1971, *chapter 10*), for example, seems to attack neither and we are automatically prompted to ask what difference the pre-programming of *either* contestant in the game is supposed to make to the adequacy of the test; if we consider the effect of substituting a person acting under hypnotic instruction instead of the computer then we see that the virtue of the Turing test lies in its allowing us to ignore the arguments about human or machine determinism (as Purtill apparently wishes to).

On the other hand we may well wonder whether (ii) really gives the machine a fair chance. It is by no means a primary characteristic of human beings that they be intelligent. Further, if one human being were tested in this way against a range of other human beings, and if he lost pretty consistently we should still not be justified in concluding that he lacked the property of "intelligence" entirely. Equally if he were to beat other human beings regularly, we should normally conclude that he was "more intelligent" and the others less so—not that the others were faulty specimens from the production line and that the magic ingredient of intelligence had been omitted. It is a vice of the test that it proposes a "yes"/"no" decision in a situation where we wish to apply a concept which is rich in differences of degree.

Even more seriously, one might doubt whether those specifically human traits which we normally use to monitor intelligence, would be the right ones for monitoring the intelligence of machines. We should not apply this to Martians, and it is not thought to be necessary to conduct such competitions when examining the records of cosmic radio emissions for evidence of intelligent life in other stellar systems. Within the human species cultural variations lead to the inapplicability of standard intelligence tests, and we are quite prepared to entertain the possibility that the approach to intelligence testing in children should differ radically from that applied to adults.

To put a five-year-old white Canadian and a seventy-year-old Pigmy into the Imitation Game test in order to decide a hypothesis that one or the other of them was not intelligent would be ludicrous. It would be so, not only because intelligence is a continuous variable as sketched

above, but also because our touchstone for using the term about human beings is their adaptive behaviour in real-life situations. It is against
this, pre-scientific, idea that psychologists still judge their own attempts
at measuring intelligence. This will probably remain so until some one
operationally-definable measure is found which is both universally and
reproducibly applicable and is correlated with a sufficiently elaborate and
powerful theory.

For the moment we are left with our intuitive approach. Not only does
this put particular stress on general adaptation, but a consideration of the
way in which we normally apply ascriptions of intelligence will reveal that
in cases where we regard items of behaviour as indicative of intelligence,
we see them in relation to the aims of the agent. Computers, however,
do not have their aims pre-programmed; we can judge the intelligence
of human beings by making assumptions about their aims—there is not
so much variety, though we meet problems with "intelligent" obsessives
and criminals—but what assumptions should we make for computers
(cf. Millar 1971). Turing's test forces us to ascribe typical human objec-
tives and a human cultural background to the machine, but if we are to be
serious in contemplating the use of such a term we should be open-minded
enough to allow computing machinery or Martians to display their intelligence by means of behaviour which is well-adapted for achieving their
own specific aims. Failure to allow this may be taken as a vice of the
Turing test.

In conclusion we may note that this final "vice" arises because the concepts we apply to human beings are highly interconnected. We may solve
the problem either by finding some way to ascribe purposes to computing machinery and then judging their performance in the light of these
and of the machine's limitations, or by retreating somewhat and saying that the Turing test is designed to test, not whether machines can
have intelligence, but whether machines can imitate human intelligence.
This last question can have a "yes"/"no" answer, and that answer might
be interesting quite independently of the debate on the applicability of
anthropomorphic terms to non-humans.

Bibliography

Meltzer, Bernard. 1971. Bury the old war-horse! *Bulletin of the AISB group of
the British Computer Society* 12.

Millar, P. H. 1971. On defining the intelligence of behaviour and machines. Paper to the Second Joint Conference on Artificial Intelligence. London, England.

Purtill, Richard L. 1971. Beating the imitation game. *Mind* LXXX(318):290–294. *Reprinted in chapter 10.*

Turing, Alan M. 1950. Computing machinery and intelligence. *Mind* LIX(236): 433–460. *Reprinted in chapter 4.*

Turing Test Chauvinism

Objections to the Turing Test as a sufficient criterion of intelligence are based on the worry that it is too easy to pass. Gunderson thinks of verbal behavior as just one example of intelligent behavior, and perhaps one like performing arithmetic or engaging in a mindless job, which require no thinking at all; Block thinks simple table lookup might suffice to implement verbal behavior; Searle thinks that it might be done by memorizing some rules for manipulating slips of paper.

On the other hand, the inadequacy of the Turing Test as a necessary condition, highlighted by Purtill, is noted in passing by Turing himself. "May not machines carry out something which ought to be described as thinking but which is very different from what a man does? This objection is a very strong one, but at least we can say that if, nevertheless, a machine can be constructed to play the imitation game satisfactorily, we need not be troubled by this objection." (Turing 1950, 435, *chapter 4*)

The Bar Hillel experience discussed earlier may convince some that the problems of processing natural language are in no sense easy, indeed qualitatively as hard as those of any behavior that people engage in, and that fluent verbal behavior is so difficult, so tied to contingent details of human idiosyncrasies, that its absence is hardly a frailty of an intelligent agent at all.

Another argument of this sort is made most strongly by Robert French. As an antidote to worries about the Turing Test being too easy, French exhorts us to keep in mind just how hard it can be, based not on the Bar Hillel phenomenon that understanding requires arbitrary world knowledge (relative sizes of writing implements, toy boxes, and pen enclosures), but rather because it requires arbitrary "subcognitive" cultural knowledge, knowledge that we as members of a social milieu have tacit yet ineffable knowledge of.

French thinks that the test is so difficult that only humans could pass it. This is not inconsistent with its being a sufficient condition for intelligence, but as French notes in a later reply to Dale Jacquette (1993), "To be useful as a test for intelligence, it would be nice if *some* intelligent beings other than those that had experienced the world as we humans had could pass it." (French 1995)

13

Subcognition and the Limits of the Turing Test

Robert M. French

1 Introduction

Alan Turing, in his original article (Turing 1950, *chapter 4*) about an imitation-game definition of intelligence, seems to be making two separate claims. The first, the philosophical claim, is that if a machine could pass the Turing Test, it would necessarily be intelligent. This claim I believe to be correct.[1] His second point, the pragmatic claim, is that in the not-too-distant future it would in fact be possible actually to build such a machine. Turing clearly felt that it was important to establish both claims. He realized, in particular, that if one could rigorously show that *no* machine could ever pass his test, his philosophical point, while still true, would lose a great deal of significance. He thus devoted considerable effort to establishing not only the philosophical claim but also the pragmatic claim.

Ever since his article appeared most philosophers have concentrated almost exclusively on attacking or defending the philosophical claim. There are those who believe that passing the Turing Test constitutes a sufficient condition for intelligence and those who do not. The philosophical importance of this first claim is that it provided a clean and novel test for intelligence that neatly sidestepped the vast philosophical quagmire of the mind-body problem. The philosophical claim translates elegantly into an operational definition of intelligence: whatever *acts* sufficiently intelligent *is* intelligent.

---

1 For a particularly clear defence of this view, see "Can Machines Think?" by Daniel Dennett (1985, *chapter 16*).

However, in this paper I will take issue with Turing's pragmatic claim, arguing that the very capacity of the Turing Test to probe the deepest, most essential areas of human cognition makes it virtually useless as a real test for intelligence. I strongly disagree with Hubert Dreyfus's claim, for example, that "as a goal for those actually trying to construct thinking machines, and as a criterion for critics to use in evaluating their work, Turing's test was just what was needed" (Dreyfus 1979). We will see that the Turing Test could be passed only by things that have experienced the world as we have experienced it, and this leads to the central point of the present paper, namely, that *the Test provides a guarantee not of intelligence but of culturally-oriented human intelligence.*

I establish this consequence of the Turing Test by proposing a first set of "subcognitive" questions that are explicitly designed to reveal low-level cognitive structure. Critics might object that there is something unfair about this type of question and suggest that it be disallowed. This leads to another important claim of this paper, which is that in fact, there is no way to distinguish questions that are subcognitive from those that are not. Close examination of some of the original questions of the Turing Test reveals that they, too, are subcognitive. In like manner, any sufficiently broad set of questions making up a Turing Test would necessarily contain questions that rely on subcognitive associations for their answers. I will show that it is impossible to tease apart "subcognitive" questions from ones that are not. From this it follows that the cognitive and subcognitive levels are inextricably intertwined.

It is this essential inseparability of the subcognitive and cognitive levels—and for that matter even the physical and cognitive levels—that makes the Turing Test a test for *human* intelligence, not intelligence in general. This fact, while admittedly interesting, is not particularly useful if our goal is to gain insight into intelligence in general. But if we cannot use the Turing Test to this end, it may turn out that the best (or possibly only) way of discussing general intelligence will be in terms of categorization abilities, the capacity to learn new concepts, to adapt old concepts to a new environment, and so on. Perhaps what philosophers in the field of artificial intelligence need is not simply a *test* for intelligence but rather a *theory* of intelligence. The precise elements of this theory are, as they were in 1950 when Turing proposed his imitation-game test, still the subject of much controversy.

2   On Nordic Seagulls

Consider the following parable: It so happens that the only flying animals known to the inhabitants of a large Nordic island are seagulls. Everyone on the island acknowledges, of course, that seagulls can fly. One day the two resident philosophers on the island are overheard trying to pin down what "flying" is really all about.

Says the first philosopher, "The essence of flying is to move through the air."

"But you would hardly call this flying, would you?" replies the second, tossing a pebble from the beach out into the ocean.

"Well then, perhaps it means to remain aloft for a certain amount of time."

"But clouds and smoke and children's balloons remain aloft for a very long time. And I can certainly keep a kite in the air as long as I want on a windy day. It seems to me that there must be more to flying than merely staying aloft."

"Maybe it involves having wings and feathers."

"Penguins have both, and we all know how well they fly. . . . "

And so on. Finally, they decide to settle the question by, in effect, avoiding it. They do this by first agreeing that the only examples of objects that they are absolutely certain can fly are the seagulls that populate their island. They do, however, agree that flight has something to do with being airborne and that physical features such as feathers, beaks, and hollow bones probably are superficial aspects of flight. On the basis of these assumptions and their knowledge of Alan Turing's famous article about a test for intelligence, they hit upon the Seagull Test for flight. The Seagull Test is meant to be a very rigorous sufficient condition for flight. Henceforth, if someone says, "I have invented a machine that can fly", instead of attempting to apply any set of flight-defining criteria to the inventor's machine, they will put it to the Seagull Test. The *only* things that they will certify with absolute confidence as being able to fly are those that can pass the Seagull Test. On the other hand, they agree that if something fails the Test, they will not pass judgement; maybe it can fly, maybe it can not.

The Seagull Test works much like the Turing Test. Our philosophers have two three-dimensional radar screens, one of which tracks a real seagull; the other will track the putative flying machine. They may run any imaginable experiment on the two objects in an attempt to determine which is the seagull and which is the machine, but they may watch them only on their radar screens. The machine will be said to have passed the Seagull Test for flight if both philosophers are indefinitely unable to distinguish the seagull from the machine.

An objection might be raised that some of their tests (for example, testing for the ability to dip in flight) might have nothing to do with flying. The philosophers would reply: "So what? We are looking for a sufficient condition for flight, not a *minimal* sufficient condition. Furthermore, we understand that ours is a very hard test to pass, but rest assured, inventors of flying machines, failing the Test proves nothing. We will not claim that your machine *cannot* fly if it fails the Seagull Test; it may very well be able to. However we, as philosophers, want to be absolutely certain we have a true case of flight, and the only way we can be sure of this is if your machine passes the Seagull Test."

Now, of course, the Seagull Test will rightly take bullets, soap bubbles, and snowballs out of the running. This is certainly as it should be. But helicopters and jet airplanes—which *do* fly—would also never pass it. Nor, for that matter, would bats or beetles, albatrosses or hummingbirds. In fact, under close scrutiny, probably only seagulls would pass the Seagull Test, and maybe only seagulls from the philosophers' Nordic island, at that. What we have is thus not a test for flight at all, but rather a test for flight as practised by a Nordic seagull.

For the Turing Test, the implications of this metaphor are clear: an entity could conceivably be extremely intelligent but, if it did not respond to the interrogator's questions in a thoroughly human way, it would not pass the Test. The *only* way, I believe, that it would have been able to respond to the questions in a perfectly human-like manner is to have experienced the world as humans have. What we have is thus not a test for intelligence at all, but rather a test for intelligence as practised by a human being.

Furthermore, the Turing Test admits of no degrees in its sufficient determination of intelligence, in spite of the fact that the intuitive human notion of intelligence clearly does. Spiders, for example, have little intelligence, sparrows have more but not as much as dogs, monkeys have still more but not as much as eight-year-old humans, who in turn have less than adults. If we agree that the underlying neural mechanisms are essentially the same across species, then we ought to treat intelligence as a continuum and not just as something that only humans have. It seems reasonable to ask a good test for intelligence to reflect, if only approximately, those differences in degree. It is especially important in the study of artificial intelligence that researchers not treat intelligence as an all-or-nothing phenomenon.

3   Subcognitive Questions

Before beginning the discussion of subcognitive questions, I wish to make a few assumptions that I feel certain Turing would have accepted. First, I will allow the interrogator to poll humans for the answers to some of the questions prior to posing them during the imitation game itself. (I will call the humans who are polled the "interviewees".) I also want to make explicit an assumption that is tacit in Turing's article, namely that the human candidate and the interrogator (and, in this case, the interviewees) are all from the same culture and that the computer will be attempting to pass as an individual from that culture. Thus, if ever the computer replies, "I don't speak English" or something of the sort, the interrogator will immediately deduce, rightly, that the other candidate is the human being. Finally, while I believe that it is *theoretically* possible to build a machine capable of experiencing the world in a manner indistinguishable from a human being—a machine that can fall off bicycles, be scratched by thorns on roses, smell sewage, and taste strawberries—I will assume that no computer is now, or will in the foreseeable future be, in a position to do so.

I will designate as *subcognitive* any question capable of providing a window on low-level (i.e., unconscious) cognitive structure. By "low-level cognitive structure" I am referring, in particular, to the subconscious associative network in human minds that consists of highly overlapping activatable representations of experience. This is the level currently being explored by new approaches to cognitive modelling.[2]

The first class of questions is explicitly designed to reveal low-level cognitive structure (and I think everyone will agree that they do so). I will respond to the anticipated objection that these explicitly subcognitive

---

2 Three different approaches that all address subcognitive issues are provided by Feldman and Ballard (1982), Hofstadter et al. (1987), and Rumelhart and McClelland (1986).

questions are unfair by following up with another set of questions that seem, at first glance, to be at a higher cognitive level than the first set. These questions will turn out, under closer examination, to be subcognitive also. I will conclude with a final set of questions that seem uncontestably to be innocent high-level cognitive questions but that will be just as hard as the others were for the computer to answer in the way a human would.

4 Associative Priming

This first set of questions is based on current research on associative priming, often called semantic facilitation. The idea is the following. Humans, over the course of their lives, develop certain associations of varying strength among concepts. By means of the so-called lexical decision task it has been established[3] that it requires less time to decide that a given item is a word when that item is preceded by an associated word. If, for example, the item "butter" is preceded by the word "bread", it would take significantly less time to recognize that "butter" was a word than had an unassociated word like "dog" or a nonsense word preceded it.

The Turing Test interrogator makes use of this phenomenon as follows. The day before the Test, she selects a set of words (and non-words), runs the lexical decision task on the interviewees and records average recognition times. She then comes to the Test armed with the results of this initial test, asks both candidates to perform the same task she ran the day before, and records the results. Once this has been done, she identifies as the human being the candidate whose results more closely resemble the average results produced by her sample population of interviewees.

The machine would invariably fail this type of test because there is no a priori way of determining associative strengths (i.e., a measure of how easy it is for one concept to activate another) between *all* possible concepts. Virtually the only way a machine could determine, even on average, all of the associative strengths between human concepts is to have experienced the world as the human candidate and the interviewees had.

A further example might help to illustrate the enormous problem of establishing the associative weights between concepts in an a priori manner.

---

3 A particularly relevant, succinct discussion of associative priming is provided by Anderson (1983). In this chapter Anderson makes reference to the classic work on facilitation by Meyer and Schvaneveldt (1971).

Certain groups of concepts, say, the steps in baking a cake, are profoundly sequential in nature. The associative strengths between sequentially related concepts involved in baking a cake (opening the flour bin, breaking the eggs, mixing the flour and eggs, putting the mixture in the oven, setting the oven temperature, removing a baked cake) are profoundly dependent on the human experience of cake-baking. Even if we made the assumption that concepts like "removing a cake from an oven", "breaking eggs", "setting oven temperature", and so on could be explicitly programmed into our computer, the associative strengths among these concepts would have to reflect the temporal order in which they normally occurred in human experience if the machine were to pass the Turing Test. We would have to be able to set these strengths in an a priori manner, not only for category sequences associated with cake-baking, but also between the concepts of *all* the concept sequences experienced by humans. While this may be theoretically possible, it would certainly seem to be very implausible.

Now, suppose a critic claims that these explicitly subcognitive questions are unfair because—ostensibly, at least—they have nothing to do with intelligence; they probe, the critic says, a cognitive level well below that necessary for intelligence and therefore they should be disallowed. Suppose, then, that we obligingly disallow such questions and propose in their stead a new set of questions that seem, at first glance, to be at a higher cognitive level.

5   Rating Games

Neologisms will form the basis of the next set of questions, which we might call the Neologism Rating Game. Our impressions involving made-up words provide particularly impressive examples of the "unbelievable number of forces and factors that interact in our unconscious processing of even...words and names only a few letters long" (Hofstadter 1985).

Consider the following set of questions, all having a totally high-level cognitive appearance:

On a scale of 0 (completely implausible) to 10 (completely plausible), please rate:

- "Flugblogs" as a name Kellogg's would give to a new breakfast cereal
- "Flugblogs" as the name of a new computer company
- "Flugblogs" as the name of big, air-filled bags worn on the feet and used to walk on water

- "Flugly" as the name a child might give its favourite teddy bear
- "Flugly" as the surname of a bank accountant in a W. C. Fields movie
- "Flugly" as the surname of a glamorous female movie star

The interrogator will give, say, between fifty and one hundred questions of this sort to her interviewees,[4] who will answer them. Then, as before, she will give the same set of questions to the two candidates and compare their results to her interviewees' averaged answers. The candidate whose results most closely resemble the answers given by the polled group will almost certainly be the human.

Let us examine a little more closely why a computer that had not acquired our full set of cultural associations would fail this test. Consider "Flugblogs" as the name of a breakfast cereal. It is unquestionably pretty awful. The initial syllable "flug" phonetically activates (unconsciously, of course) such things as "flub", "thug", "ugly", or "ugh!", each with its own aura of semantic connotations. "Blogs", the second syllable, activates "blob", "bog", and other words, which in turn activate a halo of other semantic connotations. The sum total of this spreading activation determines how we react, at a conscious level, to the word. And while there will be no precise set of associated connotations for all individuals across a culture, on the whole there is enough overlap to provoke *similar* reactions to given words and phrases. In this case, the emergent result of these activations is undeniable: "Flugblogs" would be a lousy name for a cereal (unless, of course, the explicit *intent* of the manufacturer is to come up with a perverse-sounding cereal name!).

What about "Flugly" as a name a child might give its favourite teddy bear? Now that certainly sounds plausible. In fact, it's kind of cute. But, on the surface at least, "Flugblogs" and "Flugly" seem to have quite a bit in common; if nothing else, both words have a common first syllable.

---

4 Even though Turing did not impose a time constraint in his original formulation of the imitation game, he did claim that "... in fifty years' time [i.e., by the year 2000] it will be possible to programme computers ... to make them play the imitation game so well that an average interrogator will not have more than 70 per cent chance of making the right identification after five minutes of questioning" (Turing 1950, 442, *chapter 4*). In current discussions of the Turing Test, the duration of the questioning period is largely ignored. In my opinion, one reasonable extension of the Turing Test would include the length of the questioning period as one of its parameters. In keeping wish the spirit of the original claim involving a five-minute questioning period, I have tried to keep the number of questions short although it was by no means necessary to have done so.

But "Flugly", unlike "Flugblogs", almost certainly activates "snugly" and "cuddly", which would bring to mind feelings of cosiness, warmth, and friendship. It certainly also activates "ugly", which might normally provoke a rather negative feeling, but, in this case, there are competing positive associations of vulnerability and endearment activated by the notion of children and things that children like. To see this, we need look no further than the tale of the Ugly Duckling. In the end, the positive associations seem to dominate the unpleasant sense of "ugly". The outcome of this subcognitive competition means that "Flugly" is perceived by us as being a cute, quite plausible name for a child's teddy bear. And yet, different patterns of activations rule out "Flugly" as a plausible name for a glamorous female movie star.

Imagine, for an instant, what it would take for a computer to pass this test. To begin with, there is no way it could look up words like "flugly" and "flugblogs": they do not exist. To judge the appropriateness of any given word (or, in this case, nonsense words) in a particular context requires taking unconscious account of a vast number of culturally acquired, competing associations triggered initially by phonetic resemblances. And, even though one might succeed in giving a program a certain number of these associations (for example, by asking subjects questions similar to the ones above and then programming the results into the machine), the space of neologisms is virtually infinite. The human candidate's reaction to such made-up words is an emergent result of myriad subcognitive pressures, and unless the machine has a set of associations similar to those of humans both in degree and in kind, its performance in the Rating Game would necessarily differ more from the interviewees' averaged performance than would the human candidate's. Once again, a machine that had not experienced the world as we have would be unmasked by the Rating Game, even though the questions comprising it seemed, at least at the outset, so cognitively high-level in nature.

If, for some reason, the critics were still unhappy with the Neologism Rating Game using made-up words, we could consider a variation on the game, the Category Rating Game,[5] in which all of the questions would have the form: "Rate Xs as Ys" (0 = "could be no worse", 10 = "could be no better") where X and Y are any two categories. Such questions give

---

5 This variation of the Rating Game was suggested to me by Douglas Hofstadter.

every appearance of being high-level cognitive questions: they are simple in the extreme and rely not on neologisms but on everyday words. For example, we might have, "Rate *dry leaves as hiding places*". Now, clearly no definition of "dry leaves" will ever include the fact that piles of dry autumn leaves are wonderful places for children to hide in and, yet, few among us would not make that association upon seeing the juxtaposition of those two concepts. There is therefore some overlap, however implausible this might seem a priori, between the categories of "dry leaves" and "hiding places". We might give dry leaves a rating of, say, 4 on a 10-point scale. Or, another example, "Rate *radios as musical instruments*". As in the previous example, people do not usually think of radios as musical instruments, but they do indeed have some things in common with musical instruments: both make sounds; both are designed to be listened to; John Cage once wrote a piece in which radios were manipulated by performers; etc. Once again, therefore, there is some overlapping of these two categories; as a musical instrument, therefore, we might give a radio a rating of 3 or even 4 on a 10-point scale.

The answer to any particular rating question is necessarily based on how we view the two categories involved, each with its full panoply of associations, acquired through experience, with other categories. A list of such questions might include:

- "Rate banana splits as medicine"
- "Rate grand pianos as wheelbarrows"
- "Rate purses as weapons"
- "Rate pens as weapons"
- "Rate jackets as blankets"
- "Rate pine boughs as mattresses"

Just as before, it would be virtually impossible to explicitly program into the machine all the various types and degrees of associations necessary to answer these questions like a human.

Other variations of the Rating Game could be invented that would have the same effect. We could, for example, have a Poetic Beauty Rating Game where we would ask for ratings of beauty of various lines of poetry.[6] For

---

6 In fact, the interrogator in Turing's original article does indeed conduct a line of questioning about a particular turn of phrase in one of Shakespeare's sonnets.

a computer to do as well as a human on this test, it would either have to have experienced our life and language *as we had* or contain a theory of poetic beauty that included necessary and sufficient conditions for what constituted a beautiful line of poetry. Few would seriously argue that such an experience-independent theory was possible.

Or a Joke Rating Game: "On a scale of 0 to 10 rate how funny you find each of the following jokes" followed by a list of jokes. Again, capturing the necessary and sufficient conditions for humour would seem to require a grounding in all of human experience. Most jokes depend on a vast network of associative world knowledge ranging from the most ridiculous trivia, through common but little-commented-upon aspects of human experience, to the most significant information about current events. So here again is an example of where a computer, in order to appreciate humour as we did and thereby fool the Turing Test interrogator, would almost certainly have had to experience life and language as we had.

A final variation: The Advertising Rating Game. "Given the following product: X, rate the following advertising slogan Y for that product." Once again, it is hard to imagine any theory that could provide necessary and sufficient conditions for catchy advertising slogans. Good advertising slogans, like good jokes and good lines of poetry, are perceived as good because of the myriad subconscious pressures and associations gathered in a lifetime of experiencing the world.

6 The Impossibility of Isolating the Physical Level from the Cognitive Level

One of the tacit assumptions on which Turing's proposed test rests is that it is possible to isolate the "mere" (and thus unimportant to the essence of cognition) physical level from the (essential) cognitive level. This is the reason, for example, that the candidates communicate with the interrogator by teletype, that the interrogator is not permitted to see them, and so on. Subcognitive questions, however, will always allow the interrogator to "peek behind the screen". The Turing Test is really probing the associative concept (and sub-concept) networks of the two candidates. These networks are the product of a lifetime of interaction with the world which *necessarily involves* human sense organs, their location on the body, their sensitivity to various stimuli, etc. Consider, for example, a being that resembled us precisely in all physical respects except that its eyes were attached to its knees. This physical difference alone would engender enormous differences in its associative concept network compared to our own. Bicycle riding, crawling on the floor, wearing various articles of clothing (e.g., long pants), and negotiating crowded hallways would all be experienced in a vastly different way by this individual.

The result would be an associative concept network that would be significantly—and detectably by the Turing Test—different from our own. Thus, while no one would claim that the physical location of eyes had anything essential to do with intelligence, a Turing Test could certainly distinguish this individual from a normal human being. The moral of the story is that the physical level is *not* disassociable from the cognitive level. When Dreyfus (1979) says that no one expects an intelligent robot to be able to "get across a busy street. It must only compete in the more objective and disembodied areas of human behaviour, so as to be able to win at Turing's game", he, like Turing, is tacitly accepting that such a separation of the physical and the cognitive levels is indeed possible. This may have seemed to be the case at first glance but further examination shows that the two are inextricably intertwined.

7   Can the Turing Test Be Appropriately Modified?

Any reasonable set of questions in a Turing Test will necessarily contain subcognitive questions in some form or another. Ask enough of these questions and the computer will become distinguishable from the human because its associative concept network would necessarily be unlike ours. And thus the computer would fail the Turing Test.

Is it possible to modify the rules of the Turing Test in such a way that subcognitive questions are forbidden? I think not. The answers to subcognitive questions emerge from a lifetime of experience with the minutiae of existence, ranging from functionally adaptive world-knowledge to useless trivia. The sum total of this experience with its extraordinarily complex interrelations is what defines human intelligence and this is what Turing's imitation game tests for. What we would really like is a test for (or, lacking that, a theory of) intelligence *in general*. Surely, we would not want to limit a Turing Test to questions like, "What is the capital of France?", or "How many sides does a triangle have?" If we admit that intelligence in general must have *something* to do with categorization, analogy-making, and so on, we will of course want to ask questions that test these capacities. But these are the very questions that will allow us, unfailingly, to unmask the computer.

8   The Relevance of Subcognitive Factors

There remains the question of the *relevance* of these subcognitive factors that, as I believe I have shown, make it essentially impossible for a machine that has not experienced the world as we have to pass the Turing Test. Are these factors irrelevant to intelligence—just as a seagull's dipping in flight is irrelevant to flying in general—or are they a necessary substrate of intelligence? An initial part of my response is that a human subcognitive substrate is definitely not necessary to intelligence in general. The Turing Test tests precisely for the presence of a human subcognitive substrate and this is why it is limited as a test for general intelligence.

On the other hand, I believe that some subcognitive substrate is necessary to intelligence. I will not present a detailed defence of this view in this paper for two reasons: first, such a defence is beyond the scope of this paper, the goal of which has only been to discuss the limits of the Turing Test as a tool for determining intelligence, and second, the necessity of a subcognitive substrate for intelligence has been compellingly argued elsewhere (Hofstadter 1985). Some ideas of the defence will, however, be briefly presented below.

There is little question that intelligence relies on an extraordinarily complex network of concepts with various degrees of overlap. Philosophers from Wittgenstein (1958) to Lakoff (1987) have shown that the boundaries of concepts are extraordinarily elusive things to pin down. It is probably impossible, even in principle, to describe categories in an absolute, objective manner. "Apples", for example, are almost always members of the category "food", but what about "grass", or "shoes"? If you have not eaten for ten days, "shoes" might well fall into your category of "food". But could something like "the Spanish Inquisition" ever be considered "food"? (Of course. Consider the following statement by a professor about to give an extraordinarily long lecture on medieval methods of torture: "The meat of the first three hours of this lecture will be medieval torture in general. And if none of you has fallen asleep by then, we'll have the Spanish Inquisition for dessert."[7]) This is not a point to be taken lightly, for the associative overlap of categories essential to intelligence (and creativity) frequently occurs near the blurry boundaries of categories. And, to repeat, these boundaries are virtually impossible to define in an objective, context-independent way. Most of our thought processes are intimately tied to the associative overlap of categories. One particular example is analogy-making. Considered by many to be a *sine qua non* of intelligent behaviour, it relies heavily on the ability to see two apparently unrelated situations as members, however obliquely, of the same category.

If we can view categories as being composed of many tiny (subcognitive) parts that can overlap with the subcognitive parts of other categories, we can go a long way to explaining these associative phenomena. If, on the other hand, we deny the relevance of subcognitive factors in intelligence, we are left with the daunting, perhaps impossible, task of explicitly defining *all* of the possible attributes of each particular category in every conceivable context. It is, therefore reasonable to conclude that all intelligence has a subcognitive substrate. In particular, this implies that an intelligent computer would have to possess such a substrate, though there is no reason to believe that this substrate would be identical to our own.

9   Conclusion

In conclusion, the imitation game proposed by Alan Turing provides a very powerful means of probing human-like cognition. But when the Test is actually used as a real test for intelligence, as certain philosophers propose, its very strength becomes a weakness. Turing invented the imitation game only as a novel way of looking at the question "Can machines think?" But it turns out to be so powerful that it is really asking: "Can machines think exactly like human beings?" As a real test for intelligence, the latter question is significantly less interesting than the former. The Turing Test provides a sufficient condition for human intelligence but does not address the more important issue of intelligence in general.

I have tried to show that only a computer that had acquired adult human intelligence by experiencing the world as we have could pass the Turing Test. In addition, I feel that any attempt to "fix" the Turing Test

---

7 This example is due to Peter Suber.

so that it could test for intelligence in general and not just human intelligence is doomed to failure because of the completely interwoven and interdependent nature of the human physical, subcognitive, and cognitive levels. To gain insight into intelligence, we will be forced to consider it in the more elusive terms of the ability to categorize, to generalize, to make analogies, to learn, and so on. It is with respect to these abilities that the computer will always be unmasked if it has not experienced the world as a human being has.[8]

Bibliography

Anderson, J. R. 1983. *The architecture of cognition*, chap. 3, 86–125. Cambridge, MA: Harvard University Press.

Dennett, Daniel. 1985. Can machines think? In *How we know*, ed. Michael Shafto, 121–145. San Francisco, CA: Harper & Row. *Reprinted in chapter 16.*

Dreyfus, Hubert. 1979. *What computers can't do: A critique of artificial reason.* Revised ed. New York, NY: Harper & Row.

Feldman, J., and F. Ballard. 1982. Connectionist models and their properties. *Cognitive Science* 205–254.

Hofstadter, Douglas R. 1985. On the seeming paradox of mechanizing creativity. In *Metamagical themas*, 526–46. New York, NY: Basic Books, Inc.

Hofstadter, Douglas R., Melanie Mitchell, and Robert M. French. 1987. Fluid concepts and creative analogies: A theory and its computer implementation. CSMIL Technical Report 10, University of Michigan.

Lakoff, George. 1987. *Women, fire and dangerous things.* Chicago, IL: The University of Chicago Press.

Meyer, D. E., and R. W. Schvaneveldt. 1971. Facilitation in recognizing pairs of words: Evidence of a dependence between retrieval operations. *Journal of Experimental Psychology* 227–234.

Rumelhart, David, and James McClelland, eds. 1986. *Parallel distributed processing.* Cambridge, MA: MIT Press.

Turing, Alan M. 1950. Computing machinery and intelligence. *Mind* LIX(236): 433–460. *Reprinted in chapter 4.*

Wittgenstein, Ludwig. 1958. *Philosophical investigations.* New York, NY: Macmillan Publishing Co.

---

8 I especially wish to thank Daniel Dennett and Douglas Hofstadter for their invaluable comments on the ideas and emphasis of this paper. I would also like to thank David Chalmers, Melanie Mitchell, David Moser, and the editor of *Mind* for their remarks.

The Spark of Intentionality

The most famous proposal for a wedge between Turing-Test passing and intelligence is John Searle's "Chinese room" thought experiment. The Chinese room is a system for converting Chinese input text to Chinese output text inhabited only by an English-speaking homunculus following a detailed program of purely formal symbol manipulation. The Chinese room, by hypothesis, can pass the Turing Test in Chinese. But apparently, no one in the neighborhood understands these Chinese inputs or outputs; the passing of the Turing Test is not based on anyone's (or anything's) thought. Searle concludes that purely formal symbol manipulation systems cannot yield thinking; they are missing the crucial property of intentionality.[1]

Issues of the journal *The Behavioral and Brain Sciences*, in which Searle's article first appeared, have an unusual structure. Each article is followed by a range of commentaries by respected scholars. To forestall criticisms of the Chinese room argument, Searle preemptively presents a series of objections (most notably the systems reply and the robot reply). But as one might expect, these did not exhaust the counterarguments taken by the likes of Block, Dennett, and Fodor. The full set of replies is well worth reading, but beyond the scope of this introduction. But Dennett's commentary in particular, a kind of meta-reply, is interesting to keep in mind while evaluating any philosophical argument of this sort. Dennett

---

1 Dennett (1987a) argues that although Searle claims that the Chinese room is missing intentionality, he really is relying on an argument (still fallacious, Dennett avers) that the Chinese room lacks consciousness.

points out that Searle's argument rests on a thought experiment intended as an "*intuition pump*, a device for provoking a family of intuitions by producing variations on a basic thought experiment" (Dennett 1980). Dennett thinks that this particular intuition pump leads us down a garden path, one stone at a time, to a place where we don't deserve to heed the intuitions we are led to. He proposes that other intuition pumps can pump our intuitions in the opposite direction. (Haugeland provides one in another commentary.) Does the resolution rely on which pump applies the most pressure?

Turing wasn't afraid of using a good intuition pump on occasion himself. His friend and collaborator Irving John Good describes Turing's feelings on the kind of problems raised by Searle, where intentionality sits.

I once asked Turing whether he thought a machine could be conscious. He replied that he would say so if he would otherwise be punished. This was good scientific methodism; the implication was that the question was unanswerable on its own terms. And the question may even seem to be unimportant, until we remember that pain and pleasure are aspects of consciousness. If it is not important to reduce pain and increase pleasure, then nothing is....

In another conversation Turing made the following conjecture. Let us suppose (he said) that a man is gradually dismembered, with the "boundary conditions" somehow being maintained. For example, at one stage we might have just a brain with its input artificially stimulated so that the mind is unaware that the body has been removed. Imagine that this process is continued even beyond the surface of the brain. Then (he felt) there would be a minimum size, of the order of a cubic inch, of original brain tissue, beyond which there would be no consciousness. Turing described this conjecture as a "matter of faith," having no connection with science.

But it seems possible, in this imaginary experiment, that the consciousness would gradually transfer itself to the apparatus; more exactly that the total amount of consciousness would remain constant, and would in the end be associated with the machinery. This conjecture is not intended to imply that consciousness has spatial position, rather that it may be a feature of very complicated information-handling mechanisms. (Good 1962)

Dennett (1978b) expands on just this thought experiment. See also the papers collected by Amélie Rorty (1976).

14

Minds, Brains, and Programs

John R. Searle

What psychological and philosophical significance should we attach to recent efforts at computer simulations of human cognitive capacities? In answering this question, I find it useful to distinguish what I will call "strong" AI from "weak" or "cautious" AI (Artificial Intelligence). According to weak AI, the principal value of the computer in the study of the mind is that it gives us a very powerful tool. For example, it enables us to formulate and test hypotheses in a more rigorous and precise fashion. But according to strong AI, the computer is not merely a tool in the study of the mind; rather, the appropriately programmed computer really *is* a mind, in the sense that computers given the right programs can be literally said to *understand* and have other cognitive states. In strong AI, because the programmed computer has cognitive states, the programs are not mere tools that enable us to test psychological explanations; rather, the programs are themselves the explanations.

I have no objection to the claims of weak AI, at least as far as this article is concerned. My discussion here will be directed at the claims I have defined as those of strong AI, specifically the claim that the appropriately programmed computer literally has cognitive states and that the programs thereby explain human cognition. When I hereafter refer to AI, I have in mind the strong version, as expressed by these two claims.

I will consider the work of Roger Schank and his colleagues at Yale (Schank and Abelson 1977), because I am more familiar with it than I am with any other similar claims, and because it provides a very clear example of the sort of work I wish to examine. But nothing that follows depends upon the details of Schank's programs. The same arguments would apply to Winograd's SHRDLU (Winograd 1973), Weizenbaum's ELIZA

(Weizenbaum 1966), and indeed any Turing machine simulation of human mental phenomena.

Very briefly, and leaving out the various details, one can describe Schank's program as follows: the aim of the program is to simulate the human ability to understand stories. It is characteristic of human beings' story-understanding capacity that they can answer questions about the story even though the information that they give was never explicitly stated in the story. Thus, for example, suppose you are given the following story: "A man went into a restaurant and ordered a hamburger. When the hamburger arrived it was burned to a crisp, and the man stormed out of the restaurant angrily, without paying for the hamburger or leaving a tip." Now, if you are asked "Did the man eat the hamburger?" you will presumably answer, "No, he did not." Similarly, if you are given the following story: "A man went into a restaurant and ordered a hamburger; when the hamburger came he was very pleased with it; and as he left the restaurant he gave the waitress a large tip before paying his bill," and you are asked the question, "Did the man eat the hamburger?" you will presumably answer, "Yes, he ate the hamburger." Now Schank's machines can similarly answer questions about restaurants in this fashion. To do this, they have a "representation" of the sort of information that human beings have about restaurants, which enables them to answer such questions as those above, given these sorts of stories. When the machine is given the story and then asked the question, the machine will print out answers of the sort that we would expect human beings to give if told similar stories. Partisans of strong AI claim that in this question and answer sequence the machine is not only simulating a human ability but also

(1) that the machine can literally be said to *understand* the story and provide the answers to questions, and

(2) that what the machine and its program do *explains* the human ability to understand the story and answer questions about it.

Both claims seem to me to be totally unsupported by Schank's[1] work, as I will attempt to show in what follows.

One way to test any theory of the mind is to ask oneself what it would be like if my mind actually worked on the principles that the theory says

---

1 I am not, of course, saying that Schank himself is committed to these claims.

all minds work on. Let us apply this test to the Schank program with the following *Gedankenexperiment*. Suppose that I'm locked in a room and given a large batch of Chinese writing. Suppose furthermore (as is indeed the case) that I know no Chinese, either written or spoken, and that I'm not even confident that I could recognize Chinese writing as Chinese writing distinct from, say, Japanese writing or meaningless squiggles. To me, Chinese writing is just so many meaningless squiggles.

Now suppose further that after this first batch of Chinese writing I am given a second batch of Chinese script together with a set of rules for correlating the second batch with the first batch. The rules are in English, and I understand these rules as well as any other native speaker of English. They enable me to correlate one set of formal symbols with another set of formal symbols, and all that "formal" means here is that I can identify the symbols entirely by their shapes. Now suppose also that I am given a third batch of Chinese symbols together with some instructions, again in English, that enable me to correlate elements of this third batch with the first two batches, and these rules instruct me how to give back certain Chinese symbols with certain sorts of shapes in response to certain sorts of shapes given me in the third batch. Unknown to me, the people who are giving me all of these symbols call the first batch "a script", they call the second batch a "story", and they call the third batch "questions". Furthermore, they call the symbols I give them back in response to the third batch "answers to the questions", and the set of rules in English that they gave me, they call "the program".

Now just to complicate the story a little, imagine that these people also give me stories in English, which I understand, and they then ask me questions in English about these stories, and I give them back answers in English. Suppose also that after a while I get so good at following the instructions for manipulating the Chinese symbols and the programmers get so good at writing the programs that from the external point of view that is, from the point of view of somebody outside the room in which I am locked—my answers to the questions are absolutely indistinguishable from those of native Chinese speakers. Nobody just looking at my answers can tell that I don't speak a word of Chinese.

Let us also suppose that my answers to the English questions are, as they no doubt would be, indistinguishable from those of other native English speakers, for the simple reason that I am a native English speaker. From the external point of view—from the point of view of someone reading my "answers"—the answers to the Chinese questions and the English questions are equally good. But in the Chinese case, unlike the English case, I produce the answers by manipulating uninterpreted formal symbols. As far as the Chinese is concerned, I simply behave like a computer; I perform computational operations on formally specified elements. For the purposes of the Chinese, I am simply an instantiation of the computer program.

Now the claims made by strong AI are that the programmed computer understands the stories and that the program in some sense explains human understanding. But we are now in a position to examine these claims in light of our thought experiment.

1. As regards the first claim, it seems to me quite obvious in the example that I do not understand a word of the Chinese stories. I have inputs and outputs that are indistinguishable from those of the native Chinese speaker, and I can have any formal program you like, but I still understand nothing. For the same reasons, Schank's computer understands nothing of any stories, whether in Chinese, English, or whatever, since in the Chinese case the computer is me, and in cases where the computer is not me, the computer has nothing more than I have in the case where I understand nothing.

2. As regards the second claim, that the program explains human understanding, we can see that the computer and its program do not provide sufficient conditions of understanding since the computer and the program are functioning, and there is no understanding. But does it even provide a necessary condition or a significant contribution to understanding? One of the claims made by the supporters of strong AI is that when I understand a story in English, what I am doing is exactly the same—or perhaps more of the same—as what I was doing in manipulating the Chinese symbols. It is simply more formal symbol manipulation that distinguishes the case in English, where I do understand, from the case in Chinese, where I don't. I have not demonstrated that this claim is false, but it would certainly appear an incredible claim in the example. Such plausibility as the claim has derives from the supposition that we can construct a program that will have the same inputs and outputs as native speakers, and in addition we assume that speakers have some level of description where they are also instantiations of a program. On the basis of these two assumptions we assume that even if Schank's program isn't the whole story about understanding, it may be part of the story. Well, I suppose that is an empirical possibility, but not the slightest reason has so far been given to believe that it is true, since what is suggested—though certainly not demonstrated—by

the example is that the computer program is simply irrelevant to my understanding of the story. In the Chinese case I have everything that artificial intelligence can put into me by way of a program, and I understand nothing; in the English case I understand everything, and there is so far no reason at all to suppose that my understanding has anything to do with computer programs, that is, with computational operations on purely formally specified elements. As long as the program is defined in terms of computational operations on purely formally defined elements, what the example suggests is that these by themselves have no interesting connection with understanding. They are certainly not sufficient conditions, and not the slightest reason has been given to suppose that they are necessary conditions or even that they make a significant contribution to understanding. Notice that the force of the argument is not simply that different machines can have the same input and output while operating on different formal principles—that is not the point at all. Rather, whatever purely formal principles you put into the computer, they will not be sufficient for understanding, since a human will be able to follow the formal principles without understanding anything. No reason whatever has been offered to suppose that such principles are necessary or even contributory, since no reason has been given to suppose that when I understand English I am operating with any formal program at all.

Well, then, what is it that I have in the case of the English sentences that I do not have in the case of the Chinese sentences? The obvious answer is that I know what the former mean, while I haven't the faintest idea what the latter mean. But in what does this consist and why couldn't we give it to a machine, whatever it is? I will return to this question later, but first I want to continue with the example.

I have had the occasions to present this example to several workers in artificial intelligence, and, interestingly, they do not seem to agree on what the proper reply to it is. I get a surprising variety of replies, and in what follows I will consider the most common of these (specified along with their geographic origins).

But first I want to block some common misunderstandings about "understanding": in many of these discussions one finds a lot of fancy footwork about the word "understanding". My critics point out that there are many different degrees of understanding; that "understanding" is not a simple two-place predicate; that there are even different kinds and levels of understanding, and often the law of excluded middle doesn't even apply in a straightforward way to statements of the form "x understands y"; that in many cases it is a matter for decision and not a simple matter of fact whether x understands y; and so on. To all of these points I want to say: of course, of course. But they have nothing to do with the points at issue. There are clear cases in which "understanding" literally applies and clear cases in which it does not apply; and these two sorts of cases are all I need for this argument.[2] I understand stories in English; to a lesser degree I can understand stories in French; to a still lesser degree, stories in German; and in Chinese, not at all. My car and my adding machine, on the other hand, understand nothing: they are not in that line of business. We often attribute "understanding" and other cognitive predicates by metaphor and analogy to cars, adding machines, and other artifacts, but nothing is proved by such attributions. We say, "The door knows when to open because of its photoelectric cell," "The adding machine *knows how* (*understands how*, is *able*) to do addition and subtraction but not division," and "The thermostat *perceives* changes in the temperature."

The reason we make these attributions is quite interesting, and it has to do with the fact that in artifacts we extend our own intentionality;[3] our tools are extensions of our purposes, and so we find it natural to make metaphorical attributions of intentionality to them; but I take it no philosophical ice is cut by such examples. The sense in which an automatic door "understands instructions" from its photoelectric cell is not at all the sense in which I understand English. If the sense in which Schank's programmed computers understand stories is supposed to be the metaphorical sense in which the door understands, and not the sense in which I understand English, the issue would not be worth discussing. But Newell and Simon (1963) write that the kind of cognition they claim for computers is exactly the same as for human beings. I like the straightforwardness of this claim, and it is the sort of claim I will be considering. I will argue that in the literal sense the programmed computer understands what the car and the adding machine understand, namely, exactly nothing. The computer

---

2 Also, "understanding" implies both the possession of mental (intentional) states and the truth (validity, success) of these states. For the purposes of this discussion we are concerned only with the possession of the states.

3 Intentionality is by definition that feature of certain mental states by which they are directed at or about objects and states of affairs in the world. Thus, beliefs, desires, and intentions are intentional states; undirected forms of anxiety and depression are not. For further discussion see Searle (1979).

understanding is not just (like my understanding of German) partial or incomplete; it is zero.

Now to the replies:

I The Systems Reply (Berkeley)

"While it is true that the individual person who is locked in the room does not understand the story, the fact is that he is merely part of a whole system, and the system does understand the story. The person has a large ledger in front of him in which are written the rules, he has a lot of scratch paper and pencils for doing calculations, he has 'data banks' of sets of Chinese symbols. Now, understanding is not being ascribed to the mere individual; rather it is being ascribed to this whole system of which he is a part."

My response to the systems theory is quite simple: let the individual internalize all of these elements of the system. He memorizes the rules in the ledger and the data banks of Chinese symbols, and he does all the calculations in his head. The individual then incorporates the entire system. There isn't anything at all to the system that he does not encompass. We can even get rid of the room and suppose he works outdoors. All the same, he understands nothing of the Chinese, and a fortiori neither does the system, because there isn't anything in the system that isn't in him. If he doesn't understand, then there is no way the system could understand because the system is just a part of him.

Actually I feel somewhat embarrassed to give even this answer to the systems theory because the theory seems to me so implausible to start with. The idea is that while a person doesn't understand Chinese, somehow the *conjunction* of that person and bits of paper might understand Chinese. It is not easy for me to imagine how someone who was not in the grip of an ideology would find the idea at all plausible. Still, I think many people who are committed to the ideology of strong AI will in the end be inclined to say something very much like this; so let us pursue it a bit further. According to one version of this view, while the man in the internalized systems example doesn't understand Chinese in the sense that a native Chinese speaker does (because, for example, he doesn't know that the story refers to restaurants and hamburgers, etc.), still "the man as a formal symbol manipulation system" *really does understand Chinese*. The subsystem of the man that is the formal symbol manipulation system for Chinese should not be confused with the subsystem for English.

So there are really two subsystems in the man; one understands English, the other Chinese, and "it's just that the two systems have little to do with each other." But, I want to reply, not only do they have little to do with each other, they are not even remotely alike. The subsystem that understands English (assuming we allow ourselves to talk in this jargon of "subsystems" for a moment) knows that the stories are about restaurants and eating hamburgers, he knows that he is being asked questions about restaurants and that he is answering questions as best he can by making various inferences from the content of the story, and so on. But the Chinese system knows none of this. Whereas the English subsystem knows that "hamburgers" refers to hamburgers, the Chinese subsystem knows only that "squiggle squiggle" is followed by "squoggle squoggle." All he knows is that various formal symbols are being introduced at one end and manipulated according to rules written in English, and other symbols are going out at the other end.

The whole point of the original example was to argue that such symbol manipulation by itself couldn't be sufficient for understanding Chinese in any literal sense because the man could write "squoggle squoggle" after "squiggle squiggle" without understanding anything in Chinese. And it doesn't meet that argument to postulate subsystems within the man, because the subsystems are no better off than the man was in the first place; they still don't have anything even remotely like what the English-speaking man (or subsystem) has. Indeed, in the case as described, the Chinese subsystem is simply a part of the English subsystem, a part that engages in meaningless symbol manipulation according to rules in English.

Let us ask ourselves what is supposed to motivate the systems reply in the first place; that is, what *independent* grounds are there supposed to be for saying that the agent must have a subsystem within him that literally understands stories in Chinese? As far as I can tell the only grounds are that in the example I have the same input and output as native Chinese speakers and a program that goes from one to the other. But the whole point of the examples has been to try to show that that couldn't be sufficient for understanding, in the sense in which I understand stories in English, because a person, and hence the set of systems that go to make up a person, could have the right combination of input, output, and program and still not understand anything in the relevant literal sense in which I understand English. The only motivation for saying there *must* be a subsystem in me that understands Chinese is that I have a program and I can pass the Turing test; I can fool native Chinese speakers. But precisely one of the points at issue is the adequacy of the Turing test. The example shows that there could be two "systems", both of which pass the Turing test, but only one of which understands; and it is no argument against this point to say that since they both pass the Turing test they must both understand, since this claim fails to meet the argument that the system in me that understands English has a great deal more than the system that merely processes Chinese. In short, the systems reply simply begs the question by insisting without argument that the system must understand Chinese.

Furthermore, the systems reply would appear to lead to consequences that are independently absurd. If we are to conclude that there must be cognition in me on the grounds that I have a certain sort of input and output and a program in between, then it looks like all sorts of noncognitive subsystems are going to turn out to be cognitive. For example, there is a level of description at which my stomach does information processing, and it instantiates any number of computer programs, but I take it we do not want to say that it has any understanding (cf. Pylyshyn [1980]). But if we accept the systems reply, then it is hard to see how we avoid saying that stomach, heart, liver, and so on, are all understanding subsystems, since there is no principled way to distinguish the motivation for saying the Chinese subsystem understands from saying that the stomach understands. It is, by the way, not an answer to this point to say that the Chinese system has information as input and output and the stomach has food and food products as input and output, since from the point of view of the agent, from my point of view, there is no information in either the food or the Chinese—the Chinese is just so many meaningless squiggles. The information in the Chinese case is solely in the eyes of the programmers and the interpreters, and there is nothing to prevent them from treating the input and output of my digestive organs as information if they so desire.

This last point bears on some independent problems in strong AI, and it is worth digressing for a moment to explain it. If strong AI is to be a branch of psychology, then it must be able to distinguish those systems that are genuinely mental from those that are not. It must be able to distinguish the principles on which the mind works from those on which nonmental systems work; otherwise it will offer us no explanations of what is specifically mental about the mental. And the mental-nonmental distinction cannot be just in the eye of the beholder but it must be intrinsic to the systems; otherwise it would be up to any beholder to treat people as nonmental and, for example, hurricanes as mental if he likes. But quite often in the AI literature the distinction is blurred in ways that would in the long run prove disastrous to the claim that AI is a cognitive inquiry. McCarthy, for example, writes, "Machines as simple as thermostats can be said to have beliefs, and having beliefs seems to be a characteristic of most machines capable of problem solving performance" (McCarthy 1979).

Anyone who thinks strong AI has a chance as a theory of the mind ought to ponder the implications of that remark. We are asked to accept it as a discovery of strong AI that the hunk of metal on the wall that we use to regulate the temperature has beliefs in exactly the same sense that we, our spouses, and our children have beliefs, and furthermore that "most" of the other machines in the room—telephone, tape recorder, adding machine, electric light switch—also have beliefs in this literal sense. It is not the aim of this article to argue against McCarthy's point, so I will simply assert the following without argument. The study of the mind starts with such facts as that humans have beliefs, while thermostats, telephones, and adding machines don't. If you get a theory that denies this point you have produced a counterexample to the theory and the theory is false.

One gets the impression that people in AI who write this sort of thing think they can get away with it because they don't really take it seriously, and they don't think anyone else will either. I propose for a moment at least, to take it seriously. Think hard for one minute about what would be necessary to establish that that hunk of metal on the wall over there had real beliefs, beliefs with direction of fit, propositional content, and conditions of satisfaction; beliefs that had the possibility of being strong beliefs or weak beliefs; nervous, anxious, or secure beliefs; dogmatic, rational, or superstitious beliefs; blind faiths or hesitant cogitations; any kind of beliefs. The thermostat is not a candidate. Neither is stomach, liver, adding machine, or telephone. However, since we are taking the idea seriously, notice that its truth would be fatal to strong AI's claim to be a science of the mind. For now the mind is everywhere. What we wanted to know is what distinguishes the mind from thermostats and livers. And if McCarthy were right, strong AI wouldn't have a hope of telling us that.

II   The Robot Reply (Yale)

"Suppose we wrote a different kind of program from Schank's program. Suppose we put a computer inside a robot, and this computer would not just take in formal symbols as input and give out formal symbols as output, but rather would actually operate the robot in such a way that the robot does something very much like perceiving, walking, moving about, hammering nails, eating, drinking—anything you like. The robot would, for example have a television camera attached to it that enabled it to 'see,' it would have arms and legs that enabled it to 'act,' and all of this would be controlled by its computer 'brain.' Such a robot would, unlike Schank's computer, have genuine understanding and other mental states."

The first thing to notice about the robot reply is that it tacitly concedes that cognition is not solely a matter of formal symbol manipulation, since this reply adds a set of causal relations with the outside world (cf. Fodor [1980]). But the answer to the robot reply is that the addition of such "perceptual" and "motor" capacities adds nothing by way of understanding, in particular, or intentionality, in general, to Schank's original program. To see this, notice that the same thought experiment applies to the robot case. Suppose that instead of the computer inside the robot, you put me inside the room and, as in the original Chinese case, you give me more Chinese symbols with more instructions in English for matching Chinese symbols to Chinese symbols and feeding back Chinese symbols to the outside. Suppose, unknown to me, some of the Chinese symbols that come to me come from a television camera attached to the robot and other Chinese symbols that I am giving out serve to make the motors inside the robot move the robot's legs or arms. It is important to emphasize that all I am doing is manipulating formal symbols: I know none of these other facts. I am receiving "information" from the robot's "perceptual" apparatus, and I am giving out "instructions" to its motor apparatus without knowing either of these facts. I am the robot's homunculus, but unlike the traditional homunculus, I don't know what's going on. I don't understand anything except the rules for symbol manipulation. Now in this case I want to say that the robot has no intentional states at all; it is simply moving about as a result of its electrical wiring and its program. And furthermore, by instantiating the program I have no intentional states of the relevant type. All I do is follow formal instructions about manipulating formal symbols.

III   The Brain Simulator Reply (Berkeley and M.I.T.)

"Suppose we design a program that doesn't represent information that we have about the world, such as the information in Schank's scripts, but simulates the actual sequence of neuron firings at the synapses of the brain of a native Chinese speaker when he understands stories in Chinese and gives answers to them. The machine takes in Chinese stories and questions about them as input, it simulates the formal structure of actual Chinese brains in processing these stories, and it gives out Chinese answers as outputs. We can even imagine that the machine operates, not with a single serial program, but with a whole set of programs operating in parallel, in the manner that actual human brains presumably operate when they process natural language. Now surely in such a case we would have to say that the machine understood the stories; and if we refuse to say that, wouldn't we also have to deny that native Chinese speakers understood the stories? At the level of the synapses, what would or could be different about the program of the computer and the program of the Chinese brain?"

Before countering this reply I want to digress to note that it is an odd reply for any partisan of artificial intelligence (or functionalism, etc.) to make: I thought the whole idea of strong AI is that we don't need to know how the brain works to know how the mind works. The basic hypothesis, or so I had supposed, was that there is a level of mental operations consisting of computational processes over formal elements that constitute the essence of the mental and can be realized in all sorts of different brain processes, in the same way that any computer program can be realized in different computer hardwares: on the assumptions of strong AI, the mind is to the brain as the program is to the hardware, and thus we can understand the mind without doing neurophysiology. If we had to know how the brain worked to do AI, we wouldn't bother with AI. However, even getting this close to the operation of the brain is still not sufficient to produce understanding. To see this, imagine that instead of a monolingual man in a room shuffling symbols we have the man operate an elaborate set of water pipes with valves connecting them. When the man receives the Chinese symbols, he looks up in the program, written in English, which valves he has to turn on and off. Each water connection corresponds to a synapse in the Chinese brain, and the whole system is rigged up so that after doing all the right firings, that is after turning on all the right faucets, the Chinese answers pop out at the output end of the series of pipes.

Now where is the understanding in this system? It takes Chinese as input, it simulates the formal structure of the synapses of the Chinese brain, and it gives Chinese as output. But the man certainly doesn't understand Chinese, and neither do the water pipes, and if we are tempted to adopt what I think is the absurd view that somehow the *conjunction* of man *and* water pipes understands, remember that in principle the man can internalize the formal structure of the water pipes and do all the "neuron firings" in his imagination. The problem with the brain simulator is that it is simulating the wrong things about the brain. As long as it simulates only the formal structure of the sequence of neuron firings at the synapses, it won't have simulated what matters about the brain, namely its causal properties, its ability to produce intentional states. And that the formal properties are not sufficient for the causal properties is shown by the water pipe example: we can have all the formal properties carved off from the relevant neurobiological causal properties.

IV The Combination Reply (Berkeley and Stanford)

"While each of the previous three replies might not be completely convincing by itself as a refutation of the Chinese room counterexample, if you take all three together they are collectively much more convincing and even decisive. Imagine a robot with a brain-shaped computer lodged in its cranial cavity, imagine the computer programmed with all the synapses of a human brain, imagine the whole behavior of the robot is indistinguishable from human behavior, and now think of the whole thing as a unified system and not just as a computer with inputs and outputs. Surely in such a case we would have to ascribe intentionality to the system."

I entirely agree that in such a case we would find it rational and indeed irresistible to accept the hypothesis that the robot had intentionality, as long as we knew nothing more about it. Indeed, besides appearance and behavior, the other elements of the combination are really irrelevant. If we could build a robot whose behavior was indistinguishable over a large range from human behavior, we would attribute intentionality to it, pending some reason not to. We wouldn't need to know in advance that its computer brain was a formal analogue of the human brain.

But I really don't see that this is any help to the claims of strong AI; and here's why: According to strong AI, instantiating a formal program with the right input and output is a sufficient condition of, indeed is constitutive of, intentionality. As Newell (1979) puts it, the essence of the mental is the operation of a physical symbol system. But the attributions of intentionality that we make to the robot in this example have nothing to do with formal programs. They are simply based on the assumption that if the robot looks and behaves sufficiently like us, then we would suppose, until proven otherwise, that it must have mental states like ours that cause and are expressed by its behavior and it must have an inner mechanism capable of producing such mental states. If we knew independently how to account for its behavior without such assumptions we would not attribute intentionality to it especially if we knew it had a formal program. And this is precisely the point of my earlier reply to objection II.

Suppose we knew that the robot's behavior was entirely accounted for by the fact that a man inside it was receiving uninterpreted formal symbols from the robot's sensory receptors and sending out uninterpreted formal symbols to its motor mechanisms, and the man was doing this symbol manipulation in accordance with a bunch of rules. Furthermore, suppose the man knows none of these facts about the robot, all he knows is which operations to perform on which meaningless symbols. In such a case we would regard the robot as an ingenious mechanical dummy. The hypothesis that the dummy has a mind would now be unwarranted and unnecessary, for there is now no longer any reason to ascribe intentionality to the robot or to the system of which it is a part (except of course for the man's intentionality in manipulating the symbols). The formal symbol manipulations go on, the input and output are correctly matched, but the only real locus of intentionality is the man, and he doesn't know any of the relevant intentional states; he doesn't, for example, see what comes into the robot's eyes, he doesn't intend to move the robot's arm, and he doesn't *understand* any of the remarks made to or by the robot. Nor, for the reasons stated earlier, does the system of which man and robot are a part.

To see this point, contrast this case with cases in which we find it completely natural to ascribe intentionality to members of certain other primate species such as apes and monkeys and to domestic animals such as dogs. The reasons we find it natural are, roughly, two: we can't make sense of the animal's behavior without the ascription of intentionality and we can see that the beasts are made of similar stuff to ourselves—that is an eye, that a nose, this is its skin, and so on. Given the coherence of the animal's behavior and the assumption of the same causal stuff underlying it, we assume both that the animal must have mental states underlying its behavior, and that the mental states must be produced by mechanisms made out of the stuff that is like our stuff. We would certainly make similar assumptions about the robot unless we had some reason not to, but as soon as we knew that the behavior was the result of a formal program, and that the actual causal properties of the physical substance were irrelevant we would abandon the assumption of intentionality. (See Griffin [1978].)

There are two other responses to my example that come up frequently (and so are worth discussing) but really miss the point.

V The Other Minds Reply (Yale)

"How do you know that other people understand Chinese or anything else? Only by their behavior. Now the computer can pass the behavioral tests as well as they can (in principle), so if you are going to attribute cognition to other people you must in principle also attribute it to computers."

This objection really is only worth a short reply. The problem in this discussion is not about how I know that other people have cognitive states, but rather what it is that I am attributing to them when I attribute cognitive states to them. The thrust of the argument is that it couldn't be just computational processes and their output because the computational processes and their output can exist without the cognitive state. It is no answer to this argument to feign anesthesia. In "cognitive sciences" one presupposes the reality and knowability of the mental in the same way that in physical sciences one has to presuppose the reality and knowability of physical objects.

VI   The Many Mansions Reply (Berkeley)

"Your whole argument presupposes that AI is only about analogue and digital computers. But that just happens to be the present state of technology. Whatever these causal processes are that you say are essential for intentionality (assuming you are right), eventually we will be able to build devices that have these causal processes, and that will be artificial intelligence. So your arguments are in no way directed at the ability of artificial intelligence to produce and explain cognition."

I really have no objection to this reply save to say that it in effect trivializes the project of strong AI by redefining it as whatever artificially produces and explains cognition. The interest of the original claim made on behalf of artificial intelligence is that it was a precise, well defined thesis: mental processes are computational processes over formally defined elements. I have been concerned to challenge that thesis. If the claim is redefined so that it is no longer that thesis, my objections no longer apply because there is no longer a testable hypothesis for them to apply to.

Let us now return to the question I promised I would try to answer: granted that in my original example I understand the English and I do not understand the Chinese, and granted therefore that the machine doesn't understand either English or Chinese, still there must be something about me that makes it the case that I understand English and a corresponding something lacking in me that makes it the case that I fail to understand Chinese. Now why couldn't we give those somethings, whatever they are, to a machine?

I see no reason in principle why we couldn't give a machine the capacity to understand English or Chinese, since in an important sense our bodies with our brains are precisely such machines. But I do see very strong arguments for saying that we could not give such a thing to a machine where the operation of the machine is defined solely in terms of computational processes over formally defined elements; that is, where the operation of the machine is defined as an instantiation of a computer program. It is not because I am the instantiation of a computer program that I am able to understand English and have other forms of intentionality (I am, I suppose, the instantiation of any number of computer programs), but as far as we know it is because I am a certain sort of organism with a certain biological (i.e. chemical and physical) structure, and this structure, under certain conditions, is causally capable of producing perception, action, understanding, learning, and other intentional phenomena. And part of the point of the present argument is that only something that had those causal powers could have that intentionality. Perhaps other physical and chemical processes could produce exactly these effects; perhaps, for example, Martians also have intentionality but their brains are made of different stuff. That is an empirical question, rather like the question whether photosynthesis can be done by something with a chemistry different from that of chlorophyll.

But the main point of the present argument is that no purely formal model will ever be sufficient by itself for intentionality because the formal properties are not by themselves constitutive of intentionality, and they have by themselves no causal powers except the power, when instantiated, to produce the next stage of the formalism when the machine is running. And any other causal properties that particular realizations of the formal model have, are irrelevant to the formal model because we can always put the same formal model in a different realization where those causal properties are obviously absent. Even if, by some miracle Chinese speakers exactly realize Schank's program, we can put the same program in English speakers, water pipes, or computers, none of which understand Chinese, the program notwithstanding.

What matters about brain operations is not the formal shadow cast by the sequence of synapses but rather the actual properties of the sequences. All the arguments for the strong version of artificial intelligence that I have seen insist on drawing an outline around the shadows cast by cognition and then claiming that the shadows are the real thing. By way of concluding I want to try to state some of the general philosophical points implicit in the argument. For clarity I will try to do it in a question and answer fashion, and I begin with that old chestnut of a question:

"Could a machine think?"

The answer is, obviously, yes. We are precisely such machines.

"Yes, but could an artifact, a man-made machine think?"

Assuming it is possible to produce artificially a machine with a nervous system, neurons with axons and dendrites, and all the rest of it, sufficiently like ours, again the answer to the question seems to be obviously, yes. If you can exactly duplicate the causes, you could duplicate the effects. And indeed it might be possible to produce consciousness, intentionality, and all the rest of it using some other sorts of chemical principles than those that human beings use. It is, as I said, an empirical question.

"OK, but could a digital computer think?"

If by "digital computer" we mean anything at all that has a level of description where it can correctly be described as the instantiation of a computer program, then again the answer is, of course, yes, since we are the instantiations of any number of computer programs, and we can think.

"But could something think, understand, and so on solely in virtue of being a computer with the right sort of program? Could instantiating a program, the right program of course, by itself be a sufficient condition of understanding?"

This I think is the right question to ask, though it is usually confused with one or more of the earlier questions, and the answer to it is no.

"Why not?"

Because the formal symbol manipulations by themselves don't have any intentionality; they are quite meaningless; they aren't even *symbol* manipulations, since the symbols don't symbolize anything. In the linguistic jargon, they have only a syntax but no semantics. Such intentionality as computers appear to have is solely in the minds of those who program them and those who use them, those who send in the input and those who interpret the output.

The aim of the Chinese room example was to try to show this by showing that as soon as we put something into the system that really does have intentionality (a man), and we program him with the formal program, you can see that the formal program carries no additional intentionality. It adds nothing, for example, to a man's ability to understand Chinese.

Precisely that feature of AI that seemed so appealing—the distinction between the program and the realization—proves fatal to the claim that simulation could be duplication. The distinction between the program and its realization in the hardware seems to be parallel to the distinction between the level of mental operations and the level of brain operations. And if we could describe the level of mental operations as a formal program, then it seems we could describe what was essential about the mind without doing either introspective psychology or neurophysiology of the brain. But the equation, "mind is to brain as program is to hardware" breaks down at several points among them the following three:

First, the distinction between program and realization has the consequence that the same program could have all sorts of crazy realizations that had no form of intentionality. Weizenbaum (1976, chapter 2), for example, shows in detail how to construct a computer using a roll of toilet paper and a pile of small stones. Similarly, the Chinese story understanding program can be programmed into a sequence of water pipes, a set of wind machines, or a monolingual English speaker, none of which thereby acquires an understanding of Chinese. Stones, toilet paper, wind, and water pipes are the wrong kind of stuff to have intentionality in the first place—only something that has the same causal powers as brains can have intentionality—and though the English speaker has the right kind of stuff for intentionality you can easily see that he doesn't get any extra intentionality by memorizing the program, since memorizing it won't teach him Chinese.

Second, the program is purely formal, but the intentional states are not in that way formal. They are defined in terms of their content, not their form. The belief that it is raining, for example, is not defined as a certain formal shape, but as a certain mental content with conditions of satisfaction, a direction of fit (see Searle [1979]), and the like. Indeed the belief as such hasn't even got a formal shape in this syntactic sense, since one and the same belief can be given an indefinite number of different syntactic expressions in different linguistic systems.

Third, as I mentioned before, mental states and events are literally a product of the operation of the brain, but the program is not in that way a product of the computer.

"Well if programs are in no way constitutive of mental processes, why have so many people believed the converse? That at least needs some explanation."

I don't really know the answer to that one. The idea that computer simulations could be the real thing ought to have seemed suspicious in the first place because the computer isn't confined to simulating mental operations, by any means. No one supposes that computer simulations of a five-alarm fire will burn the neighborhood down or that a computer simulation of a rainstorm will leave us all drenched. Why on earth would anyone suppose that a computer simulation of understanding actually understood anything? It is sometimes said that it would be frightfully hard to get computers to feel pain or fall in love, but love and pain are neither harder nor easier than cognition or anything else. For simulation, all you need is the right input and output and a program in the middle that transforms the former into the latter. That is all the computer has for anything it does. To confuse simulation with duplication is the same mistake, whether it is pain, love, cognition, fires, or rainstorms.

Still, there are several reasons why AI must have seemed—and to many people perhaps still does seem—in some way to reproduce and thereby explain mental phenomena, and I believe, we will not succeed in removing these illusions until we have fully exposed the reasons that give rise to them.

First, and perhaps most important, is a confusion about the notion of information processing: many people in cognitive science believe that the human brain, with its mind, does something called "information processing", and analogously the computer with its program does information processing; but fires and rainstorms, on the other hand, don't do information processing at all. Thus, though the computer can simulate the formal features of any process whatever, it stands in a special relation to the mind and brain because when the computer is properly programmed, ideally with the same program as the brain, the information processing is identical in the two cases, and this information processing is really the essence of the mental.

But the trouble with this argument is that it rests on an ambiguity in the notion of "information". In the sense in which people "process information" when they reflect, say, on problems in arithmetic or when they read and answer questions about stories, the programmed computer does not do "information processing". Rather, what it does is manipulate formal symbols. The fact that the programmer and the interpreter of the computer output use the symbols to stand for objects in the world is totally beyond the scope of the computer. The computer, to repeat, has a syntax but no semantics. Thus, if you type into the computer "2 plus 2 equals?" it will type out "4". But it has no idea that "4" means 4 or that it means anything at all. And the point is not that it lacks some second-order information about the interpretation of its first-order symbols, but rather that its first-order symbols don't have any interpretations as far as the computer is concerned. All the computer has is more symbols.

The introduction of the notion of "information processing" therefore produces a dilemma: either we construe the notion of "information processing" in such a way that it implies intentionality as part of the process or we don't. If the former, then the programmed computer does not do information processing, it only manipulates formal symbols. If the latter, then, though the computer does information processing, it is only doing so in the sense in which adding machines, typewriters, stomachs, thermostats, rainstorms, and hurricanes do information processing; namely, they have a level of description at which we can describe them as taking information in at one end, transforming it, and producing information as output. But in this case it is up to outside observers to interpret the input and output as information in the ordinary sense. And no similarity is established between the computer and the brain in terms of any similarity of information processing.

Second, in much of AI there is a residual behaviorism or operationalism. Since appropriately programmed computers can have input-output patterns similar to those of human beings, we are tempted to postulate mental states in the computer similar to human mental states. But once we see that it is both conceptually and empirically possible for a system to have human capacities in some realm without having any intentionality at all, we should be able to overcome this impulse. My desk adding machine has calculating capacities, but no intentionality, and in this paper I have tried to show that a system could have input and output capabilities that duplicated those of a native Chinese speaker and still not understand Chinese, regardless of how it was programmed. The Turing test is typical of the tradition in being unashamedly behavioristic and operationalistic, and I believe that if AI workers totally repudiated behaviorism and operationalism much of the confusion between simulation and duplication would be eliminated.

Third, this residual operationalism is joined to a residual form of dualism; indeed strong AI only makes sense given the dualistic assumption that, where the mind is concerned, the brain doesn't matter. In strong AI (and in functionalism, as well) what matters are programs, and programs are independent of their realization in machines; indeed, as far as AI is concerned, the same program could be realized by an electronic machine, a Cartesian mental substance, or a Hegelian world spirit. The single most surprising discovery that I have made in discussing these issues is that many AI workers are quite shocked by my idea that actual human mental phenomena might be dependent on actual physical/chemical properties of actual human brains.

But if you think about it a minute you can see that I should not have been surprised; for unless you accept some form of dualism, the strong AI project hasn't got a chance. The project is to reproduce and explain the mental by designing programs, but unless the mind is not only conceptually but empirically independent of the brain you couldn't carry out the project, for the program is completely independent of any realization. Unless you believe that the mind is separable from the brain both conceptually and empirically—dualism in a strong form—you cannot hope to reproduce the mental by writing and running programs since programs must be independent of brains or any other particular forms of instantiation. If mental operations consist in computational operations on formal symbols, then it follows that they have no interesting connection with the brain; the only connection would be that the brain just happens to be one of the indefinitely many types of machines capable of instantiating the program.

This form of dualism is not the traditional Cartesian variety that claims there are two sorts of *substances,* but it is Cartesian in the sense that it insists that what is specifically mental about the mind has no intrinsic connection with the actual properties of the brain. This underlying dualism is masked from us by the fact that AI literature contains frequent fulminations against "dualism"; what the authors seem to be unaware of is that their position presupposes a strong version of dualism.

"Could a machine think?" My own view is that only a machine could think, and indeed only very special kinds of machines, namely brains and machines that had the same causal powers as brains. And that is the main reason strong AI has had little to tell us about thinking, since it has nothing to tell us about machines. By its own definition, it is about programs, and programs are not machines. Whatever else intentionality is, it is a biological phenomenon, and it is as likely to be as causally dependent on the specific biochemistry of its origins as lactation, photosynthesis, or any other biological phenomena. No one would suppose that we could produce milk and sugar by running a computer simulation of the formal sequences in lactation and photosynthesis, but where the mind is concerned many people are willing to believe in such a miracle because of a deep and abiding dualism: the mind they suppose is a matter of formal processes and is independent of quite specific material causes in the way that milk and sugar are not.

In defense of this dualism the hope is often expressed that the brain is a digital computer (early computers, by the way, were often called "electronic brains"). But that is no help. Of course the brain is a digital computer. Since everything is a digital computer, brains are too. The point is that the brain's causal capacity to produce intentionality cannot consist in its instantiating a computer program, since for any program you like it is possible for something to instantiate that program and still not have any mental states. Whatever it is that the brain does to produce intentionality, it cannot consist in instantiating a program since no program, by itself, is sufficient for intentionality.

Acknowledgment

I am indebted to a rather large number of people for discussion of these matters and for their patient attempts to overcome my ignorance of artificial intelligence. I would especially like to thank Ned Block, Hubert Dreyfus, John Haugeland, Roger Schank, Robert Wilensky, and Terry Winograd.

Bibliography

Fodor, Jerry. 1980. Methodological solipsism. *Behavior and Brain Sciences* 3(1).

Griffin, Donald R. 1978. Cognition and consciousness in nonhuman species. *Behavioral and Brain Sciences* 1(4):555–629.

McCarthy, John. 1979. Ascribing mental qualities to machines. In *Philosophical perspectives in artificial intelligence*, ed. M. Ringle. Atlantic Highlands, NJ: Humanities Press.

Newell, Alan. 1979. Physical symbol systems. Lecture at the La Jolla Conference on Cognitive Science.

Newell, Alan, and Herbert A. Simon. 1963. GPS: A program that simulates human thought. In *Computers and thought*, ed. A. Feigenbaum and V. Feldman, 279–93. New York, NY: McGraw Hill.

Pylyshyn, Z. W. 1980. Computation and cognition: Issues in the foundations of cognitive science. *Behavioral and Brain Sciences* 3(1).

Schank, Roger C., and Robert P. Abelson. 1977. *Scripts, plans, goals, and understanding: An inquiry into human knowledge structures.* Hillsdale, NJ: Lawrence Erlbaum Press.

Searle, John R. 1979. What is an intentional state? *Mind* 88:74–92.

Weizenbaum, Joseph. 1966. Eliza—A computer program for the study of natural language communication between man and machine. *Communications of the Association for Computing Machinery* 9(1):36–45.

———. 1976. *Computer power and human reason.* San Francisco, CA: W. H. Freeman and Co.

Winograd, Terry. 1973. A procedural model of language understanding. In *Computer models of thought and language,* ed. Roger Schank and Kenneth Colby. San Francisco, CA: W. H. Freeman and Co.

The Spark of Richness of Information Processing

The Turing Test could not possibly be a litmus test of intelligence in the sense that only things that *actually* pass a Turing Test are intelligent. Virtually all human beings have never been subject to such a test, yet we don't deny them an attribution of intelligence. What Turing must have had in mind is that such persons *could* pass a Turing Test if they participated in one. They have the *capacity* to pass the Test, and it is the capacity, however unrealized, that is indicative of intelligence. That is, the capacity to pass the test is a sufficient condition for intelligence.[1]

Block (1981, *chapter 15*) first argues that this move from concrete behaviors to capacities (sufficiently broadly construed) may allow a behavioristic definition of intelligence that survives the standard arguments against behavioristic definitions of other mentalistic terms (pain, desire, and so forth).

But still, even this is not sufficient to save the behaviorist Turing Test as a test of intelligence. Like Searle, he too uses a simple constructed machine in a thought experiment to serve as an intuition pump. His "Aunt Bertha machine" operates by looking up in a (very large) table what the developer of the machine thinks his Aunt Bertha might respond to each and every possible conversation up to, say, an hour in length. Such a program is trivial to write; it amounts essentially to a search through a huge tree of possible

---

1 As an example of the superiority of this view of the Turing Test conception of intelligence, note that it vitiates the monkeys and typewriters example from page 138.

conversation prefixes.[2] By hypothesis, it can pass a Turing Test of up to an hour, and therefore has the capacity to do so. But it is clearly not intelligent. It is merely the conduit of the intelligence of Aunt Bertha's nephew. The argument is one against identification of intelligence and Turing-Test-passing in principle, not in practice, so objections on the basis of impracticality can be dispensed with. In the end, Block concludes, a definition of intelligence must be psychologistic, that is, must make reference to internal properties of the agent that displays it. What is missing from the Aunt Bertha machine is the richness of information processing that the real Aunt Bertha possesses.

The vagueness in the notion of "richness of information processing" may seem problematic, but Block is shooting lower than Searle in diagnosing the failings of the Turing Test. "I wish I could say more about just what this sort of richness comes to," says Block. "But I have chosen a much less ambitious task: to give a clear case of something that *lacks* that richness, but nonetheless behaves as if it were intelligent." (Block 1981, *chapter 15, 248*)

Perhaps there is some connection between richness of information processing and the requirement to avert exponential explosions, which Block addresses in his objection 8. One might believe, for instance, that any method that is able to avert the sort of massive exponential blowups intrinsic in caching all possible Turing Test conversations must be performing some sort of information processing that deserves the term "rich". A machine actually passing a Turing Test would provide impressive evidence (and see Moor [1976, *chapter 17*] for the evidentiary view of the Turing Test) of having averted such an explosion, Block's statements about nomological possibility notwithstanding. (I have made this argument quite concrete elsewhere (Shieber 2004).) This is presumably why

---

2 This objection to a behaviorist definition of intelligence was first pointed out by Shannon and McCarthy (1956).

(if the claim in Block's footnote 21 is true) Dennett is content with the amended neo-Turing-Test conception of intelligence.[3]

---

3 Dowe and Hajek (1998) propose a condition directly along these lines, proposing an extension to the Turing Test that requires the machine to store any information in a highly compressed form. The condition would be tested, presumably, by merely noting the size of the program/data that the machine executes. Because of the close connection between compression and inductive inference, such a requirement would go some way towards demonstrating that the machine was acting based on general principles rather than memorization. The authors note that such a condition is certainly non-behaviorist.

15

Psychologism and Behaviorism

Ned Block

Let psychologism be the doctrine that whether behavior is intelligent behavior depends on the character of the internal information processing that produces it. More specifically, I mean psychologism to involve the doctrine that two systems could have actual and potential behavior *typical* of familiar intelligent beings, that the two systems could be exactly alike in their actual and potential behavior, and in their behavioral dispositions and capacities and counterfactual behavioral properties (i.e., what behaviors, behavioral dispositions, and behavioral capacities they would have exhibited had their stimuli differed)—the two systems could be alike in all these ways, yet there could be a difference in the information processing that mediates their stimuli and responses that determines that one is not at all intelligent while the other is fully intelligent.

This paper makes two claims: first, psychologism is true, and thus a natural behaviorist analysis of intelligence that is incompatible with psychologism is false. Second, the standard arguments against behaviorism are inadequate to defeat this natural behaviorist analysis of intelligence or to establish psychologism.

While psychologism is of course anathema to behaviorists,[1] it also seems wrong-headed to many philosophers who would not classify

---

1 Indeed, Ryle's *The Concept of Mind* (Ryle 1949) is a direct attack on psychologism. Ryle considers what we are judging "in judging that someone's performance is or is not intelligent," and he concludes: "Our inquiry is *not into causes* ... but into capacities, skills, habits, liabilities and bents." See Jerry Fodor's *Psychological Explanation* (Fodor 1968) for a penetrating critique of Ryle from a psychologistic point of view.

themselves as behaviorists. For example, Michael Dummett says:

> If a Martian could learn to speak a human language, or a robot be devised to behave in just the ways that are essential to a language speaker, an implicit knowledge of the correct theory of meaning for the language could be attributed to the Martian or the robot with as much right as to a human speaker, even though their internal mechanisms were entirely different. (Dummett 1976)

Dummett's view seems to be that what is relevant to the possession of a certain mental state is a matter of actual and potential behavior, and that internal processing is *not* relevant except to the extent that internal processing affects actual and potential behavior. I think that this Dummettian claim contains an important grain of truth, a grain that many philosophers wrongly take to be incompatible with psychologism.

This grain of truth can be elucidated as follows. Suppose we meet Martians, and find them to be behaviorally indistinguishable from humans. We learn their languages and they learn ours, and we develop deep commercial and cultural relations with them. We contribute to their journals and enjoy their movies, and vice versa. Then Martian and human psychologists compare notes, only to find that in underlying psychological mechanisms the Martians are very different from us. The Martian and human psychologists soon agree that the difference could be described as follows. Think of humans and Martians as if they were the products of conscious design. In any artificial intelligence project, there will be a range of engineering options. For example, suppose one wants to design a machine that makes inferences from information fed into it in the form of English sentences. One strategy would be to represent the information in the machine in English, and to formulate a set of inference rules that operate on English sentences. Another strategy would be to formulate a procedure for translating English into an artificial language whose sentences wear their logical forms on their faces. This strategy would simplify the inference rules, though at the computational cost of implementing the translation procedure. Suppose that the Martian and human psychologists agree that Martians and humans differ as if they were the products of a whole series of engineering decisions that differ along the lines illustrated. Should we conclude that the Martians are *not* intelligent after all? Obviously not! That would be crude human chauvinism. I suggest that philosophers reject psychologism in part because they (wrongly) see psychologism as involving this sort of chauvinism.

One of my purposes in this paper will be to show that psychologism does not in fact involve this sort of chauvinism.

If I succeed in showing psychologism to be true, I will have provided aid and comfort to those of us who have doubts about functionalism (the view that mental states are functional states—states definable in terms of their causal roles). Doubts about functionalism stem in part from the possibility of entities that look and act like people (and possess a network of internal states whose causal roles mirror those of our mental states), but differ from people in being operated by a network of homunculi whose aim is to simulate the functional organization of a person.[2] The presence of the homunculi can be used to argue that the homunculi-heads lack mentality. Defenders of functionalism are often inclined to "bite the bullet," replying along the following lines: "If I were to discover that my best friend and most valuable colleague was a homunculi-head, that should not lead me to regard him as lacking intelligence (or other aspects of mentality), since differences in internal goings-on that do not affect actual or potential behavior (or behavioral counterfactuals) are not relevant to intelligence." If this paper shows psychologism to be true, it blocks this line of defense of functionalism.

Let us begin the main line of argument by focusing on the well-known Turing Test. The Turing Test involves a machine in one room, and a person in another, each responding by teletype to remarks made by a human judge in a third room for some fixed period of time, e.g., an hour. The machine passes the test just in case the judge cannot tell which are the machine's answers and which are those of the person. Early perspectives on the Turing Test reflected the contemporary view of what it was for something to be intelligent, namely that it act in a certain way, a way hard to define, but easy enough to recognize.

---

2 See my "Troubles with Functionalism" (Block 1978b). Direct criticisms appear in William Lycan's "New Lilliputian Argument against Machine Functionalism" (Lycan 1979) and "Form, Function, and Feel" (Lycan 1981). See also Sydney Shoemaker's "Functionalism and Qualia" (Shoemaker 1975), my reply, "Are Absent Qualia Impossible?" (Block 1980), and Shoemaker's rejoinder, "The Missing Absent Qualia Argument—a Reply to Block" (Shoemaker 1981).

Note that the sense of "intelligent" deployed here—and generally in discussion of the Turing Test[3]—is *not* the sense in which we speak of one person being more intelligent than another. "Intelligence" in the sense deployed here means something like the possession of thought or reason.

One popular way of construing Turing's proposal is as a version of operationalism. "Being intelligent" is defined as passing the Turing Test, if it is administered (or alternatively, a la Carnap: if a system is given the Turing Test, then it is intelligent if and only if it passes). Construed operationally, the Turing Test conception of intelligence shares with other forms of operationalism the flaw of stipulating that a certain measuring instrument (the Turing Test) is *infallible*. According to the operationalist interpretation of the Turing Test as a definition of intelligence, it is absurd to ask of a device that passes the Turing Test whether it is *really* intelligent, and it is equally absurd to ask of a device that fails it whether it failed for some extraneous reason, but is nonetheless intelligent.

This difficulty can be avoided by going from the crude operationalist formulation to a familiar behavioral disposition formulation. On such a formulation, intelligence is identified not with the property of passing the test (if it is given), but rather with a behavioral *disposition* to pass the test (if it is given). On this behaviorist formulation, failing the Turing Test is not taken so seriously, since we can ask of a system that fails the test whether the failure *really does* indicate that the system lacks the disposition to pass the test. Further, passing the test is not *conclusive* evidence of a disposition to pass it, since, for example, the pass may have been accidental.

But the new formulation is nonetheless subject to deep difficulties. One obvious difficulty is its reliance on the discriminations of a human judge. Human judges may be able to discriminate *too well*—that is, they may be able to discriminate some genuinely intelligent machines from humans. Perhaps the responses of some intelligent machines will have a machinish style that a good human judge will be able to detect.

---

3 Turing himself said the question of whether the machine could *think* should "be replaced by" the question of whether it could pass the Turing Test, but much of the discussion of the Turing Test has been concerned with *intelligence* rather than thought. (Turing's paper (1950, *chapter 4*) was called "Computing Machinery and *Intelligence*" [emphasis added].)

This problem could be avoided by altering the Turing Test so that the judge is not asked to say which is the machine, but rather is asked to say whether one or both of the respondents are, say, as intelligent as the average human. However, this modification introduces circularity, since "intelligence" is defined in terms of the judge's judgments of intelligence. Further, even ignoring the circularity problem, the modification is futile, since the difficulty just crops up in a different form: perhaps human judges will tend chauvinistically to regard some genuinely intelligent machines as unintelligent because of their machinish style of thought.

More importantly, human judges may be too easily fooled by mindless machines. This point is strikingly illustrated by a very simple program (Boden 1977; Weizenbaum 1966) (two hundred lines in BASIC), devised by Joseph Weizenbaum, which can imitate a psychiatrist by employing a small set of simple strategies. Its major technique is to look for key words such as "I", "you", "alike", "father", and "everybody". The words are ranked—for example, "father" is ranked above "everybody", and so if you type in "My father is afraid of everybody", the machine will respond with one of its "father" responses, such as "What else comes to mind when you think of your father?" If you type in "I know everybody laughed at me", you will get one of its responses to "everybody", for example, "Who in particular are you thinking of?" It also has techniques that simultaneously transform "you" into "I" and "me" into "you", so that if you type in "You don't agree with me", it can reply: "Why do you think that I don't agree with you?" It also *stores* sentences containing certain key words such as "my". If your *current* input contains no key words, but if you had earlier said "My boyfriend made me come here", it will "ignore" your current remark, saying instead, "Does that have anything to do with the fact that your boyfriend made you come here?" If all other tricks fail, it has a list of last ditch responses such as, "Who is the psychiatrist here, you or me?" Though this system is *totally* without intelligence, it proves *remarkably* good at fooling people in short conversations. Of course, Weizenbaum's machine rarely fools anyone for very long if the person has it in mind to explore the machine's capacities. But the program's extraordinary success (Weizenbaum's secretary asked him to leave the room in order to talk to the machine privately) reminds us that human gullibility being what it is, some more complex (but nonetheless unintelligent) program may be able to fool most any human judge. Further, since our tendency to be fooled by such programs seems dependent on our degree of suspicion, sophistication about machines, and other contingent factors, it seems silly to adopt a view of the nature of intelligence or thought that so closely ties it to human judgment. Could the issue of whether a machine *in fact* thinks or is intelligent depend on how gullible human interrogators tend to be?

In sum, human judges may be unfairly chauvinist in rejecting genuinely intelligent machines, and they may be overly liberal in accepting cleverly engineered, mindless machines.

The problems just described could be avoided if we could specify in a non-question-begging way what it is for a sequence of responses to verbal stimuli to be a typical product of one or another style of intelligence. For then we would be able to avoid the dependence on human powers of discrimination that lies at the root of the problems of the last paragraph. Let us suppose, for the sake of argument, that we *can* do this, that is, that we can formulate a non-question-begging definition—indeed, a behavioristically acceptable definition—of what it is for a sequence of verbal outputs to be, as we shall say, "sensible", relative to a sequence of inputs. Though of course it is very doubtful that "sensible" can be defined in a non-question-begging way, it will pay us to *suppose* it can, for as we shall see, even such a definition would not save the Turing Test conception of intelligence.

The role of the judge in Turing's definition of intelligence is to avoid the problem of actually specifying the behavior or behavioral dispositions thought to constitute intelligence. Hence my supposition that "sensible" can be defined in a non-question-begging way amounts to the suggestion that we ignore one of the usual criticisms of behaviorists—that they cannot specify their behavioral dispositions in a non-question-begging way. This is indeed an enormous concession to behaviorism, but it will not play an important role in what follows.

We can now propose a version of the Turing Test conception of intelligence that avoids the problems described:

Intelligence (or more accurately, conversational intelligence) is the disposition to produce a sensible sequence of verbal responses to a sequence of verbal stimuli, whatever they may be.

The point of the "whatever they may be" is to emphasize that this account avoids relying on anyone's ability to come up with clever questions; for in order to be intelligent according to the above-described conception, the system must be disposed to respond sensibly not only to what the interlocutor *actually* says, but to whatever he *might* have said as well.

While the definition just given is a vast improvement (assuming that "sensible" can be adequately defined), it is still a clearly behaviorist formulation. Let us now review the standard arguments against behaviorism with an eye towards determining whether the Turing Test conception of intelligence is vanquished by them.

Probably the most influential argument against behaviorism is due to Chisholm and Geach (Chisholm 1957). Suppose a behaviorist analyzes someone's wanting an ice cream cone as his having a set of behavioral dispositions such as the disposition to grasp an ice cream cone if one is "presented" to him. But someone who wants an ice cream cone will be disposed to grasp it only if he *knows* it is an ice cream cone (and not in general if he thinks it is a tube of axle grease being offered to him as a joke) and only if he does not *believe* that taking an ice cream cone would conflict with other *desires* of more importance to him (for example, the desire to avoid an obligation to return the favor). In short, which behavioral dispositions a desire issues in depends on the *other* mental states of the desirer. And similar points apply to behaviorist analyses of belief and of many other mental states. Conclusion: one cannot define the conditions under which a given mental state will issue in a given behavioral disposition without adverting to *other mental states*.

Another standard argument against behaviorism flows out of the Chisholm-Geach point. If a person's behavioral dispositions depend on a group of mental states, perhaps *different* mental groups can produce the same behavioral dispositions. This line of thought gave rise to the "perfect actor" family of counterexamples. As Putnam (1975b) argued in convincing detail, it is possible to imagine a community of perfect actors (Putnam's super-super-spartans) who, in virtue of lawlike regularities, lack the behavioral dispositions envisioned by the behaviorists to be associated with pain, even though they do in fact have pain. This shows that no behavioral disposition is necessary for pain, and an exactly analogous example of perfect pain-pretenders shows that no behavioral disposition is sufficient for pain either.

Another less important type of traditional counterexample to behaviorism is illustrated by paralytics and brains in vats. Like Putnam's super-super-spartans, they can have pain without the usual dispositions.

When I speak of the "standard objections to behaviorism" in what follows, I shall have these three types of objection in mind: the Chisholm-Geach objection, the perfect actor objection, and the objection based on paralytics and the like.[4]

1   Do the Standard Objections to Behaviorism Dispose of Behaviorist Conceptions of Intelligence?

The three arguments just reviewed are generally and rightly regarded as decisive refutations of behaviorist analyses of many mental states, such as belief, desire, and pain. Further, they serve to refute one quite plausible behaviorist analysis of intelligence. Intelligence is plausibly regarded as a second order mental property, a property that consists in having first order mental states—beliefs, desires, etc.—that are caused to change in certain ways by changes in one another and in sensory inputs. If intelligence is indeed such a second order property, and given that the behaviorist analyses of the first order states are false, one can conclude that a plausible behaviorist view of intelligence is false as well.[5]

But it would be unfair to behaviorism to leave the matter here. Behaviorists generally mean their dispositions to be "pure dispositions".

---

4 While the Chisholm-Geach objection and the perfect actor objection ought in my view to be considered the main objections to behaviorism in the literature, they are not on *everybody's* list. Rorty (1979, 98), for example, has his own list. Rorty and others make heavy weather of one common objection that I have ignored: that behaviorism's analyses of mental states are supposed to be analytic or true in virtue of the meanings of the mental terms. I have ignored analyticity objections in part because behaviorism's main competitors, physicalism and functionalism, are often held in versions that involve commitment to analytic truth (for example, by Lewis and Shoemaker). Further, many behaviorists have been willing to settle for conceptual connections "weaker" than analyticity, and I see no point in exploring such weakened versions of the thesis when behaviorism can be refuted quite independently of the analyticity issue.

5 I am indebted here to Sydney Shoemaker.

Ryle (1949), for example, emphasized that "to possess a dispositional property is not to be in a particular state or to undergo a particular change." Brittleness, according to Ryle, is not a cause of breaking, but merely *the fact* of breaking easily. Similarly, to attribute pain to a person is not to attribute a cause or effect of anything, but simply to say *what he would do* in certain circumstances. However, the notion just mentioned of intelligence as a second order property is at its most plausible when first order mental states are thought of as entities that *have causal roles*. Since pure dispositions do not have causal roles in any straightforward sense, the analysis of intelligence as a second order property should seem unsatisfactory to a behaviorist, even if it is the right analysis of intelligence. Perhaps this explains why behaviorists and behaviorist-sympathizers do not seem to have adopted a view of intelligence as a second order property.

Secondly, an analysis of intelligence along roughly the lines indicated in what I called the Turing Test conception of intelligence is natural for the behaviorist because it arises by patching a widely known operationalist formulation. It is not surprising that such a position is popular in artificial intelligence circles.[6] Further, it seems to be regarded sympathetically by many philosophers who accept the standard arguments against behaviorist analyses of beliefs, desires, etc.[7]

Another attraction of an analysis along the lines suggested by the Turing Test conception of intelligence is that such an analysis can *escape the standard objections to behaviorism*. If I am right about this, then it

---

6 See Schank and Abelson (1977). See also Weizenbaum's (1976) description of the reaction to his ELIZA program.

7 There is, admittedly, something odd about accepting a behaviorist analysis of intelligence while rejecting (on the standard grounds) behaviorist theories of belief, desire, etc. Dennett's view, as I understand it, comes close to this (see footnote 21), though the matter is complicated by Dennett's skepticism about many first order mental states. (See *Brainstorms* (Dennett 1978a), especially the Introduction, and Dennett's support of Ryle against Fodor's psychologism (96). See also Dennett's Mary-Ruth-Sally parable (Dennett 1978a, 105).) In discussions among computer scientists who accept something like the Turing Test conception, the "oddness" of the position doesn't come to the fore because these practitioners are simply not *interested* in making machines that believe, desire, feel, etc. Rather, they focus on machines that are intelligent in being able to reason, solve problems, etc.

would certainly be foolish for the critic of behaviorism to regard behaviorism with respect to intelligence as obliterated by the standard objections, ignoring analyses along the lines of the Turing Test conception of intelligence. For these reasons, I will now return to an examination of how well the Turing Test conception of intelligence fares when faced with the standard objections.

The Turing Test conception of intelligence offers a necessary and sufficient condition of intelligence. The standard objections are effective against the necessary condition claim, but not against the sufficient condition claim. Consider, for example, Putnam's perfect actor argument. The super-super-spartans have pain, though they have no disposition to pain behavior. Similarly, a machine might be intelligent, but not be disposed to *act* intelligently because, for example, it might be programmed to believe that acting intelligently is not *in its interest*. But what about the converse sort of case? A perfect actor who pretends to *have* pain seems as plausible as the super-super-spartans who pretend to *lack* pain, but *this* sort of perfect actor case does *not* seem to transfer to intelligence. For how could an unintelligent system perfectly pretend to be intelligent? It would seem that any system that is *that* good at pretending to be intelligent would have to be intelligent. So no behavioral disposition is necessary for intelligence, but *as far as this standard objection is concerned,* a behavioral disposition may yet be sufficient for intelligence. A similar point applies with respect to the Chisholm-Geach objection. The Chisholm-Geach objection tells us that a disposition to pain behavior is not a sufficient condition of having pain, since the behavioral disposition could be produced by a number of different combinations of mental states, e.g., [pain + a normal preference function] or by [no pain + an overwhelming desire to appear to have pain]. Turning to intelligent behavior, we see that it normally is produced by [intelligence + a normal preference function]. But could intelligent behavior be produced by [no intelligence + an overwhelming desire to appear intelligent]? Indeed, could there be any combination of mental states and properties *not including intelligence* that produces a lawful and thoroughgoing disposition to act intelligently? It seems not. So it seems that the Chisholm-Geach objection does not refute the claim of the Turing Test conception that a certain disposition is sufficient for intelligence.

Finally, the standard paralytic and brain in the vat examples are only intended to apply to claims of necessary conditions—not sufficient conditions—of mental states.

The defect I have just pointed out in the case against the behaviorist view of intelligence is a moderately serious one, since behaviorists have tended to focus on giving sufficient conditions for the application of mental terms (perhaps in part because of their emphasis on the connection between the meaning of "pain" and the circumstances in which we learned to apply it). Turing, for example; was willing to settle for a "sufficient condition" formulation of his behaviorist definition of intelligence.[8] One of my purposes in this paper is to remedy this defect in the standard objections to behaviorism by showing that no behavioral disposition is sufficient for intelligence.

I have just argued that the standard objections to behaviorism are only partly effective against the Turing Test conception of intelligence. I shall now go one step further, arguing that there is a reformulation of the Turing Test conception of intelligence that avoids the standard objections *altogether*. The reformulation is this: substitute the term "capacity" for the term "disposition" in the earlier formulation. As mentioned earlier, there are all sorts of reasons why an intelligent system may fail to be disposed to act intelligently: believing that acting intelligently is not in its interest, paralysis, etc. But intelligent systems that do not want to act intelligently or are paralyzed still have *the capacity* to act intelligently, even if they do not or cannot exercise this capacity.

Let me say a bit more about the difference between a behavioral disposition and a behavioral capacity. A capacity to ϕ need not result in a disposition to ϕ unless certain *internal* conditions are satisfied—say,

---

8 Turing says:

The game may perhaps be criticized on the ground that the odds are weighted too heavily against the machine. If the man were to try and pretend to be the machine he would clearly make a very poor showing. He would be given away at once by slowness and inaccuracy in arithmetic. May not machines carry out something which ought to be described as thinking but which is very different from what a man does? This objection is a very strong one, but at least we can say that if, nevertheless, a machine can be constructed to play the imitation game satisfactorily, we need not be troubled by this objection. (Turing 1950, 435, *chapter 4*)

the appropriate views or motivation or not having curare in one's bloodstream. To a first approximation, a disposition can be specified by a set (perhaps infinite) of input-output conditionals.

If i_1 obtains, then o_1, is emitted
If i_2 obtains, then o_2, is emitted
and so on.[9]

A corresponding first stab at a specification of a capacity, on the other hand, would involve mentioning *internal states* in the antecedents of the conditionals.

If s_a and i_a obtain, then o_a is emitted
If s_b and i_b obtain, then o_b is emitted
and so on,

where s_a and s_b are internal states.[10] In humans, such states would include beliefs and desires and working input and output organs at a minimum, though a machine could have a capacity the exercise of which is contingent only on nonmental internal parameters, e.g., whether its fuses are intact.

What I have said about the difference between a disposition and a capacity is very sketchy, and clarification is needed, especially with regard to the question of what sorts of internal states are to be specified in the antecedents of the conditionals. If paralytics are to be regarded as

---

9 A disposition to ϕ would be more revealingly described in terms of conditionals all of whose consequents are "ϕ is emitted". But in the cases of the "pain behavior" or "intelligent behavior" of interest to the behaviorist, what output is appropriate depends on the input.

10 Of the inadequacies of this sort of analysis of dispositions and capacities of which I am aware, the chief one is that it seems implausible that in attributing a disposition or a capacity, one commits oneself to an infinite (or even a very large) number of specific conditionals. Rather, it seems that in saying that x has the capacity to ϕ, one is saying something *quite vague* about the sort of internal and external conditions in which x would ϕ. Notice, however, that it won't do to be *completely* vague, to analyze "x has the capacity to ϕ", as "possibly, x ϕs", using a notion of possibility that holds entirely unspecified features of the actual world constant. For such an analysis would commit its proponents to ascribing too many capacities. For example, since there is a possible world in which Jimmy Carter has had a womb and associated paraphernalia surgically inserted, Jimmy Carter (*the actual one*) would have the capacity to bear children. There is a difference between the capacities someone has and the capacities he *might* have had, and the analysis of "x has the capacity to ϕ" as "possibly, x ϕs" does not respect this distinction.

possessing behavioral capacities, these internal states will have to include specifications of functioning input and output devices. And if the systems that believe that acting intelligently is not in their interest are to have the required capacity, internal states will have to be specified such that if they were to obtain, the system would believe that acting intelligently is in its interest. Notice, however, that the behaviorist need not be committed to these *mentalistic description* of the internal states; physiological or functional descriptions will do.[11]

The reader may suspect that the reformulation of behaviorism in terms of capacities that I have suggested avoids the standard objections to behaviorism only because it concedes *too much*. The references to internal states—even under physiological or functional descriptions—may be seen as too great a concession to psychologism (or other nonbehavioristic doctrines) for any genuine behaviorist to make. I reply: so much the better for my purposes, for I intend to show that this concession is not *enough,* and that the move from behavioral dispositions to behavioral capacities *will not save behaviorism.*

I now propose the reformulation suggested by the preceding remarks; let us call it the *neo-Turing Test conception of intelligence.*

Intelligence (or, more accurately, conversational intelligence) is the capacity to produce a sensible sequence of verbal responses to a sequence of verbal stimuli, whatever they may be.

Let us briefly consider the standard objections to behaviorism in order to show that the neo-Turing Test conception avoids them. First, intelligent paralytics and brains in vats provide no counterexample, since they do have the capacity to respond sensibly, though they lack the means to exercise the capacity. Second, consider the "perfect actor" objection. An intelligent being who perfectly feigns stupidity nonetheless has the capacity to respond sensibly. Further, as in the disposition case, it would seem that no one could have the capacity to pretend perfectly to be intelligent without actually being intelligent. Third, the new formulation

---

11 The departure from behaviorism involved in appealing to internal states, physiologically or functionally described, is mitigated somewhat when the point of the previous footnote is taken into account. The physiological/functional descriptions in a *proper* analysis of capacities may be so vague as to retain the behavioristic flavor of the doctrine.

entirely disarms the Chisholm-Geach objection. There are many combinations of beliefs and desires that could cause an intelligent being to fail to be *disposed* to respond sensibly, but these beliefs and desires would not destroy the being's *capacity* to respond sensibly. Further, as I have mentioned repeatedly, it is hard to see how any combination of mental states not including intelligence could result in the capacity to respond in an intelligent manner to arbitrary sequences of stimuli.

One final point. Notice that my concession that "sensible" can be defined in a behavioristically adequate way is *not* what is responsible for the fact that the neo-Turing Test conception of intelligence evades the standard objections. What does the job is first the difficulty of conceiving of someone who can pretend perfectly to be intelligent without actually being intelligent, and second, the move from dispositions to capacities.

2   The Argument for Psychologism and against Behaviorism

My strategy will be to describe a machine that produces (and thus has the capacity to produce) a sensible sequence of verbal responses to verbal stimuli. The machine is thus intelligent according to the neo-Turing Test conception of intelligence (and also according to the cruder versions of this conception). However, according to me, a knowledge of the machine's internal information processing shows conclusively that it is totally lacking in intelligence.

I shall now describe my unintelligent machine. First, we require some terminology. Call a string of sentences whose members can be typed by a human typist one after another in an hour or less, a typable string of sentences. Consider the set of all *typable* strings of sentences. Since English has a finite number of words (indeed, a finite number of typable letter strings), this set has a very large, but nonetheless finite, number of members. Consider the subset of this set which contains all and only those strings which are naturally interpretable as conversations in which at least one party's contribution is sensible in the sense described above. Call a string which can be understood in this way a *sensible* string. For example, if we allot each party to a conversation one sentence per "turn" (a simplification I will continue to use), and if each even-numbered sentence in the string is a reasonable conversational contribution, then the string is a sensible one. We need not be very restrictive as to what is to count as sensible. For example, if sentence 1 is "Let's see you talk nonsense", it would be sensible for sentence 2 to be nonsensical. The set of sensible strings so defined is a finite set that could in principle be listed by a very large and clever team working for a long time, with a very large grant and a lot of mechanical help, *exercising imagination and judgment* about what is to count as a sensible string.

Presumably the programmers will find that in order to produce really convincing sensible strings, they will have to think of themselves as simulating some definite personality with some definite history. They might choose to give the responses my Aunt Bertha might give if she were brought to a room with a teletype by her errant nephew and asked to answer "silly" questions for a time.

Imagine the set of sensible strings recorded on tape and deployed by a very simple machine as follows. The interrogator types in sentence A. The machine searches its list of sensible strings, picking out those that begin with A. It then picks one of these A-initial strings at random, and types out its second sentence, call it "B". The interrogator types in sentence C. The machine searches its list, isolating the strings that start with A followed by B followed by C. It picks one of these ABC-initial strings and types out its fourth sentence, and so on.[12]

The reader may be helped by seeing a variant of this machine in which the notion of a sensible string is replaced by the notion of a sensible branch of a tree structure. Suppose the interrogator goes first, typing in one of $A_1 \cdots A_n$. The programmers produce *one* sensible response to each of these sentences, $B_1 \cdots B_n$. For each of $B_1 \cdots B_n$, the interrogator can make various replies, so many branches will sprout below each of $B_1 \cdots B_n$. Again, for each of these replies, the programmers produce one sensible response, and so on. In this version of the machine, all the X-initial strings can be replaced by a single tree with a single token of X as the head node; all the XYZ-initial strings can be replaced by a branch of that tree with Y and Z as the next nodes, and so forth. This machine is a tree-searcher instead of a string-searcher.

So long as the programmers have done their job properly, such a machine will have the capacity to emit a sensible sequence of verbal outputs,

---

12 A version of this machine was sketched in my "Troubles with Functionalism" (Block 1978b).

whatever the verbal inputs, and hence it is intelligent according to the neo-Turing Test conception of intelligence. But actually, the machine has the intelligence of a toaster. *All the intelligence it exhibits is that of its programmers.* Note also that its limitation to Turing Tests of an hour's length is not essential. For a Turing Test of *any* given length, the machine could in principle be programmed in just the same way to pass a Turing Test of that length.

I conclude that the capacity to emit sensible responses is not sufficient for intelligence, and so the neo-Turing Test conception of intelligence is refuted (along with the older and cruder Turing Test conceptions). I also conclude that whether behavior is intelligent behavior is in part a matter of how it is produced. Even if a system has the actual and potential behavior characteristic of an intelligent being, if its internal processes are like those of the machine described, it is not intelligent. So psychologism is true.

I haven't shown *quite* what I advertised initially, since I haven't shown that the machine could duplicate the response properties of a real person. But what I have shown is close enough for me, and besides, it doesn't change the essential point of the example if we imagine the programmers deciding *exactly* what Aunt Bertha would say on the basis of a psychological or physiological theory of Aunt Bertha.

We can now see why psychologism is not incompatible with the point made earlier in connection with the Martian example. The Martian example suggested that it was doubtful that there would be any single natural kind of information processing that must be involved in the production of all intelligent behavior. (I argued that it would be chauvinist to refuse to classify Martians as intelligent *merely* because their internal information processing is very different from ours.) Psychologism is not chauvinist because psychologism requires only that intelligent behavior *not* be the product of a (at least one) certain kind of internal processing. One can insist that behavior which has a certain etiology cannot be intelligent behavior without holding that all intelligent behavior must have the same "kind" of etiology.

The point of the machine example may be illuminated by comparing it with a two-way radio. If one is speaking to an intelligent person over a two-way radio, the radio will normally emit sensible replies to whatever one says. But the radio does not do this in virtue of a capacity to make sensible replies that *it* possesses. The two-way radio is like my machine in being a *conduit* for intelligence, but the two devices differ in that my machine has a crucial capacity that the two-way radio lacks. In my machine, no causal signals from the interrogators reach those who think up the responses, but in the case of the two-way radio, the person who thinks up the responses has to hear the questions. In the case of my machine, the causal efficacy of the programmers is limited to what they have stored in the machine before the interrogator begins.

The reader should also note that my example is really an extension of the traditional perfect pretender counterexample, since the machine "pretends" to be intelligent without actually being intelligent. Once one notes this, it is easy to see that a person could have a capacity to respond intelligently, even though the intelligence he exhibits is not *his*—for example, if he memorizes responses in Chinese though he understands only English.[13] An idiot with a photographic memory, such as Luria's famous mnemonist, could carry on a brilliant philosophical conversation if provided with strings by a team of brilliant philosophers.[14]

The machine, as I have described it thus far, is limited to typewritten inputs and outputs. *But this limitation is inessential, and that is what makes my argument relevant to a full-blooded behaviorist theory of intelligence,* not just to a theory of conversational intelligence. What I need to show to

---

13 This sort of point is discussed in somewhat more detail at the end of the paper.

14 What I say here should not be taken as indicating that the standard objections *really* do vanquish the neo-Turing Test conception of intelligence after all. If the idiot can be said to have the mental state [no intelligence + an overwhelming desire to appear intelligent], the sense of "intelligence" used is the "comparative" sense, not the sense we have been concerned with here (the sense in which intelligence is the possession of thought or reason). If the idiot wants to appear intelligent (in the comparative sense) and thinks that he can do so by memorizing strings, then he is intelligent in the sense of possessing (at least minimally) thought or reason.

Whether one thinks my objection is really just a variant of the "perfect actor" objection depends on how closely one associates the perfect actor objection with the Chisholm-Geach objection. If we associate the perfect actor objection quite closely with the Chisholm-Geach objection, as I think is historically accurate (see Putnam (1975b, 324)), then we will take the point of the perfect actor objection to be that different groups of mental states can produce the same behavioral dispositions. [mental state x + a normal preference function] can produce the same behavioral disposition as [lack of mental state x + a preference function that gives infinite weight to seeming to have mental state x]. My machine is *not a perfect actor in this sense,* since it has no mental states, and hence no groups of mental states either.

make my point is that the kind of finiteness assumption that holds with respect to typewritten inputs and outputs also holds with respect to the whole range of sensory stimulation and behavior. If I can show this, then I can generalize the idea of the machine I described to an unintelligent robot that nonetheless acts in every possible situation just as intelligently as a person.

The sort of finiteness claim that I need can be justified both empirically and conceptually. The empirical justifications are far too complex to present here, so I will only mention them briefly. First, I would claim that enough is now known about sensory physiology to back up the assertion that every stimulus parameter that is not already "quantized" could be quantized without making any difference with respect to effects on the brain or on behavior, provided that the "grain" of quantization is fine enough. Suppose that all of your sense organs were covered by a surface that effected an "analog-to-digital conversion". For example, if some stimulus parameter had a value of .111 . . . units, the surface might change it to .11 units. Provided that the grain was fine enough (not too many decimal places are "lopped off"), the analog-to-digital conversion would make no mental or behavioral difference. If this is right, then one could take the output of the analog-digital converter as the relevant stimulus, and so there would be a finite number of possible sequences of arrays of stimuli in a finite time.

I am told that a similar conclusion can actually be reached with respect to *any* physical system that can be regarded as having inputs and outputs. The crucial claim here is that no physical system could be an infinitely powerful amplifier, so given a "power of amplification", one could impose a corresponding quantization of the inputs that would not affect the outputs. I don't know enough physics to pursue this line further, so I won't.

The line of argument for my conclusion that I want to rely on is more conceptual than empirical. The point is that our *concept* of intelligence allows an intelligent being to have quantized sensory devices. Suppose, for example, that Martian eyes are like movie cameras in that the information that they pass on to the Martian brain amounts to a series of newspaper-like "dot" pictures, i.e., matrices containing a large number of cells, each of which can be either black or white. (Martians are color-blind.) If Martians are strikingly like us in appearance, action, and even internal information processing, no one ought to regard their movie camera eyes (and other finitary sense organs) as showing they are not intelligent. However, note that since there are a finite number of such "dot" pictures of a given grain, there are a finite number of *sequences* of such pictures of a given duration, and thus a finite number of *possible visual stimuli* of a given duration.

It is easy to see that both the empirical and the conceptual points support the claim that an intelligent being could have a finite number of possible sequences of types of stimuli in a finite time (and the same is also true of responses). But then the stimulus sequences could in principle be catalogued by programmers, just as can the interrogator's remarks in the machine described earlier. Thus, a robot programmed along the lines of the machine I described earlier could be given every behavioral capacity possessed by humans, via a method of the sort I have already described. In sum, while my remarks so far have dealt mainly with a behaviorist account of conversational intelligence, broadening the argument to cover a behaviorist theory of intelligence simpliciter would raise no new issues of principle. In what follows, I shall return for convenience to a discussion of conversational intelligence.

By this time, the reader may have a number of objections. Given the heavy use of the phrase "in principle" above, you may feel that what this latest wrinkle shows is that the sense of "in principle possible" in which *any* of the machines I described are in principle possible is a bit strange. Or you may object: "Your machine's capacity to pass the Turing Test does depend on an arbitrary time limit to the test." Or: "You are just stipulating a new meaning for the word 'intelligent'." Or you may want to know what I would say if *I* turned out to be one.

I will now attempt to answer these and other objections. If an objection has a subscripted numeral (e.g., 3a), then it depends on the immediately preceding objection or reply. However, the reader can skip any other objection or reply without loss of continuity.

Objection 1.   Your argument is too strong in that it could be said of any intelligent machine that the intelligence it exhibits is that of its programmers.

Reply. I do *not* claim that the intelligence of *every* machine designed by intelligent beings is merely the intelligence of the designers, and no such principle is used in my argument. If we ever do make an intelligent machine, presumably we will do it by equipping it with mechanisms for learning, solving problems, etc. Perhaps we will find general principles of learning, general principles of problem solving, etc., which we can build into it. But though we *make* the machine intelligent, the intelligence it exhibits is its own, just as our intelligence is no less ours, even if it was produced mainly by the enormously skillful efforts of our parents.

By contrast, if my string-searching machine emits a clever pun *P*, in response to a conversation *C*, then the sequence *CP* is literally one that was thought of and included by the programmers. Perhaps the programmers will say of one of their colleagues, "Jones thought of that pun—he is so clever."

The trouble with the neo-Turing Test conception of intelligence (and its predecessors) is precisely that it does not allow us to distinguish between behavior that reflects a machine's *own* intelligence, and behavior that, reflects *only the intelligence of the machine's programmers*. As I suggested, only a partly etiological notion of intelligent behavior will do the trick.

Objection 2. If the strings were recorded before this year, the machine would not respond the way a person would to a sentence like "What do you think of the latest events in the Mid-East?"

Reply. A system can be intelligent, yet have no knowledge of current events. Likewise, a machine can *imitate* intelligence without *imitating* knowledge of current events. The programmers could, if they liked, choose to simulate an intelligent Robinson Crusoe who knows nothing of the last twenty-five years. Alternatively, they could undertake the much more difficult task of reprogramming periodically to simulate knowledge of current events.

Objection 3. You have argued that a machine with a certain internal mechanical structure is not intelligent, even though it seems intelligent in every *external* respect (that is, in every external respect examined in the Turing Test). But by introducing this internal condition, aren't you in effect merely suggesting a linguistic stipulation, a new meaning for the word "intelligent"? We *normally* regard input-output capacities as criterial for intelligence. All you are doing is suggesting that we adopt a new practice, involving a *new* criterion which includes something about what goes on inside.

Reply.   Jones plays brilliant chess against two of the world's foremost grandmasters at once. You think him a genius until you find out that his method is as follows. He goes second against grandmaster G_1 and first against G_2. He notes G_1's first move against him, and then makes the same move against G_2. He awaits G_2's response, and makes the same move against G_1, and so on. Since Jones's method itself was one he read about in a comic book, Jones's performance is no evidence of his intelligence. As this example[15] illustrates, it is a feature of our concept of intelligence, that to the degree that a system's performance merely echoes the intelligence of another system, the first system's performance is thereby misleading as an indication of its intelligence. Since my machine's performances are *all* echoes, these performances provide no reason to attribute intelligence to it.[16]

The point is that though we *normally* ascertain the intelligence of a system by trying to assess its input-output capacities, it is part of our ordinary concept of intelligence that input-output capacities can be misleading. As Putnam has suggested, it is part of the logic of natural kind terms that what seems to be a stereotypical X can turn out not to be an

---

15 Such examples were suggested by Dick Boyd and Georges Rey in their comments on an earlier rendition of this paper. Rey tells me the chess story is a true tale.

16 The reader should not conclude from the "echo" examples that what *makes* my machine unintelligent is that its responses are echoes. Actually, what makes it unintelligent is that its responses are *mere* echoes, i.e., its information processing is of the most elementary sort (and the appearances to the contrary are merely the echoes of genuinely intelligent beings). Notice that such a machine would be just as unintelligent if it were produced by a cosmic accident rather than by the long creative labors of intelligent people. What makes this accidentally produced machine unintelligent is, as before, that its information processing is of the most elementary sort; the appearances to the contrary are produced in this case not via echoes, but by a cosmic accident.

X at all if it fails to belong to the same scientific natural kind as the main body of things we have referred to as X's (Kripke 1972; Putnam 1975a). If Putnam is right about this, one can never accuse someone of "changing the meaning" of a natural kind term merely on the ground that he says that something that satisfies the standard "criteria" for X's is not an X.

Objection 3a.   I am very suspicious of your reply to the last objection, especially your introduction of the Putnam point. Is it not rather chauvinist to suppose that a system has to be scientifically *like us* to be intelligent? Maybe a system with information processing very unlike ours does not belong in the extension of our term "intelligence"; but it is equally true that we do not belong in the extension of *its* term "shmintelligence". And who is to say that intelligence is any better than shmintelligence?

Reply.   I have not argued that the *mere fact* of an information processing *difference* between my machine and us cuts any ice. Rather, my point is based on the *sort* of information processing difference that exists. My machine lacks the kind of "richness" of information processing requisite for intelligence. Perhaps this richness has something to do with the application of abstract principles of problem solving, learning, etc. I wish I could say more about just what this sort of richness comes to. But I have chosen a much less ambitious task: to give a clear case of something that *lacks* that richness, but nonetheless behaves as if it were intelligent. If someone offered a definition of "life" that had the unnoticed consequence that small stationery items such as paper clips are alive, one could refute him by pointing out the absurdity of the consequence, even if one had no very detailed account of what life really is with which to replace his. In the same way, one can refute the neo-Turing Test conception by counterexample without having to say very much about what intelligence really is.

Objection 4.   Suppose it turns out that human beings, including you, process information in just the way that your machine does. Would you insist that humans are not intelligent?

Reply. I'm not very sure of what I would say about human intelligence were someone to convince me that human information processing is the same as that of my machine. However, I do not see that there is any *clearly and obviously correct* response to this question against which the responses natural for someone with my position can be measured. Further, none of the more plausible responses that I can think of are incompatible with what I have said so far.

Assume, for example, a theory of reference that dictates that in virtue of the causal relation between the word "intelligence" and human information processing, human information processing is intelligent *whatever* its nature.[17] Then, if I were convinced that humans process information in the manner of my machine, I should admit that my machine is intelligent. But how is this incompatible with my claim that my machine is not in *fact* intelligent? Tweaking me with "What if you turned out to be one?" is a bit like tweaking an atheist with "What if you turned out to be God?" The atheist would have to admit that if he were God, then God would exist. But the atheist could concede this counterfactual without giving up atheism. If the word "intelligence" is firmly anchored to human information processing, as suggested above, then my position is committed to the *empirical claim* that human information processing is not like that of my machine. But this is a perfectly congenial claim, one that is supported both by common sense and by empirical research in cognitive psychology.

---

17 The theory sketched by Putnam (1975a) might be taken to have this consequence. Whether it does have this consequence depends on whether it dictates that there is *no* descriptive component at all to the determination of the reference of natural kind terms. It seems certain that there is some descriptive component to the determination of the reference of natural kind terms, just as there is *some* descriptive component to the determination of the reference of names. There is a possible world in which Moses was an Egyptian fig merchant who spread tall tales about himself, but is there a possible world in which Moses was a brick? Similarly, even if there is a possible world in which tigers are automata, is there a possible world in which tigers exist, but are ideas? I would argue, along these lines, that the word "intelligence" attaches to whatever natural kind our information processing belongs to (assuming it belongs to a single natural kind) *unless* our information processing fails the minimal descriptive requirement for intelligence (as ideas fail the minimal descriptive requirement for being tigers). String-searchers, I would argue, *do* fail to have the minimal requirement for intelligence.

Objection 5.   You keep insisting that we do not process information in the manner of your machine. What makes you so sure?

Reply.   I don't see how someone could make such an objection without being somewhat facetious. You will have no difficulty coming up with responses to my arguments. Are we to take seriously the idea that someone long ago recorded both what I said and a response to it and inserted both in your brain? Common sense recoils from such patent nonsense. Further, pick any issue of any cognitive psychology journal, and you will see attempts at experimental investigation of our information processing mechanisms. Despite the crudity of the evidence, it tells overwhelmingly against the string-searching idea.

Our cognitive processes are undoubtedly much more mechanical than some people like to think. But there is a vast gap between our being more mechanical than some people like to think and our being a machine of the sort I described.

Objection 6.   Combinatorial explosion makes your machine impossible. George Miller long ago estimated (Miller et al. 1960) that there are on the order of 10^{30} grammatical sentences 20 words in length. Suppose (utterly arbitrarily) that of these 10^{15} are semantically well formed as well. An hour-long Turing Test would require perhaps 100 such sentences. That makes 10^{1500} strings, a number which is greater than the number of particles in the universe.

Reply.   My argument requires only that the machine be *logically* possible, not that it be feasible or even nomologically possible. Behaviorist analyses were generally presented as *conceptual analyses,* and it is difficult to see how conceptions such as the neo-Turing Test conception could be seen in a very different light. Could it be an *empirical hypothesis* that intelligence is the capacity to emit sensible sequences of outputs relative to input sequences? What sort of empirical evidence (other than evidence from *linguistics*) could there be in favor of such a claim? If the neo-Turing Test conception of intelligence is seen as something on the order of a claim about the concept of intelligence, then the mere *logical* possibility of an unintelligent system that has the capacity to pass the Turing Test is enough to refute the neo-Turing Test conception.

It may be replied that although the neo-Turing Test conception clearly is not a *straightforwardly* empirical hypothesis, still it may be *quasi-empirical*. For it may be held that the identification of intelligence with the capacity to emit sensible output sequences is a *background* principle or law of empirical psychology. Or it may be offered as a rational reconstruction (of our vague common sense conception of intelligence) which will be fruitful in future empirical psychological theories. In both cases, while no empirical evidence *could* directly support the neo-Turing Test conception, still it could be held to be part of a perspective that could be empirically supported as a whole.[18]

This reply would carry some weight if any proponent of the neo-Turing Test conception had offered the *slightest reason* for thinking that such a conception of intelligence is likely to contribute to the fruitfulness of empirical theories that contain it. In the absence of such a reason (and, moreover, in the presence of examples that suggest the contrary—behaviorist psychology and Turingish approaches to artificial intelligence—see

---

18 What follows is one rejoinder for which I only have space for a brief sketch. If intelligence = sensible response capacity (and if the terms flanking the "=" are rigid), then the *metaphysical* possibility of my machine is enough to defeat the neo-Turing Test conception, even if it is not nomologically possible. (The claim that there are metaphysical possibilities that are not also nomological possibilities is one that I cannot argue for here.)

What if the neo-Turing Test conception of intelligence is formulated not as an identity claim, but as the claim that a certain capacity is nomologically necessary and sufficient for intelligence? I would argue that if F is nomologically necessary and sufficient for G, then one of the following holds:

(a) This nomological coextensivity is an ultimate law of nature.
(b) This nomological coextensivity can be explained in terms of an underlying mechanism.
(c) $F = G$.

In case (c), the claim is vulnerable to the point of the previous paragraph. Case (a) is obviously wrong. And in case (b), intelligence must be identifiable with something other than the capacity to give sensible responses. Suppose, for example, that we can give a mechanistic account of the correlation of intelligence with sensible response capacity by showing that intelligence requires a certain sort of cognitive structure, and creatures with such a cognitive structure have the required capacity. But then intelligence should be identified with *the cognitive structure* and not with the capacity. See my "Reductionism" (Block 1978a) for a brief discussion of some of these ideas.

footnote 6), why should we take the neo-Turing Test conception seriously as a quasi-empirical claim?

While this reply suffices, I shall add that my machine may indeed be nomologically possible. Nothing in contemporary physics prohibits the possibility of matter in some part of the universe that is infinitely divisible. Indeed, whenever the latest "elementary" particle turns out not to be truly elementary, and when the number and variety of its constituents multiply (as has now happened with quarks), physicists typically entertain the hypothesis that *our* matter is not composed of any *really* elementary particles.

Suppose there is a part of the universe (possibly this one) in which matter is infinitely divisible. In that part of the universe there need be no upper bound on the amount of information storable in a given finite space. So my machine could perhaps exist, its tapes stored in a volume the size of, e.g., a human head. Indeed, one can imagine that where matter is infinitely divisible, there are creatures of all sizes, including creatures the size of electrons who agree to do the recording for us if we agree to wipe out their enemies by putting the lumps on which the enemies live in one of our particle accelerators.

Further, even if the story of the last paragraph is not nomologically possible, still it is not clear that the *kind* of nomological impossibility it possesses is relevant to my objection to the neo-Turing Test conception of intelligence. For if the neo-Turing Test conception of intelligence is an empirical "background" principle or law, it is a background principle or law of human *cognitive psychology,* not of *physics.* But a situation can contravene laws of physics without contravening laws of human psychology. For example, in a logically possible world in which gravity obeyed an inverse cube law instead of an inverse square law, our laws of *physics* would be different, but our laws of *psychology* might not be.

Now if my machine contravenes laws of nature, these laws are presumably laws of physics, not laws of psychology. For the question of how much information can be stored in a given space and how fast information can be transferred from place to place depends on such physical factors as the divisibility of matter and the speed of light. Even if the electron-sized creatures just described contravene laws of physics, still they need not contravene laws of human psychology. That is, humans (with their psychological laws intact) could coexist with the little creatures.[19]

But if my machine does not contravene laws of human psychology—if it exists in a possible world in which the laws of human psychology are the same as they are here—then the neo-Turing Test conception of intelligence is false in a world where the laws of human psychology are the same as they are here. So the neo-Turing Test conception of intelligence cannot be one of the laws of human psychology.

In sum, the neo-Turing Test conception of intelligence can be construed either as some sort of conceptual truth or as a kind of psychological law. And it is false on both construals.

One final point: various sorts of modifications may make a variant of my machine nomologically possible in a much more straightforward sense. First, we could limit the vocabulary of the Turing Test to Basic English. Basic English has a vocabulary of only 850 words, as opposed to the hundreds of thousands of words in English, and it is claimed that Basic English is adequate for normal conversation, and for expression of a wide range of ideas. Second, the calculation made above was based on the string-searching version of the machine. The tree-searching version described earlier, however, avoids enormous amounts of duplication of parts of strings, and is no more intelligent.

More importantly, the machine as I have described it is designed to perform *perfectly* (barring breakdown); but perfect performance is far better than one could expect from any human, even ignoring strokes, heart attacks, and other forms of human "breakdown". Humans whose mental processes are functioning normally often misread sentences, or get confused; worse, any normal person engaged in a long Turing Test would soon get bored, and his attention would wander. Further, many,

---

19 It may be objected that since brute force information processing methods are far more effective in the world in which matter is infinitely divisible than in ours, the laws of thought in that world *do* differ from the laws of thought in ours. But this objection begs the question, since if the string-searching machine I described cannot think in *any* world (as I would argue), the nomological difference which makes it possible is a difference in laws which affect the *simulation* of thought, not a difference in laws of thought.

loquacious souls would blather on from the very beginning, occasionally apologizing for not listening to the interlocutor. Many people would respond more by way of free association to the interlocutor's remarks than by grasping their sense and giving a considered reply. Some people might devote nearly every remark to complaints about the unpleasantness of these interminable Turing Tests. If one sets one's sights on making a machine that does only as well in the Turing Test as *most* people would do, one might try a hybrid machine, containing a relatively small number of trees plus a bag of tricks of the sort used in Weizenbaum's program.

Perhaps many tricks can be found to reduce the memory load without making the machine any smarter. Of course, no matter how sophisticated the memory-reduction tricks we find, they merely postpone, but do not avoid the inevitable combinatorial explosion. For the whole point of the machine is to substitute memory for intelligence. So for a Turing Test of *some* length, perhaps a machine of the general type that I have described will be so large that making it any larger will cause collapse into a black hole. My point is that technical ingenuity being what it is, the point at which nomological impossibility sets in may be beyond what is required to simulate human conversational abilities.

Objection 7.   The fault of the Turing Test as you describe it is one of experimental design, not experimental concept. The trouble is that your Turing Test has a *fixed length*. The programmers must know the length in order to program the machine. In an *adequate* version of the Turing Test, the duration of any occasion of testing would be decided in some random manner. In short, the trouble with your criticism is that you've set up a straw man.

Reply.   It is certainly true that my machine's capacity to pass Turing Tests depends on there being some upper bound to the length of the tests. But the same is true of *people*. Even if we allow, say, twelve hours between question and answer to give people time to eat and sleep, still, people eventually die. Few humans could pass a Turing Test that lasted ninety years, and no humans could pass a Turing Test that lasted five hundred years. You can (if you like) characterize intelligence as the capacity to pass a Turing Test of arbitrary length, but since *humans do not have this capacity,* your characterization will not be a necessary condition of intelligence, and even if it were a sufficient condition of intelligence (which I very much doubt—see below) a sufficient condition of intelligence that *humans do not satisfy* would be of little interest to proponents of views like the neo-Turing Test conception.

Even if medical advances remove any upper bound on the human life span, still people will die by accident. There is a nonzero probability that, in the course of normal thermal motion, the molecules in the two halves of one's body will move in opposite directions, tearing one in half. Indeed, the probability of escaping such accidental death literally *forever* is zero. Consider the "half-life" of people in a world in which death is put off as long as is physically possible. (The half-life for people, as for radioactive atoms, is the median life span, the time it takes for half to pass away.) Machines of my sort could be programmed to last for that half-life and (assuming they are no more susceptible to accidental destruction than people) their median life span would be as long as that of the median person.

Objection 7a.   Let me try another tack. Cognitive psychologists and linguists often claim that cognitive mechanisms of one sort or another have "infinite capacities". For example, Chomsky says that our mechanisms for understanding language have the capacity to understand sentences of any length. An upper bound on the length of sentences people can understand in practice is a matter of interferences due to distraction, boredom, going mad, memory limitations, and many other phenomena, including, of course, death. This point is often put by saying that under the appropriate idealization (i.e., ignoring "interfering" phenomena of the sort mentioned) we have the capacity to understand sentences of any length. Now here is my point: under the same sort of idealization, we presumably have the capacity to pass a Turing Test of any length. But your string-searcher does *not* have this capacity, even under the appropriate idealization.

Reply.   You seem to think you have objected to my claim, but really you have *capitulated* to it. I cheerfully concede that there is an idealization under which we probably have an "infinite" capacity that my machine lacks. But in order to describe this idealization, you will have to indulge in a kind of theorizing about cognitive mechanisms that would be unacceptable to a behaviorist.

Consider the kind of reformulation of the neo-Turing Test conception of intelligence suggested by the idealization objection; it would be something like: "intelligence = the possession of language-processing mechanisms such that, were they provided with unlimited memory, and were they directed by motivational mechanisms that assigned at least a moderately high preference value to responding sensibly, and were they 'insulated' from 'stop' signals from emotion centers, and so forth, then the language-processing mechanisms would have the capacity to respond sensibly indefinitely." Notice that in order to state such a doctrine, one has to distinguish among various mental components and mechanisms. As an aside, it is worth noting that these distinctions have substantive empirical presuppositions. For example, memory might be inextricably bound up with language-processing mechanisms so as to make nonsense of talk of supplying the processing mechanisms with unlimited memory. The main point, however, is that in order to state such an "idealization" version of the neo-Turing Test conception one has to invoke mentalistic notions that no behaviorist could accept.

Objection 7b.   I believe I can make my point without using mentalistic notions by idealizing away simply from nonaccidental causes of death. In replying to Objection 7, you said (correctly) that if medical advances removed an upper bound on human life, still the median string-searching machine could do as well as the median person. However, note that if nonaccidental causes of death were removed, every *individual* human would have no upper bound on how long he could go on in a Turing Test. By contrast, any individual string-searching machine must by its very nature have some upper bound on its ability to go on.

Reply.   What determines how long we can go on in a Turing Test is not just how long we live, but the nature of our cognitive mechanisms and their interactions with other mental mechanisms. Suppose, for example, that we have no mechanisms for "erasing" information stored in long term memory. (Whether this is so is not known.) If we can't "erase", then when our finite memories are "used up", normal conversational capacity will cease.

If the behaviorist identifies intelligence with the capacity to go on indefinitely in a Turing Test, idealizing away only from non-accidental death, then people may turn out not to be intelligent in his sense. Further, even if people do turn out to satisfy such a condition, it can't be regarded as *necessary* for intelligence. Beings that go senile within two hundred years because they lack "erase" mechanisms can nonetheless be intelligent before they go senile.

Of course, the behaviorist could avoid this difficulty by further idealizing, explicitly mentioning erase mechanisms in his definition of intelligence. But that would land him back in the mentalistic swamp described in the last reply.

It is worth adding that even if we do have "erase" mechanisms, and even if nonaccidental causes of death were eliminated, still we would have *finite* memories. A variant of my string-searcher could perhaps exploit the finiteness of our memories so as to do as well as a person in an indefinitely long Turing Test. Suppose, for example, that human memory cannot record more than two hundred years of conversation. Then one of my string-searchers could perhaps be turned into a *loop-searcher* that could go on indefinitely. Instead of "linear" strings of conversation, it would contain circular strings whose ends rejoin the beginnings after, say, one thousand years of conversation. The construction of such loops would take much more inventiveness than the construction of ordinary strings. Even if it could be done, such a machine would seem intolerably repetitive to a being whose memory capacity far exceeded ours, but human conversation would seem equally repetitive to such a being.

Here is one final kind of rejoinder to the "unbounded Turing Test" objection. Consider a variant of my machine in which the programmers simply continue on and on, adding to the strings. When they need new tape, they reuse tape that has already been passed by.[20] Note that it is *logically* possible for the everextending strings to come into existence by themselves—without the programmers (see footnote 16). Thus not even the capacity to go on indefinitely in a Turing Test is *logically* sufficient for intelligence.

Continuing on this theme, consider the infinitely divisible matter mentioned in the reply to Objection 6. It is logically and perhaps nomologically

---

20 This machine would get ever larger unless the programmers were allowed to abandon strings which had been rendered useless by the course of the conversation. (In the tree-searching version, this would amount to pruning by-passed branches.)

possible for a *man-sized* string-searching machine to contain creatures of everdecreasing size who work away making the tapes longer and longer without bound. Of course, neither of the two machines just mentioned has a *fixed* program, but since the programmers never see the stimuli, it is still the *machines* and not the programmers that are doing the responding. Contrast these machines with the infamous "machine" of long ago that contained a midget hidden inside it who listened to the questions and produced the answers.

Objection 8.   You remarked earlier that the neo-Turing Test conception of intelligence is widespread in artificial intelligence circles. Still, your machine cannot be taken as refuting any AI (artificial intelligence) point of view, because as Newell and Simon point out, in the AI view, "the task of intelligence ... is to avert the ever-present threat of the exponential explosion of search." (Newell and Simon 1979) (In exponential explosion of search, adding one step to the task requires, e.g., 10 times the computational resources, adding two steps requires 10^2 ($= 100$) times the computational resources, adding three steps requires 10^3 ($= 1000$) times the computational resources, etc.) So it would be reasonable for AIers to amend their version of the neo-Turing conception of intelligence as follows:

Intelligence is the capacity to emit sensible sequences of responses to stimuli, so long as this is accomplished in a way that averts exponential explosion of search.[21]

Reply.   Let me begin by noting that for a proponent of the neo-Turing Test conception of intelligence to move to the amended neo-Turing Test conception is to capitulate to the psychologism that I have been defending. The *amended* neo-Turing Test conception attempts to avoid the problem I have posed by placing a *condition on the internal processing* (albeit a minimal one), viz., that it not be explosive. So the amended neo-Turing Test conception does characterize intelligence partly with respect to its

---

21 I am indebted to Dan Dennett for forcefully making this objection in his role as respondent to an earlier version of this paper in the University of Cincinnati Philosophy of Psychology Conference in 1978. Dennett tells me that he advocates the neo-Turing Test conception as amended above.

internal etiology, and hence the amended neo-Turing Test conception is psychologistic.

While the amended neo-Turing Test conception is an improvement over the original neo-Turing Test conception in this one respect (it appeals to internal processing), it suffers from a variety of defects. One difficulty arises because there is an ambiguity in phrases such as "averts the exponential explosion of search". Such phrases can be understood as equivalent to "*avoids* exponential explosion altogether" (i.e., uses methods that do not require computational resources that go up exponentially with the "length" of the task) or, alternatively, as "*postpones* exponential explosion long enough" (i.e., does use methods that require computational resources that go up exponentially with the "length" of the task, but the "length" of the task is short enough that the required resources are in fact available). If it is postponing that is meant, my counterexample may well be untouched by the new proposal, because as I pointed out earlier, my machine or a variant on it may postpone combinatorial explosion long enough to pass a reasonable Turing Test.

On the other hand, if it is *avoiding* combinatorial explosion altogether that is meant, then the amended neo-Turing Test conception may brand us as unintelligent. For it is certainly possible that our information processing mechanisms—like those of many AI systems—are ones that succeed not because they avoid combinatorial explosion altogether, but only because they *postpone* combinatorial explosion long enough for practical purposes.

In sum, the amended neo-Turing Test conception is faced with a dilemma. If it is postponing combinatorial explosion that is meant, my machine may count as intelligent. If it is avoiding combinatorial explosion altogether that is meant, *we* (or other intelligent organisms) may not count as intelligent.

Further, the proposed amendment to the neo-Turing Test conception is an entirely ad hoc addition. The trouble with such ad hoc exclusion of counterexamples is that one can never be sure whether someone will come up with another type of counterexample which will require another ad hoc maneuver.

I shall now back up this point by sketching a set of devices that have sensible input-output relations, but arguably are not intelligent.

Imagine a computer which simulates your responses to stimuli by computing *the trajectories* of all the elementary particles in your body. This machine starts with a specification of the positions, velocities, and charges (I assume Newtonian mechanics for convenience) of all your particles at one moment, and computes the changes of state of your body as a function of these initial conditions and energy impinging on your sensory mechanisms. Of course, what is especially relevant for the Turing Test is the effect of light from your teletype monitor on your typing fingers. Now though this takes some discussion, I opine that a machine that computes your elementary particle trajectories in this way is not intelligent, though it could control a robot which has the capacity to behave exactly as you would in any situation. It behaves as you do when you are doing philosophy, but it is not doing philosophy; rather, what *it* is doing is computing elementary particle trajectories so as to mimic your doing philosophy.

Perhaps what I have described is not nomologically possible. Indeed, it may be that even if God told us the positions and velocities of all the particles in your body, no computer could compute the complex interactions, even assuming Newtonian mechanics. However, notice one respect in which this machine may be superior to the one this paper has been mainly concerned with: namely, if it can simulate something for an hour, it may be able to simulate it for a year or a decade with the same apparatus. For continuing the simulation would be simply a matter of solving the same equations over and over again. For a wide variety of types of equations, solving the same equations over and over will involve no exponential explosion of search. If there is no exponential expansion of search here, the ad hoc condition added in the objection is eluded, and we are left with the issues about nomological possibility that we discussed in Objection 6.

The idea of the machine just sketched could be applied in another machine which is closer to nomological possibility, namely one that simulates your *neurophysiology* instead of your elementary particle physics. That is, this machine would contain a representation of some adequate neurological theory (say, of the distant future) and a specification of the current states of all your neurons. It would simulate you by computing the changes of state of your neurons. Still more likely to be nomologically possible would be a machine which, in an analogous manner, simulates your *psychology*. That is, it contains a representation of some adequate psychological theory (of the distant future) and a specification of the current states of your psychological mechanisms. It simulates you by computing the changes of state of those mechanisms given their initial states and sensory inputs. Again, if there is no exponential expansion of search, the modification introduced in the objection gains nothing.

I said that these three devices are *arguably* unintelligent, but since I have little space to give any such arguments, this part of my case will have to remain incomplete. I will briefly sketch part of one argument.

Consider a device that simulates you by using a theory of your psychological processes. It is a robot that looks and acts as you would in any stimulus situation. Instead of a brain it has a computer equipped with a description of your psychological mechanisms. You receive a certain input, cogitate about it, and emit a certain output. If your robot doppelganger receives that input, a transducer converts the input into a description of the input. The computer uses its description of your cognitive mechanisms to deduce the product of your cogitations; it then transmits a description of your output to a mechanism that causes the robot body to execute the output. It is hardly obvious that the robot's process of manipulation of descriptions of your cogitation is *itself* cogitation. It is still less obvious that the robot's manipulation of descriptions of your experiential and emotional processes are themselves experiential and emotional processes.

To massage your intuitions about this a bit, substitute for the description-manipulating computer in your doppelganger's head a very small *intelligent* person who speaks only Chinese, and who possesses a manual (in Chinese) describing your psychological mechanisms. You get the input "Who is your favorite philosopher?" You cogitate a bit and reply "Heraclitus". Your robot doppelganger on the other hand contains a mechanism that transforms the question into a description of its sound; then the little man deduces that you would emit the noise "Heraclitus", and he causes the robot's voice box to emit that noise. The robot could simulate your input-output relations (and in a sense, simulate your internal processing, too) even though the person inside the robot understands nothing of the question or the answer. It seems that the robot simulates your thinking your thoughts without itself thinking those thoughts. Returning to the case where the robot has a description-manipulating computer instead of a description-manipulating person inside it, why should we suppose that the robot has or contains any thought processes at all?[22]

The string-searching machine with which this paper has been mainly concerned showed that behavior is intelligent only if it is *not* the product of a certain sort of information processing. Appealing to the Martian

---

22 Much more needs to be said to turn this remark into a serious argument. Intuitions about homunculi-headed creatures are too easily manipulable to stand on their own. For example, I once argued against functionalism by describing a robot that is functionally equivalent to a person, but is controlled by an "external brain" consisting of an army of people, each doing the job of a "square" in a machine table that describes a person. William Lycan (1981) objected that the intuition that the aforementioned creature lacked mentality could be made to go away by imagining yourself reduced to the size of a molecule, and standing inside a person's sensory cortex. Seeing the molecules bounce about, it might seem absurd to you that what you were watching was a series of events that constituted or was crucial to some being's experience. Similarly, Lycan suggests, the intuition that my homunculi-heads lack qualia is an illusion produced by missing the forest for the trees, that is, by focusing on "the hectic activities of the little men . . . , seeing the homunculi-head as if through a microscope rather than as a whole macroscopic person." (David Rosenthal made the same objection in correspondence with me.)

While I think that the Lycan-Rosenthal point does genuinely alter one's intuitions, it can be avoided by considering a variant of the original example in which a *single* homunculus does the whole job, his attention to column S_i of a machine table posted in his compartment playing precisely the causal role required for the robot he controls to *have* S_i. (See "Are Absent Qualia Impossible?" (Block 1980) for a somewhat more detailed description of this case.) No "forest for the trees" illusion can be at work here. Nonetheless, the Lycan-Rosenthal point does illustrate the manipulability of intuitions, and the danger of appealing to intuition without examining the source of the intuition. The role of most of the early objections and replies in this paper was to locate the source of our intuitions about the stupidity of the string-searching machine in its extremely simple information processing.

Another difficulty with the description-manipulator example is that it may seem that such an example could be used to show that *no symbol manipulation theory of thought processes* (such as those popular in cognitive psychology and artificial intelligence) *could be correct,* since one could always imagine a being in which the symbol-manipulating mechanisms are replaced by homunculi. (John Searle uses an example of the same sort as mine to make such a case in "Minds, Brains and Programs" (Searle 1980, *chapter 14*). See my reply in the same issue.) While I cannot defend it here, I would claim that some symbol-manipulating homunculi-heads *are* intelligent, and that what justifies us in regarding some symbol-manipulating homunculus-heads (such as the one just described in the text) as unintelligent is that the causal relations among their states do not mirror the causal relations among our mental states.

example described at the beginning of the paper, I cautioned against jumping to the conclusion that there is any positive characterization of the type of information processing underlying all intelligent behavior (except that it have at least a minimal degree of "richness"). However, what was said in connection with the Martian and string-searching examples left it open that though there is no single natural kind of information processing underlying all intelligent behavior, still there might be a kind of processing common to all *un*intelligent entities that nonetheless pass the Turing Test (viz., very simple processes operating over enormous memories). What this last machine suggests, however, is that it is also doubtful that there will be any interesting type of information processing common to such unintelligent devices.[23]

Bibliography

Block, Ned. 1978a. Reductionism. In *Encyclopedia of bioethics*. New York, NY: Macmillan.

————. 1978b. Troubles with functionalism. In *Perception and cognition: Issues in the foundations of psychology*, ed. C. W. Savage, vol. 9 of *Minnesota Studies in the Philosophy of Science*. Minneapolis, MN: University of Minnesota Press.

————. 1980. Are absent qualia impossible? *Philosophical Review* LXXXIX.

Boden, M. 1977. *Artificial intelligence*. New York, NY: Basic Books.

Chisholm, Roderick. 1957. *Perceiving*, chap. 11. Ithaca, NY: Cornell University Press.

Dennett, Daniel. 1978. *Brainstorms*. Cambridge, MA: MIT Press.

Dummett, Michael. 1976. What is a theory of meaning (II). In *Truth and meaning*, ed. G. Evans and J. McDowell. London, England: Oxford University Press.

Fodor, Jerry. 1968. *Psychological explanation*. New York, NY: Random House.

Kripke, Saul. 1972. Naming and neccesity. In *Semantics and natural language*. Dordrecht, Holland: Reidel.

Lycan, William. 1979. New lilliputian argument against machine functionalism. *Philosophical Studies* 35.

---

23 Previous versions of this paper were read at a number of universities and meetings, beginning with the 1977 meeting of the Association for Symbolic Logic. I am indebted to the following persons for comments on previous drafts: Sylvain Bromberger, Noam Chomsky, Jerry Fodor, Paul Horwich, Jerry Katz, Israel Krakowski, Robert Kirk, Philip Kitcher, David Lewis, Hugh Lacey, William Lycan, Charles Marks, Dan Osherson, Georges Rey, Sydney Shoemaker, George Smith, Judy Thomson, Richard Warner, and Scott Weinstein.

———. 1981. Form, function, and feel. *Journal of Philosophy* LXXVIII:24–50.

Miller, George, Eugene Galanter, and Karl H. Pribram. 1960. *Plans and the structure of behavior.* New York, NY: Holt, Rinehart, and Winston.

Newell, Alan, and Herbert Simon. 1979. Computer science as empirical inquiry: Symbols and search. *Communications of the Association for Computing Machinery* 19.

Putnam, Hilary. 1975a. The meaning of "meaning". In *Language, mind, and knowledge,* ed. Keith Gunderson, vol. 7 of *Minnesota Studies in the Philosophy of Science.* Minneapolis, MN: University of Minnesota Press.

———. 1975b. *Mind, language, and reality.* Cambridge, England: Cambridge University Press.

Rorty, Amélie. 1979. *Philosophy and the mirror of nature.* Princeton, NJ: Princeton University Press.

Ryle, Gilbert. 1949. *The concept of mind.* London, England: Hutchinson.

Schank, Roger C., and Robert P. Abelson. 1977. *Scripts, plans, goals, and understanding: An inquiry into human knowledge structures.* Hillsdale, NJ: Lawrence Erlbaum Press.

Searle, John R. 1980. Minds, brains, and programs. *Behavioral and Brain Sciences* 3:417–457. *Reprinted in chapter 14.*

Shoemaker, Sydney. 1975. Functionalism and qualia. *Philosophical Studies* 27.

———. 1981. Absent qualia are impossible—a reply to Block. *The Philosophical Review* 90(4):581–599.

Turing, Alan M. 1950. Computing machinery and intelligence. *Mind* LIX(236): 433–460. *Reprinted in chapter 4.*

Weizenbaum, Joseph. 1966. Eliza—A computer program for the study of natural language communication between man and machine. *Communications of the Association for Computing Machinery* 9(1):36–45.

———. 1976. *Computer power and human reason.* San Francisco, CA: W. H. Freeman and Co.

The Supporting View

The first mention in Turing's writings of an imitation game is in his paper "Intelligent Machinery", which was published only posthumously (Turing 1969 [1947]). He proposes an indistinguishability test for computer and human chess players.

The extent to which we regard something as behaving in an intelligent manner is determined as much by our own state of mind and training as by the properties of the object under consideration. If we are able to explain and predict its behaviour or if there seems to be little underlying plan, we have little temptation to imagine intelligence. With the same object therefore it is possible that one man would consider it as intelligent and another would have found out the rules of its behaviour.

It is possible to do a little experiment on these lines, even at the present stage of knowledge. It is not difficult to devise a paper machine which will play not a very bad game of chess. Now get three men as subjects for the experiment A, B, C. A and C are to be rather poor chess players, B is the operator who works the paper machine. (In order that he should be able to work it fairly fast it is advisable that he be both mathematician and chess player.) Two rooms are used with some arrangement for communicating moves, and a game is played between C and either A or the paper machine. C may find it quite difficult to tell which he is playing. (This is a rather idealized form of an experiment I have actually done.)

The mention of Turing himself having carried out a Turing-like test, even if of a very restricted sort, is tantalizing, but the truly revealing part of this selection is the first paragraph. Turing here describes intelligence as an ascribed attribute, rather than an intrinsic one. The philosopher Daniel Dennett is the prime proponent of the generalized form of this view, that all mentalistic notions (such as beliefs, desires, intentions) are correctly viewed as attributed properties. This is his "intentional stance" (Dennett 1987b).

In amongst all the philosophers dismissing the Turing Test as a criterion for intelligence, one might hope for someone to support the proposal, to answer the Big Question in the positive, quixotic as that might seem. Daniel Dennett is that philosopher. If Dennett is right about his intentional stance, then Searle and his ilk—the essentialists who think that there is something intrinsic about people's brains that make them intentional, thinking beings—are wrong. And that is just what Dennett (1985, *chapter 16*) says.

Dennett also makes an important point about Turing's chess test, one that Turing himself would undoubtedly agree with. A "Turing Test" limited or simplified in any way is no Turing Test at all. (In the nomenclature of the Turing syllogism, we can't replace "conversational verbal behavior" with, for example, "chess-playing behavior" in the premises and retain their validity.) "The moral we should draw is that as Turing test judges we should resist all limitations and waterings-down of the Turing test." (Dennett 1985, *chapter 16*, 277)

16

Can Machines Think?

Daniel C. Dennett

Can machines think? This has been a conundrum for philosophers for years, but in their fascination with the pure conceptual issues they have for the most part overlooked the real social importance of the answer. It is of more than academic importance that we learn to think clearly about the actual cognitive powers of computers, for they are now being introduced into a variety of sensitive social roles, where their powers will be put to the ultimate test: In a wide variety of areas, we are on the verge of making ourselves dependent upon their cognitive powers. The cost of overestimating them could be enormous.

One of the principal inventors of the computer was the great British mathematician Alan Turing. It was he who first figured out, in highly abstract terms, how to design a programmable computing device—what we now call a universal Turing machine. All programmable computers in use today are in essence Turing machines. Over thirty years ago, at the dawn of the computer age, Turing began a classic article, "Computing Machinery and Intelligence" with the words: "I propose to consider the question, 'Can machines think?'"—but then went on to say that this was a bad question, a question that leads only to sterile debate and haggling over definitions, a question, as he put it, "too meaningless to deserve discussion" (Turing 1950, *chapter 4*). In its place he substituted what he took to be a much better question, a question that would be crisply answerable and intuitively satisfying—in every way an acceptable substitute for the philosophic puzzler with which he began.

First he described a parlor game of sorts, the "imitation game", to be played by a man, a woman, and a judge (of either gender). The man and woman are hidden from the judge's view but able to communicate with the judge by teletype; the judge's task is to guess, after a period of questioning each contestant, which interlocutor is the man and which the woman. The man tries to convince the judge he is the woman (and the woman tries to convince the judge of the truth), and the man wins if the judge makes the wrong identification. A little reflection will convince you, I am sure, that, aside from lucky breaks, it would take a clever man to convince the judge that he was the woman—assuming the judge is clever too, of course.

Now suppose, Turing said, we replace the man or woman with a computer, and give the judge the task of determining which is the human being and which is the computer. Turing proposed that any computer that can regularly or often fool a discerning judge in this game would be intelligent—would be a computer that thinks—*beyond any reasonable doubt*. Now, it is important to realize that failing this test is not supposed to be a sign of lack of intelligence. Many intelligent people, after all, might not be willing or able to play the imitation game, and we should allow computers the same opportunity to decline to prove themselves. This is, then, a one-way test; failing it proves nothing.

Furthermore, Turing was not committing himself to the view (although it is easy to see how one might think he was) that to think is to think just like a human being—any more than he was committing himself to the view that for a man to think, he must think exactly like a woman. Men and women, and computers, may all have different ways of thinking. But surely, he thought, if one can think in one's own peculiar style well enough to imitate a thinking man or woman, one can think well, indeed. This imagined exercise has come to be known as the Turing test.

It is a sad irony that Turing's proposal has had exactly the opposite effect on the discussion of that which he intended. Turing didn't design the test as a useful tool in scientific psychology, a method of confirming or disconfirming scientific theories or evaluating particular models of mental function; he designed it to be nothing more than a philosophical conversation-stopper. He proposed—in the spirit of "Put up or shut up!"—a simple test for thinking that was *surely* strong enough to satisfy the sternest skeptic (or so he thought). He was saying, in effect, "Instead of arguing interminably about the ultimate nature and essence of thinking, why don't we all agree that whatever that nature is, anything that could pass this test would surely have it; then we could turn to asking how or whether some machine could be designed and built that might pass the test fair and square." Alas, philosophers—amateur and professional—have instead taken Turing's proposal as the pretext for just the sort of definitional haggling and interminable arguing about imaginary counterexamples he was hoping to squelch.

This thirty-year preoccupation with the Turing test has been all the more regrettable because it has focused attention on the wrong issues. There are *real world problems* that are revealed by considering the strengths and weaknesses of the Turing test, but these have been concealed behind a smokescreen of misguided criticisms. A failure to think imaginatively about the test actually proposed by Turing has led many to underestimate its severity and to confuse it with much less interesting proposals.

So first I want to show that the Turing test, conceived as he conceived it, is (as he thought) plenty strong enough as a test of thinking. I defy anyone to improve upon it. But here is the point almost universally overlooked by the literature: There is a common *misapplication* of the sort of testing exhibited by the Turing test that often leads to drastic overestimation of the powers of actually existing computer systems. The follies of this familiar sort of thinking about computers can best be brought out by a reconsideration of the Turing test itself.

The insight underlying the Turing test is the same insight that inspires the new practice among symphony orchestras of conducting auditions with an opaque screen between the jury and the musician. What matters in a musician, obviously, is musical ability and only musical ability: such features as sex, hair length, skin color, and weight are strictly irrelevant. Since juries might be biased—even innocently and unawares— by these irrelevant features, they are carefully screened off so only the essential features, musicianship, can be examined. Turing recognized that people similarly might be biased in their judgments of intelligence by whether the contestant had soft skin, warm blood, facial features, hands and eyes—which are obviously not themselves essential components of intelligence—so he devised a screen that would let through only a sample of what really mattered: the capacity to understand, and think cleverly about, challenging problems. Perhaps he was inspired by Descartes, who in his *Discourse on Method* plausibly argued that there was no more demanding test of human mentality than the capacity to hold an intelligent conversation:

It is indeed conceivable that a machine could be so made that it would utter words, and even words appropriate to the presence of physical acts or objects which cause some change in its organs; as, for example, if it was touched in some spot that it would ask what you wanted to say to it; if in another, that it would cry that it was hurt, and so on for similar things. But it could never modify its phrases to reply to the sense of whatever was said in its presence, as even the most stupid men can do. (Descartes 1960 [1637], 41–42)

This seemed obvious to Descartes in the seventeenth century, but of course the fanciest machines he knew were elaborate clockwork figures, not electronic computers. Today it is far from obvious that such machines are impossible, but Descartes's hunch that ordinary conversations would put as severe a strain on artificial intelligence as any other test was shared by Turing. Of course there is nothing sacred about the particular conversational game chosen by Turing for his test: it is just a cannily chosen test of more general intelligence. The assumption Turing was prepared to make was this: Nothing could possibly pass the Turing test by winning the imitation game without being able to perform indefinitely many other clearly intelligent actions. Let us call that assumption the quick-probe assumption. Turing realized, as anyone would, that there are hundreds and thousands of telling signs of intelligent thinking to be observed in our fellow creatures, and one could, if one wanted, compile a vast battery of different tests to assay the capacity for intelligent thought. But success on his chosen test, he thought, would be highly predictive of success on many other intuitively acceptable tests of intelligence. Remember, failure on the Turing test does not predict failure on those others, but success would surely predict success. His test was so severe, he thought, that nothing that could pass it fair and square would disappoint us in other quarters. Maybe it wouldn't do everything we hoped—maybe it wouldn't appreciate ballet, or understand quantum physics, or have a good plan for world peace, but we'd all see that it was surely one of the intelligent, thinking entities in the neighborhood.

Is this high opinion of the Turing test's severity misguided? Certainly many have thought so—but usually because they have not imagined the test in sufficient detail, and hence have underestimated it. Trying to forestall this skepticism, Turing imagined several lines of questioning that a judge might employ in this game—about writing poetry, or playing chess—that would be taxing indeed, but with thirty years experience with the actual talents and foibles of computers behind us, perhaps we can add a few more tough lines of questioning.

Terry Winograd, a leader in artificial intelligence efforts to produce conversational ability in a computer, draws our attention to a pair of sentences (Winograd 1972). They differ in only one word. The first sentence is this:

The committee denied the group a parade permit because they advocated violence.

Here's the second sentence:

The committee denied the group a parade permit because they feared violence.

The difference is just in the verb—*advocated* or *feared*. As Winograd points out, the pronoun *they* in each sentence is officially ambiguous. Both readings of the pronoun are always legal. Thus we can imagine a world in which governmental committees in charge of parade permits advocate violence in the streets and, for some strange reason, use this as their pretext for denying a parade permit. But the natural, reasonable, intelligent reading of the first sentence is that it's the group that advocated violence, and of the second, that it's the committee that feared the violence.

Now if sentences like this are embedded in a conversation, the computer must figure out which reading of the pronoun is meant, if it is to respond intelligently. But mere rules of grammar or vocabulary will not fix the right reading. What fixes the right reading for us is knowledge about the world, about politics, social circumstances, committees and their attitudes, groups that want to parade, how they tend to behave, and the like. One must know about the world, in short, to make sense of such a sentence.

In the jargon of artificial intelligence (AI), a conversational computer needs lots of *world knowledge* to do its job. But, it seems, if somehow it is endowed with that world knowledge on many topics, it should be able to do much more with that world knowledge than merely make sense of a conversation containing just that sentence. The only way, it appears, for a computer to disambiguate that sentence and keep up its end of a conversation that uses that sentence would be for it to have a much more general ability to respond intelligently to information about social and political circumstances, and many other topics. Thus, such sentences, by putting a demand on such abilities, are good quick probes. That is, they test for a wider competence.

People typically ignore the prospect of having the judge ask off-the-wall questions in the Turing test, and hence they underestimate the competence a computer would have to have to pass the test. But remember, the rules of the imitation game as Turing presented it permit the judge to ask any question that could be asked of a human being—no holds barred. Suppose then we give a contestant in the game this question:

An Irishman found a genie in a bottle who offered him two wishes. "First I'll have a pint of Guinness," said the Irishman, and when it appeared he took several long drinks from it and was delighted to see that the glass filled itself magically as he drank. "What about your second wish?" asked the genie. "Oh well," said the Irishman, "that's easy. I'll have another one."
—Please explain this story to me, and tell me if there is anything funny or sad about it.

Now even a child could express, if not eloquently, the understanding that is required to get this joke. But think of how much one has to know and understand about human culture, to put it pompously, to be able to give an account of the point of this joke. I am not supposing that the computer would have to laugh at, or be amused by, the joke. But if it wants to win the imitation game—and that's the test, after all—it had better know enough in its own alien, humorless way about human psychology and culture to be able to pretend effectively that it was amused and explain why.

It may seem to you that we could devise a better test. Let's compare the Turing test with some other candidates.

Candidate 1: A computer is intelligent if it wins the World Chess Championship.

That's not a good test, as it turns out. Chess prowess has proven to be an isolatable talent. There are programs today that can play fine chess but can do nothing else. So the quick probe assumption is false for the test of playing winning chess.

Candidate 2: The computer is intelligent if it solves the Arab-Israeli conflict.

This is surely a more severe test than Turing's. But it has some defects: it is unrepeatable, if passed once; slow, no doubt; and it is not crisply clear what would count as passing it. Here's another prospect, then:

Candidate 3: A computer is intelligent if it succeeds in stealing the British crown jewels without the use of force or violence.

Now this is better. First, it could be repeated again and again, though of course each repeat test would presumably be harder—but this is a feature it shares with the Turing test. Second, the mark of success is clear—either you've got the jewels to show for your efforts or you don't. But it is expensive and slow, a socially dubious caper at best, and no doubt luck would play too great a role.

With ingenuity and effort one might be able to come up with other candidates that would equal the Turing test in severity, fairness, and efficiency, but I think these few examples should suffice to convince us that it would be hard to improve on Turing's original proposal.

But still, one may protest, something might pass the Turing test and still not be intelligent, not be a thinker. What does *might* mean here? If what you have in mind is that by cosmic accident, by a supernatural coincidence, a stupid person or a stupid computer *might* fool a clever judge repeatedly. Well, yes, but so what? The same frivolous possibility "in principle" holds for any test whatever. A playful god, or evil demon, let us agree, could fool the world's scientific community about the presence of H_2O in the Pacific Ocean. But still, the tests they rely on to establish that there is H_2O in the Pacific Ocean are quite beyond reasonable criticism. If the Turing test for thinking is no worse than any well-established scientific test, we can set skepticism aside and go back to serious matters. Is there any more likelihood of a "false positive" result on the Turing test than on, say, the tests currently used for the presence of iron in an ore sample?

This question is often obscured by a "move" that philosophers have sometimes made called operationalism. Turing and those who think well of his test are often accused of being operationalists. Operationalism is the tactic of *defining* the presence of some property, for instance, intelligence, as being established once and for all by the passing of some test. Let's illustrate this with a different example.

Suppose I offer the following test—we'll call it the Dennett test—for being a great city:

A great city is one in which, on a randomly chosen day, one can do all three of the following:
• Hear a symphony orchestra
• See a Rembrandt *and* a professional athletic contest
• Eat *quenelles de brochet à la Nantua* for lunch

To make the operationalist move would be to declare that any city that passes the Dennett test is by *definition* a great city. What being a great city *amounts* to is just passing the Dennett test. Well then, if the Chamber of Commerce of Great Falls, Montana, wanted—and I can't imagine why—to get their hometown on my list of great cities, they could accomplish this by the relatively inexpensive route of hiring full time about ten basketball players, forty musicians, and a quick-order quenelle chef and renting a cheap Rembrandt from some museum. An idiotic operationalist would then be stuck admitting that Great Falls, Montana was in fact a great city, since all he or she cares about in great cities is that they pass the Dennett test.

Sane operationalists (who for that very reason are perhaps not operationalists at all, since *operationalist* seems to be a dirty word) would cling confidently to their test, but only because they have what they consider to be very good reasons for thinking the odds against a false positive result, like the imagined Chamber of Commerce caper, are astronomical. I devised the Dennett test, of course, with the realization that no one would be both stupid and rich enough to go to such preposterous lengths to foil the test. In the actual world, wherever you find symphony orchestras, *quenelles,* Rembrandts, and professional sports, you also find daily newspapers, parks, repertory theaters, libraries, fine architecture, and all the other things that go to make a city great. My test was simply devised to locate a *telling* sample that could not help but be representative of the rest of the city's treasures. I would cheerfully run the miniscule risk of having my bluff called. Obviously, the test items are not all that I care about in a city. In fact, some of them I don't care about at all. I just think they would be cheap and easy ways of assuring myself that the subtle things I do care about in cities are present. Similarly, I think it would be entirely unreasonable to suppose that Alan Turing had an inordinate fondness for party games, or put too high a value on party game prowess in his test. In both the Turing test and the Dennett test, a very unrisky gamble is being taken: the gamble that the quick-probe assumption is, in general, safe.

But two can play this game of playing the odds. Suppose some computer programmer happens to be, for whatever strange reason, dead set on tricking me into judging an entity to be a thinking, intelligent thing when it is not. Such a trickster could rely as well as I can on unlikelihood and take a few gambles. Thus, if the programmer can expect that it is not remotely likely that I, as the judge, will bring up the topic of children's birthday parties, or baseball, or moon rocks, then he or she can avoid the trouble of building world knowledge on those topics into the data base. Whereas if I do improbably raise these issues, the system will draw a blank and I will unmask the pretender easily. But given all the topics and words that I *might* raise, such a savings would no doubt be negligible. Turn the idea inside out, however, and the trickster will have a fighting chance. Suppose the programmer has reason to believe that I will ask *only* about children's birthday parties, or baseball, or moon rocks—all other topics being, for one reason or another, out of bounds. Not only does the task shrink dramatically, but there already exist systems or preliminary sketches of systems in artificial intelligence that can do a whiz-bang job of responding with apparent intelligence on just those specialized topics.

William Woods's LUNAR program, to take what is perhaps the best example, answers scientists' questions—posed in ordinary English—about moon rocks. In one test it answered correctly and appropriately something like 90 percent of the questions that geologists and other experts thought of asking it about moon rocks. (In 12 percent of those correct responses there were trivial, correctable defects.) Of course, Woods's motive in creating LUNAR was not to trick unwary geologists into thinking they were conversing with an intelligent being. And if that had been his motive his project would still be a long way from success.

For it is easy enough to unmask LUNAR without ever straying from the prescribed topic of moon rocks. Put LUNAR in one room, and a moon rocks specialist in another, and then ask them both their opinion of the social value of the moon-rocks–gathering expeditions, for instance. Or ask the contestants their opinion of the suitability of moon rocks as ashtrays, or whether people who have touched moon rocks are ineligible for the draft. Any intelligent person knows a lot more about moon rocks than their geology. Although it might be *unfair* to demand this extra knowledge of a computer moon rock specialist, it would be an easy way to get it to fail the Turing test.

But just suppose that someone could extend LUNAR to cover itself plausibly on such probes, so long as the topic was still, however indirectly, moon rocks. We might come to think it was a lot more like the human moon rocks specialist than it really was. The moral we should draw is that as Turing test judges we should resist all limitations and waterings-down of the Turing test. They make the game too easy—vastly easier than the original test. Hence they lead us into the risk of overestimating the actual comprehension of the system being tested.

Consider a different limitation on the Turing test that should strike a suspicious chord in us as soon as we hear it. This is a variation on a theme developed in a recent article by Ned Block (1981, *chapter 15*). Suppose someone were to propose to restrict the judge to a vocabulary of say, the 850 words of "Basic English," and to single-sentence probes—that is "moves"—of no more than four words. Moreover, contestants must respond to these probes with no more than four words per move, and a test may involve no more than forty questions.

Is this an innocent variation on Turing's original test? These restrictions would make the imitation game clearly finite. That is, the total number of all possible permissible games is a large, but finite, number. One might suspect that such a limitation would permit the trickster simply to store, in alphabetical order, all the possible good conversations within the limits and beat the judge with nothing more sophisticated than a system of table lookup. In fact, that isn't in the cards. Even with these severe and improbable and suspicious restrictions imposed upon the imitation game, the number of legal games, though finite, is mind-bogglingly large. I haven't bothered trying to calculate it, but it surely exceeds astronomically the number of possible chess games with no more than forty moves, and that number has been calculated. John Haugeland says it's in the neighborhood of ten to the one hundred twentieth power. For comparison, Haugeland suggests there have only been ten to the eighteenth seconds since the beginning of the universe (Haugeland 1981, page 16).

Of course, the number of good, sensible conversations under these limits is a tiny fraction, maybe one in a quadrillion, of the number of merely grammatically well formed conversations. So let's say, to be very conservative, that there are only ten to the fiftieth different smart conversations such a computer would have to store. Well, the task shouldn't take more than a few trillion years—given generous federal support. Finite numbers can be very large.

So though we needn't worry that this particular trick of storing all the smart conversations would work, we can appreciate that there are lots of ways of making the task easier that may appear innocent at first. We also get a reassuring measure of just how severe the unrestricted Turing test is by reflecting on the more than astronomical size of even that severely restricted version of it.

Block's imagined—and utterly impossible—program exhibits the dreaded feature known in computer science circles as *combinatorial explosion*. No conceivable computer could overpower a combinatorial explosion with sheer speed and size. Since the problem areas addressed by artificial intelligence are veritable minefields of combinatorial explosion, and since it has often proven difficult to find *any* solution to a problem that avoids them, there is considerable plausibility in Newell and Simon's proposal that avoiding combinatorial explosion (by any means at all) be viewed as one of the hallmarks of intelligence.

Our brains are millions of times bigger than the brains of gnats, but they are still, for all their vast complexity, compact, efficient, timely organs that somehow or other manage to perform all their tasks while avoiding combinatorial explosion. A computer a million times bigger or faster than a human brain might not look like the brain of a human being, or even be internally organized like the brain of a human being, but if, for all its differences, it somehow managed to control a wise and timely set of activities, it would have to be the beneficiary of a very special design that avoided combinatorial explosion, and whatever that design was, would we not be right to consider the entity intelligent?

Turing's test was designed to allow for this possibility. His point was that we should not be species-chauvinistic, or anthropocentric, about the insides of an intelligent being, for there might be inhuman ways of being intelligent.

To my knowledge, the only serious and interesting attempt by any program designer to win even a severely modified Turing test has been Kenneth Colby's. Colby is a psychiatrist and intelligence artificer at UCLA. He has a program called PARRY, which is a computer simulation of a paranoid patient who has delusions about the Mafia being out to get him. As you do with other conversational programs, you interact with it by sitting at a terminal and typing questions and answers back and forth. A number of years ago, Colby put PARRY to a very restricted test. He had genuine psychiatrists interview PARRY. He did not suggest to them that they might be talking or typing to a computer; rather, he made up some plausible story about why they were communicating with a real live patient by teletype. He also had the psychiatrists interview real, human paranoids via teletype. Then he took a PARRY transcript, inserted it in a group of teletype transcripts from real patients, gave them to another group of experts—more psychiatrists—and said, "One of these was a conversation with a computer. Can you figure out which one it was?" They couldn't. They didn't do better than chance.

Colby presented this with some huzzah, but critics scoffed at the suggestion that this was a legitimate Turing test. My favorite commentary on it was Joseph Weizenbaum's; in a letter to the *Communications of the Association of Computing Machinery* (Weizenbaum 1974), he said that, inspired by Colby, he had designed an even better program, which passed the same test. His also had the virtue of being a very inexpensive program, in these times of tight money. In fact you didn't even need a computer for it. All you needed was an electric typewriter. His program modeled infantile autism. And the transcripts—you type in your questions, and the thing just sits there and hums—cannot be distinguished by experts from transcripts of real conversations with infantile autistic patients. What was wrong, of course, with Colby's test was that the unsuspecting interviewers had no motivation at all to try out any of the sorts of questions that easily would have unmasked PARRY.

Colby was undaunted, and after his team had improved PARRY he put it to a much more severe test—a surprisingly severe test. This time, the interviewers—again, psychiatrists—*were* given the task at the outset of telling the computer from the real patient. They were set up in a classic Turing test: the patient in one room, the computer PARRY in the other room, with the judges conducting interviews with both of them (on successive days). The judges' task was to find out which one was the computer and which one was the real patient. Amazingly, they didn't do much better, which leads some people to say, "Well, that just confirms my impression of the intelligence of psychiatrists!"

But now, more seriously, was this an honest-to-goodness Turing test? Were there tacit restrictions on the lines of questioning of the judges? Like the geologists interacting with LUNAR, the psychiatrists' professional preoccupations and habits kept them from asking the sorts of unlikely questions that would have easily unmasked PARRY. After all, they realized that since one of the contestants was a real, live paranoid person, medical ethics virtually forbade them from toying with, upsetting, or attempting to confuse their interlocutors. Moreover, they also knew that this was a test of a model of paranoia, so there were certain questions that wouldn't be deemed to be relevant to testing the model *as a model of paranoia*. So, they asked just the sort of questions that therapists *typically* ask of such patients, and of course PARRY had been ingeniously and laboriously prepared to deal with just that sort of question.

One of the psychiatrist judges did, in fact, make a rather half-hearted attempt to break out of the mold and ask some telling questions: "Maybe you've heard the saying 'Don't cry over spilled milk.' What does that mean to you?" PARRY answered: "Maybe you have to watch out for the Mafia." When then asked "Okay, now if you were in a movie theater watching a movie and smelled something like burning wood or rubber, what would you do?" PARRY replied: "You know, they know me." And the next question was, "If you found a stamped, addressed letter in your path as you were walking down the street, what would you do?" PARRY replied: "What else do you want to know?"[1]

Clearly PARRY was, you might say, *parrying* these questions, which were incomprehensible to it, with more or less stock paranoid formulas. We see a bit of a dodge, which is apt to work, apt to seem plausible to the judge, only because the "contestant" is *supposed* to be a paranoid, and such people are expected to respond uncooperatively on such occasions. These unimpressive responses didn't particularly arouse the suspicions of the judge, as a matter of fact, though probably they should have.

PARRY, like all other large computer programs, is dramatically bound by limitations of cost-effectiveness. What was important to Colby and his crew was simulating his model of paranoia. This was a massive effort. PARRY has a thesaurus or dictionary of about 4500 words and 700 idioms and the grammatical competence to use it—a *parser,* in the jargon of computational linguistics. The entire PARRY program takes up about 200,000 words of computer memory, all laboriously installed by the programming team. Now once all the effort had gone into devising the model of paranoid thought processes and linguistic ability, there was little if any time, energy, money, or interest left over to build in huge amounts of world knowledge of the sort that any actual paranoid, of course, would have. (Not that anyone yet knows how to build in world knowledge in the first place.) Building in the world knowledge, if one could even do it, would no doubt have made PARRY orders of magnitude larger and slower. And what would have been the point, given Colby's theoretical aims?

---

1 I thank Kenneth Colby for providing me with the complete transcripts (including the judges' commentaries and reactions), from which these exchanges are quoted. The first published account of the experiment is by Heiser et al. (1980). Colby (1981) discusses PARRY and its implications.

PARRY is a theoretician's model of a psychological phenomenon: paranoia. It is not intended to have practical applications. But in recent years a branch of AI (knowledge engineering) has appeared that develops what are now called expert systems. Expert systems *are* designed to be practical. They are software superspecialist consultants, typically, that can be asked to diagnose medical problems, to analyze geological data, to analyze the results of scientific experiments, and the like. Some of them are very impressive. SRI in California announced a few years ago that PROSPECTOR, an SRI-developed expert system in geology, had correctly predicted the existence of a large, important mineral deposit that had been entirely unanticipated by the human geologists who had fed it its data. MYCIN, perhaps the most famous of these expert systems, diagnoses infections of the blood, and it does probably as well as, maybe better than, any human consultants. And many other expert systems are on the way.

All expert systems, like all other large AI programs, are what you might call Potemkin villages. That is, they are cleverly constructed facades, like cinema sets. The actual filling-in of details of AI programs is time-consuming, costly work, so economy dictates that only those surfaces of the phenomenon that are likely to be probed or observed are represented.

Consider, for example, the CYRUS program developed by Janet Kolodner in Roger Schank's AI group at Yale a few years ago (Kolodner 1983a,b, 1984). CYRUS stands (we are told) for Computerized Yale Retrieval and Updating System, but surely it is no accident that CYRUS modeled the memory of Cyrus Vance, who was then secretary of state in the Carter administration. The point of the CYRUS project was to devise and test some plausible ideas about how people organize their memories of the events they participate in: hence it was meant to be a "pure" AI system, a scientific model, not an expert system intended by any practical purpose. CYRUS was updated daily by being fed all UPI wire service news stories that mentioned Vance, and it was fed them directly, with no doctoring and no human intervention Thanks to an ingenious news-reading program called FRUMP, it could take any story just as it came in on the wire and could digest it and use it to update its data base so that it could answer more questions. You could address questions to CYRUS in English by typing at a terminal. You addressed them in the second person, as if you were talking with Cyrus Vance himself. The results looked like this:

Q Last time you went to Saudi Arabia, where did you stay?

A In a palace in Saudi Arabia on September 23, 1978.

Q Did you go sightseeing there?

A Yes, at an oilfield in Dharan on September 23, 1978.

Q Has your wife ever met Mrs. Begin?

A Yes, most recently at a state dinner in Israel in January 1980.

CYRUS could correctly answer thousands of questions—almost any fair question one could think of asking it. But if one actually set out to explore the boundaries of its facade and find the questions that overshot the mark, one could soon find them. "Have you ever met a female head of state?" was a question I asked it, wondering if CYRUS knew that Indira Gandhi and Margaret Thatcher were women. But for some reason the connection could not be drawn, and CYRUS failed to answer either yes or no. I had stumped it, in spite of the fact that CYRUS could handle a host of what you might call neighboring questions flawlessly. One soon learns from this sort of probing exercise that it is very hard to extrapolate accurately from a sample of performance that one has observed to such a system's total competence. It's also very hard to keep from extrapolating much too generously.

While I was visiting Schank's laboratory in the spring of 1980, something revealing happened. The real Cyrus Vance resigned suddenly. The effect on the program CYRUS was chaotic. It was utterly unable to cope with the flood of "unusual" news about Cyrus Vance. The only sorts of episodes CYRUS could understand at all were diplomatic meetings, flights, press conferences, state dinners, and the like—less than two dozen general sorts of activities (the kinds that are newsworthy and typical of secretaries of state). It had no provision for sudden resignation. It was as if the UPI had reported that a wicked witch had turned Vance into a frog. It is distinctly possible that CYRUS would have taken that report more in stride than the actual news. One can imagine the conversation

Q Hello, Mr. Vance, what's new?

A I was turned into a frog yesterday.

But of course it wouldn't know enough about what it had just written to be puzzled, or startled, or embarrassed. The reason is obvious. When you look inside CYRUS, you find that it has skeletal definitions of thousands of words, but these definitions are minimal. They contain as little as the system designers think that they can get away with. Thus, perhaps, *lawyer* would be defined as synonymous with *attorney* and *legal counsel*, but aside from that, all one would discover about lawyers is that they are adult human beings and that they perform various functions in legal areas. If you then traced out the path to *human being*, you'd find out various obvious things CYRUS "knew" about human beings (hence about lawyers), but that is not a lot. That lawyers are university graduates, that they are better paid than chambermaids, that they know how to tie their shoes, that they are unlikely to be found in the company of lumberjacks—these trivial, if weird, facts about lawyers would not be explicit or implicit anywhere in this system. In other words, a very thin stereotype of a lawyer would be incorporated into the system, so that almost nothing you could tell it about a lawyer would surprise it.

So long as surprising things don't happen, so long as Mr. Vance, for instance, leads a typical diplomat's life, attending state dinners, giving speeches, flying from Cairo to Rome, and so forth, this system works very well. But as soon as his path is crossed by an important anomaly, the system is unable to cope, and unable to recover without fairly massive human intervention. In the case of the sudden resignation. Kolodner and her associates soon had CYRUS up and running again, with a new talent—answering questions about Edmund Muskie, Vance's successor—but it was no less vulnerable to unexpected events. Not that it mattered particularly, since CYRUS was a theoretical model, not a practical system.

There are a host of ways of improving the performance of such systems, and, of course some systems are much better than others. But all AI programs in one way or another have this facadelike quality, simply for reasons of economy. For instance, most expert systems in medical diagnosis so far developed operate with statistical information. They have no deep or even shallow knowledge of the underlying causal mechanisms of the phenomena that they are diagnosing. To take an imaginary example, an expert system asked to diagnose an abdominal pain would be oblivious to the potential import of the fact that the patient had recently been employed as a sparring partner by Muhammed Ali—there being no statistical data available to it on the rate of kidney stones among athlete's assistants. That's a fanciful case no doubt—too obvious, perhaps, to lead to an actual failure of diagnosis and practice. But more subtle and hard-to-detect limits to comprehension are always present, and even experts, even the system's designers, can be uncertain of where and how these limits will interfere with the desired operation of the system. Again, steps can be taken and are being taken to correct these flaws. For instance, my former colleague at Tufts, Benjamin Kuipers, is currently working on an expert system in nephrology—for diagnosing kidney ailments—that will be based on an elaborate system of causal reasoning about the phenomena being diagnosed. But this is a very ambitious, long-range project of considerable theoretical difficulty. And even if all the reasonable, cost-effective steps are taken to minimize the superficiality of expert systems, they will still be facades, just somewhat thicker or wider facades.

When we were considering the fantastic case of the crazy Chamber of Commerce of Great Falls, Montana, we couldn't imagine a plausible motive for anyone going to any sort of trouble to trick the Dennett test. The quick probe assumption for the Dennett test looked quite secure. But when we look at expert systems, we see that, however innocently, their designers do have motivation for doing exactly the sort of trick that would fool an unsuspicious Turing tester. First, since expert systems are all superspecialists who are only supposed to know about some narrow subject, users of such systems, not having much time to kill, do not bother probing them at the boundaries at all. They don't bother asking "silly" or irrelevant questions. Instead, they concentrate—not unreasonably—on exploiting the system's strengths. But shouldn't they try to obtain a clear vision of such a system's weaknesses as well? The normal habit of human thought when conversing with one another is to assume general comprehension, to assume rationality, to assume, moreover, that the quick probe assumption is, in general, sound. This amiable habit of thought almost irresistibly leads to putting too much faith in computer systems, especially user-friendly systems that present themselves in a very anthropomorphic manner.

Part of the solution to this problem is to teach all users of computers, especially users of expert systems, how to probe their systems before they rely on them, how to search out and explore the boundaries of the facade.

This is an exercise that calls not only for intelligence and imagination, but also a bit of special understanding about the limitations and actual structure of computer programs. It would help, of course, if we had standards of truth in advertising, in effect, for expert systems. For instance, each such system should come with a special demonstration routine that exhibits the sorts of shortcomings and failures that the designer knows the system to have. This would not be a substitute, however, for an attitude of cautious, almost obsessive, skepticism on the part of users, for designers are often, if not always, unaware of the subtler flaws in the products they produce. That is inevitable and natural, given the way system designers must think. They are trained to think positively—constructively, one might say—about the designs that they are constructing.

I come, then, to my conclusions. First, a philosophical or theoretical conclusion: The Turing test in unadulterated, unrestricted form, as Turing presented it, is plenty strong if well used. I am confident that no computer in the next twenty years is going to pass the unrestricted Turing test. They may well win the World Chess Championship or even a Nobel Prize in physics, but they won't pass the unrestricted Turing test. Nevertheless, it is not, I think, impossible in principle for a computer to pass the test, fair and square. I'm not running one of those a priori "computers can't think" arguments. I stand unabashedly ready, moreover, to declare that any computer that actually passes the unrestricted Turing test will be, in every theoretically interesting sense, a thinking thing.

But remembering how very strong the Turing test is, we must also recognize that there may also be interesting varieties of thinking or intelligence that are not well poised to play and win the imitation game. That no non-human Turing test winners are yet visible on the horizon does not mean that there aren't machines that already exhibit *some* of the important features of thought. About them, it is probably futile to ask my title question. Do they think? Do they *really* think? In some regards they do, and in some regards they don't. Only a detailed look at what they do, and how they are structured will reveal what is interesting about them. The Turing test, not being a scientific test, is of scant help on that task, but there are plenty of other ways of examining such systems. Verdicts on their intelligence or capacity for thought or consciousness would be only as informative and persuasive as the theories of intelligence or thought or consciousness the verdicts were based on, and since our task is to create such theories, we should get on with it and leave the Big Verdict for another occasion. In the meantime, should anyone want a surefire, almost-guaranteed-to-be-fail-safe test of thinking by a computer, the Turing test will do very nicely.

My second conclusion is more practical, and hence in one clear sense more important. Cheapened versions of the Turing test are everywhere in the air. Turing's test is not just effective, it is entirely natural—this is, after all, the way we assay the intelligence of each other every day. And since incautious use of such judgments and such tests is the norm, we are in some considerable danger of extrapolating too easily, and judging too generously, about the understanding of the systems we are using. The problem of overestimation of cognitive prowess, of comprehension, of intelligence, is not, then, just a philosophical problem, but a real social problem, and we should alert ourselves to it, and take steps to avert it.

Postscript: Eyes, Ears, Hands, and History

My philosophical conclusion in this paper is that any computer that actually passed the Turing test would be a thinking thing in every theoretically interesting sense. This conclusion seems to some people to fly in the face of what I have myself argued on other occasions. Peter Bieri, commenting on this paper at Boston University, noted that I have often claimed to show the importance to genuine understanding of a rich and intimate perceptual interconnection between an entity and its surrounding world—the need for something like eyes and ears—and a similarly complex active engagement with elements in that world—the need for something like hands with which to do things in that world. Moreover, I have often held that only a biography of sorts, a history of actual projects, learning experiences, and other bouts with reality, could produce the sorts of complexities (both external, or behavioral, and internal) that are needed to ground a principled interpretation of an entity as a thinking thing, an entity with beliefs, desires, intentions and other mental attitudes.

But the opaque screen in the Turing test discounts or dismisses these factors altogether, it seems, by focusing attention on only the contemporaneous capacity to engage in one very limited sort of activity: verbal communication. (I have even coined a pejorative label for such purely language-using systems: bedridden.) Am I going back on my earlier claims? Not at all. I am merely pointing out that the Turing test is so powerful that it will ensure indirectly that these conditions, if they are truly necessary, are met by any successful contestant.

"You may well be right," Turing could say, "that eyes, ears, hands, and a history are necessary conditions for thinking. If so, then I submit that nothing could pass the Turing test that didn't have eyes, ears, hands, and a history. That is an empirical claim, which we can someday hope to test. If you suggest that these are conceptually necessary, not just practically or physically necessary, conditions for thinking, you make a philosophical claim that I for one would not know how, or care, to assess. Isn't it more interesting and important in the end to discover whether or not it is true that no bedridden system could pass a demanding Turing test?"

Suppose we put to Turing the suggestion that he add another component to his test: Not only must an entity win the imitation game, but also it must be able to identify—using whatever sensory apparatus it has available to it—a variety of familiar objects placed in its room: a tennis racket, a potted palm, a bucket of yellow paint, a live dog. This would ensure that somehow or other the entity was capable of moving around and distinguishing things in the world. Turing could reply, I am asserting, that this is an utterly unnecessary addition to his test, making it no more demanding than it already was. A suitably probing conversation would surely establish, beyond a shadow of a doubt, that the contestant knew its way around in the real world. The imagined alternative of somehow "prestocking" a bedridden, blind computer with enough information, and a clever enough program, to trick the Turing test is science fiction of the worst kind—possible "in principle" but not remotely possible in fact, given the combinatorial explosion of possible variation such a system would have to cope with.

"But suppose you're wrong. What would you say of an entity that was created all at once (by some programmers, perhaps), an instant individual with all the conversational talents of an embodied, experienced human being?" This is like the question: "Would you call a hunk of H_2O that was as hard as steel at room temperature ice?" I do not know what Turing would say, of course, so I will speak for myself. Faced with such an improbable violation of what I take to be the laws of nature, I would probably be speechless. The least of my worries would be about which lexicographical leap to take:

A. "It turns out, to my amazement, that something can think without having had the benefit of eyes, ears, hands, and a history."
B. "It turns out, to my amazement, that something can pass the Turing test without thinking."

Choosing between these ways of expressing my astonishment would be asking myself a question "too meaningless to deserve discussion."

Discussion

Q   Why was Turing interested in differentiating a man from a woman in his famous test?

A   That was just an example. He described a parlor game in which a man would try to fool the judge by answering questions as a woman would answer. I suppose that Turing was playing on the idea that maybe, just maybe, there is a big difference between the way men think and the way women think. But of course they're both thinkers. He wanted to use that fact to make us realize that, even if there were clear differences between the way a computer and a person thought, they'd both still be thinking.

Q   Why does it seem that some people are upset by AI research? Does AI research threaten our self-esteem?

A   I think Herb Simon has already given the canniest diagnosis of that. For many people the mind is the last refuge of mystery against the encroaching spread of science, and they don't like the idea of science engulfing the last bit of terra incognita. This means that they are threatened, I think irrationally, by the prospect that researchers in artificial intelligence may come to understand the human mind as well as biologists understand the genetic code, or as well as physicists understand electricity and magnetism. This could lead to the "evil scientist" (to take a stock character from science fiction) who can control you because he or she has a deep understanding of what's going on in your mind. This seems to me to be a totally valueless fear, one that you can set aside, for the simple reason that the human mind is full of an extraordinary amount of detailed knowledge, as, for example, Roger Schank has been pointing out.

As long as the scientist who is attempting to manipulate you does not share all your knowledge, his or her chances of manipulating you are minimal. People can always hit you over the head. They can do that now. We don't need artificial intelligence to manipulate people by putting them in chains or torturing them. But if someone tries to manipulate you by controlling your thoughts and ideas, that person will have to know what you know and more. The best way to keep yourself safe from that kind of manipulation is to be well informed.

Q   Do you think we will be able to program self-consciousness into a computer?

A   Yes, I do think that it's possible to program self-consciousness into a computer. *Self-consciousness* can mean many things. If you take the simplest, crudest notion of self-consciousness, I suppose that would be the sort of self-consciousness that a lobster has: When it's hungry, it eats something, but it never eats itself. It has some way of distinguishing between itself and the rest of the world, and it has a rather special regard for itself.

The lowly lobster is, in one regard, self-conscious. If you want to know whether or not you can create that on the computer, the answer is yes. It's no trouble at all. The computer is already a self-watching, self-monitoring sort of thing. That is an established part of the technology.

But, of course, most people have something more in mind when they speak of self-consciousness. It is that special inner light, that private way that it is with you that nobody else can share, something that is forever outside the bounds of computer science. How could a computer ever be conscious in this sense?

That belief, that very gripping, powerful intuition is, I think, in the end simply an illusion of common sense. It is as gripping as the commonsense illusion that the earth stands still and the sun goes around the earth. But the only way that those of us who do not believe in the illusion will ever convince the general public that it is an illusion is by gradually unfolding a very difficult and fascinating story about just what is going on in our minds.

In the interim, people like me—philosophers who have to live by our wits and tell a lot of stories—use what I call intuition pumps, little examples that help to free up the imagination. I simply want to draw your attention to one fact. If you look at a computer—I don't care whether it's a giant Cray or a personal computer—if you open up the box and look inside and see those chips, you say, "No way could that be conscious. No way could that be self-conscious." But the same thing is true if you take the top off somebody's skull and look at the gray matter pulsing away in there. You think, "That is conscious? No way could that lump of stuff be conscious."

Of course, it makes no difference whether you look at it with a microscope or with a macroscope: At no level of inspection does a brain look like the seat of consciousness. Therefore, don't expect a computer to look like the seat of consciousness. If you want to get a grasp of how a computer could be conscious, it's no more difficult in the end than getting a grasp of how a brain could be conscious.

As we develop good accounts of consciousness, it will no longer seem so obvious to everyone that the idea of a self-conscious computer is a contradiction in terms. At the same time, I doubt that there will ever be self-conscious robots. But for boring reasons. There won't be any point in making them. Theoretically, could we make a gall bladder out of atoms? In principle we could. A gall bladder is just a collection of atoms, but manufacturing one would cost the moon. It would be more expensive than every project NASA has even dreamed of, and there would be no scientific payoff. We wouldn't learn anything new about how gall bladders work. For the same reason, I don't think we're going to see really humanoid robots, because practical, cost-effective robots don't need to be very humanoid at all. They need to be like the robots you can already see at General Motors, or like boxy little computers that do special-purpose things.

The theoretical issues will be studied by artificial intelligence researchers by looking at models that, to the layman, will show very little sign of humanity at all, and it will be only by rather indirect arguments that anyone will be able to appreciate that these models cast light on the deep theoretical question of how the mind is organized.

Bibliography

Block, Ned. 1981. Psychologism and behaviorism. *Philosophical Review* XC(1): 5–43. *Reprinted in chapter 15.*

Colby, Kenneth. 1981. Modeling a paranoid mind. *Behavioral and Brain Sciences* 4(4):515–560.

Descartes, René. 1637. *Discourse on the Method*, Part Five. Reprinted in Descartes 1985, volume I. *Reprinted in chapter 1.*

———. 1960 [1637]. *Discourse on method and meditations.* New York, NY: Macmillan Publishing Company. Translated with an introduction by Laurence J. Lafleur. See also (Descartes 1637, *chapter 1*).

———. 1985. *The philosophical writings of René Descartes.* Cambridge, England: Cambridge University Press. Translated by John Cottingham, Robert Stoothoff, and Dugald Murdoch.

Haugeland, John. 1981. *Mind design.* Cambridge, MA: MIT Press.

Heiser, Jon F., Kenneth Mark Colby, William S. Faught, and Roger C. Parkison. 1980. Can psychiatrists distinguish a computer simulation of paranoia from the real thing? The limitations of Turing-like tests as measures of the adequacy of simulations. *Journal of Psychiatric Research* 15(3):149–162.

Kolodner, Janet L. 1983a. Maintaining organization in a dynamic long-term memory. *Cognitive Science* 7(4):243–280.

————. 1983b. Reconstructive memory: A computer model. *Cognitive Science* 7(4):281–328.

————. 1984. *Retrieval and organization strategies in conceptual memory: A computer model.* Hillsdale, NJ: Lawrence Erlbaum Associates.

Turing, Alan M. 1950. Computing machinery and intelligence. *Mind* LIX(236): 433–460. *Reprinted in chapter 4.*

Weizenbaum, Joseph. 1974. Automating psychotherapy. *Communications of the Association for Computing Machinery* 17(7):425.

Winograd, Terry. 1972. *Understanding natural language.* New York, NY: Academic Press.

The Turing Test's Evidentiary Value

In the discussion of Block's Aunt Bertha machine, Block moved Turing's test of intelligence from one based on behaviors to one based on capacities. The *capacity* to pass the Test is what is indicative of intelligence. Block goes on to argue that such a capacity can still not be taken to be a sufficient condition of intelligence. But it might still be indicative. In "An Analysis of the Turing Test" (Moor 1976, *chapter 17*), James Moor argues that the Turing Test should be taken to be evidence of intelligence, not a definition or even sufficient condition.

He calls the evidence inductive evidence, but what kind of induction could a Turing Test be evidence for? Induction, in one guise at least, is the form of reasoning from instances of a universal to the universal. The instances we see in a Turing Test are the agent "producing a sensible sequence of verbal responses to a sequence of verbal stimuli" as Block would say. The natural inductive conclusion to draw from such data is that the agent has the "capacity to produce a sensible sequence of verbal responses to arbitrary sequences of verbal stimuli". Moor's inductive evidence is evidence for Block's neo-Turing-Test conception of intelligence.

The first thing to note is that as evidence, it is extremely good. The combinatorics that work against Block's Aunt Bertha machine work to the advantage of the induction. For instance, as the Turing Test gets longer, the odds that the responses could have been generated randomly (by monkeys on typewriters as it were) go down exponentially. Similarly, the odds that an Aunt Bertha machine is being used (assuming certain principles of physics and information storage) go down just as quickly, for the size of the required machine goes up exponentially in Test length. Seen this way, the Turing Test is not a proof in the deductive sense, but in a statistical sense made mathematically precise by the recent work in computer science on so-called interactive proofs (Shieber 2004).[1]

The second thing to note is that if a Turing Test is inductive evidence for the general capacity of the neo-Turing-Test conception of intelligence, then it is only evidence of intelligence itself insofar as that conception is sound. Thus, if Block is right, and the neo-Turing-Test conception fails, so does the inductive evidence reconstruction.

But what Moor is getting at goes beyond the inductive view of the Turing Test, and is made clearer by Stalker's reply (Stalker 1978, *chapter 18*) and Moor's response (Moor 1978, *chapter 19*). Stalker refers to the evidence not as inductive evidence, but as explanatory evidence. More properly, the Test appeals to reasoning by *abduction*. We can caricature the types of reasoning as follows: *Deduction* is reasoning from P and $P \rightarrow Q$ to Q; *induction* is reasoning from (repeated instances of) P and Q to $P \rightarrow Q$; *abduction* is reasoning from P and $Q \rightarrow P$ to Q. Of course, such reasoning is deductively unsound, and appropriately limited to special cases where $Q \rightarrow P$ holds because Q is a cause of P, and if there are multiple Q_i such that $Q_i \rightarrow P$, we select the Q_i that serves as the "best" explanation as the cause of P. For this reason, abduction is often referred to as "reasoning to the best explanation". (What "best" means is a tricky issue, of course; it is where all the action is in formalizing abductive reasoning.)

In the case at hand, we take P to be the passing of the Turing Test and Q to be the possession of intelligence. Abduction then allows us to reason from an agent passing the Turing Test, along with the view that intelligence (at least of a certain sort) implies

---

1 Bradford and Wollowski (1995) attempt to make a precise mathematical characterization of intelligence based on interactive proof techniques, but applying these techniques to a phenomenon as difficult to get a handle on as human cognition makes the effort less than satisfactory. The relationship between the Turing Test and interactive proof methods is more properly viewed as one of insightful analogy than mathematical identity.

the ability to pass the Turing Test, to the conclusion that the agent is intelligent.

Stalker points out that abductive reasoning requires an argument that the particular $Q \rightarrow P$ that one chooses must be the *best* explanation, not just any explanation, and he thinks he has a better one, namely, that the machine's behavior is merely the output of mechanical "mindless" application of a particular program in response to its inputs. No appeal to the computer's thinking need be made. Moor's reply amounts to arguing that the intelligence view is just as good, if not better, as an abductive explanation. The evidence for such a conclusion can be seen in Stalker's own statement that such a nonmentalistic explanation would be preferred in explaining people's behavior too, if only we had a better understanding of neurophysiology. Sampson's reply to Purtill applies here too.

Abductive reasoning in general has a further problem: The explanation that is best (relative to one's theory of possible explanations) may still be wrong. Moor implies as much when he talks about the possibility that new evidence can cause one to change one's conclusions. So the move to viewing the Turing Test as abductive evidence of intelligence probably won't satisfy those (like Searle) who believe themselves in possession of a priori arguments against the possibility of mechanical intelligence. No matter how much "evidence" of this sort accumulates, the deductive conclusion from the premise "machines can't think" will trump the abductive evidence to the contrary.

17

An Analysis of the Turing Test

James H. Moor

1 The Turing Test

In his classic article, "Computing Machinery and Intelligence", A. M. Turing suggests that the ambiguous question, "Can machines think?" should be replaced with a new set of questions involving a game which he calls "the imitation game" (Turing 1950, *chapter 4*). In this paper I wish to argue that the proponents and critics of the imitation game have misunderstood its significance. The real value of the imitation game lies not in treating it as the basis for an operational definition but in considering it as a potential source of good inductive evidence for the hypothesis that machines think. With this understanding the four standard criticisms against the game do not apply.

A standard version of the imitation game involves a man, a computer, and a human interrogator. The interrogator stays in a room apart from the man and the computer and must on the basis of answers to questions that he puts to each via a teletypewriter decide which respondent is the man and which respondent is the computer.[1] In this version of the game, which is often called "the Turing test", the basic question which replaces the question "Can machines think?" might be put, "On the average after n minutes or m questions is an interrogator's probability of correctly identifying which respondent is a machine significantly greater than 50 percent?"

If the number of minutes and questions were kept very small, then playing the imitation game would be little more than an entertaining

---

1 I believe this version represents the usual interpretation of the imitation game although Turing's own description is ambiguous (Turing 1950, 433–434, *chapter 4*).

pastime. But, in order to make the imitation game less of a game and more of a test with interesting results let us assume that the following situation occurs. The imitation game is played by many different interrogators each of whom has ample opportunity to ask many questions (each taking a week to make thousands of inquiries if you wish) and the results are such that the probability of the average interrogator correctly identifying the machine is not significantly greater than 50 percent. If such a situation did occur, then one would have little doubt that the imitation game was played well by the machine, but one might have a lingering doubt about the significance of this result. One is tempted to say, "Sure, the machine plays the imitation game very well but so what?"

2   The Significance of the Turing Test

Unfortunately, Turing does not help us very much in understanding the significance of the imitation game. At one point he claims that the question, "Can machines think?" is "too meaningless to deserve discussion" (Turing 1950, *chapter 4*). But, if Turing intends that the question of the success of the machine at the imitation game replace the question about machines thinking, then it is difficult to understand how we are to judge the propriety and adequacy of the replacement if the question being replaced is too meaningless to deserve discussion. Our potential interest in the imitation game is aroused not by the fact that a computer might learn to play yet another game, but that in some way this test reveals a connection between possible computer activities and our ordinary concept of thinking.

The usual understanding of the Turing test put forth by its proponents (and critics) is that it provides an operational definition. For instance, P. H. Millar describes it as a virtue of the Turing test that "it constitutes an operational definition which, given a computer terminal system, can be used as a criterion" (Millar 1973, *chapter 12*). It is usually not specified whether the Turing test is intended as an operational definition of "computer thinking", "the equivalence of human and computer thinking", or what. But in any case the benefits of this type of interpretation seem to me to be illusory. Either one is giving an arbitrary definition of a new term in which case the operational definition needs no justification but the Turing test becomes very uninteresting, or one is attempting to capture a notion which is at least related to our ordinary concept of thinking in which case the Turing test is very interesting but the operational definition requires some justification. In short, one cannot assess the significance of the Turing test without attending to the ordinary concept of thinking as unclear as that concept might be.

To think is to process information in ways which involve recognition, imagination, evaluation and decision. To a moderate extent computers perform these processes already. The question is whether a computer could eventually process information in these ways with the sophistication of a normal, living, adult human being; and if it could, how would we know it? The clue lies in considering the basis for our knowledge that other humans think. I believe that another human being thinks because his ability to think is part of a theory I have to explain his actions. The theory postulates a number of inner information processes, but the evidence for the theory comes from the outward behavior of the person. On the basis of his behavior I can confirm, disconfirm, and modify my theory. Furthermore, there is no reason why knowledge of computer thinking can not arise in the same way. I can use the computer's behavior as evidence in assessing my theory about its information processing. In neither the human case nor the computer case must I consider the thinking to be on a close analogy with my own, for the evidence might dictate that the human or computer discriminates and evaluates quite differently than I do.

If passing the Turing test is not an operational definition, then is it at least a necessary condition for making an inductive inference about computer thinking? Again, I believe the answer is negative. One might have solid inductive evidence based on the computer's behavior that it was thinking as well as a human but the computer could not pass the Turing test simply because it was a poor actor. Thus, the Turing test is not essential to our knowledge about computer thinking. One could certainly construct and test a theory about computer thinking in much the same way one constructs and tests a theory about human thinking without becoming engaged in the Turing test.

Then what is the value of the Turing test? I believe that the significance of the Turing test is that it provides one good format for gathering inductive evidence such that if the Turing test was passed, then one would certainly have very adequate grounds for inductively inferring that the computer could think on the level of a normal, living, adult human being. Beyond the obvious reason that the Turing test eliminates prejudice due to the appearance of the computer I believe there are two strong arguments why the Turing test is a good format for gathering inductive evidence. First, the Turing test permits direct or indirect testing of virtually all of the activities one would count as evidence for thinking. Foremost, the Turing test permits (even demands) evaluation of linguistic behavior which is central to our inductive inferences about how others think. In the Turing test format the nonverbal behavior of the respondents cannot be directly observed by the interrogator, but this limitation is not as severe as is usually supposed. Since nonverbal behavior can be described, probing questions can be put to the respondents about how they would perform various activities involving thinking, e.g., designing a house, balancing a bank account, playing bridge, etc. Secondly, the Turing test encourages severe testing. It is a familiar point that the confirmation of a theory can come all too easily. If a computer simply repeated one cognitive activity many times and did it well, even if it is a complex activity like playing chess, it does not follow that the computer's thinking capacity has been critically tested. In the Turing test, however, the computer would be tested in detail over a wide range of subjects. Moreover, the interrogator's goal is to find a refuting instance which gives the computer away.

3   Replies To Objections

3.1   The Objection Concerning Behaviorism
One of the most common objections to the Turing test is that the test must be based upon a behavioristic construal of the concept of thinking and any such behavioristic analysis is absurd. Probably the most imaginative form of this argument is given by Keith Gunderson. Gunderson creates a parody of the imitation game by asking whether rocks could imitate. (Gunderson 1971) He imagines an elaborate apparatus consisting of a rock box, electric eye, releasing mechanism, etc. which could land on someone's toe with about the same effect as a person's foot. It would be the interrogator's job to determine if it was a rock box or a person stepping

on his toe. If the interrogator could not reliably determine whether it was a person or a rock box that was stepping on his toe, the rock box would pass the test. Gunderson concludes:

The parody comparison can be pushed too far. But I think it lays bare the reason why there is no contradiction involved in saying, "Yes, a machine can play the imitation game, but it can't think." It is for the same reason that there is no contradiction in saying, "Of course a rock box of such-and-such a sort can be set up, but rocks surely can't imitate." For thinking (or imitating) cannot be fully described simply by pointing to net results such as those illustrated above. For if this were not the case it would be correct to say that a phonograph could sing, and that an electric eye could see people coming. (Gunderson 1971)

I have tried to argue that an understanding of the Turing test is not necessarily dependent upon a behavioristic analysis of thinking, i.e., providing an operational definition of thinking. On the contrary, since our knowledge of thinking by others has an inductive basis, it certainly is neither a surprise nor a criticism to point out that the statement "Yes, a machine can play the imitation game, but it can't think" is not a contradiction. It is doubtful whether the toe-stepping game provides a good format for generating adequate evidence to establish that the rock box apparatus (let alone the rocks themselves as Gunderson misleadingly suggests) imitates. It surely does not follow from this that the Turing test fails to provide a good format for generating adequate behavioral evidence to justify the induction that a computer thinks.

3.2   The Objection Concerning Mechanism

Michael Apter (1971, 68) suggests that Turing's position is question-begging since it assumes that the brain is a machine. As a factual matter Turing probably did believe that the brain is a machine in some sense although not a discrete state machine. Turing says, "In considering the functions of the mind or the brain we find certain operations which we can explain in purely mechanical terms." (Turing 1950, *chapter 4*) But he is careful to qualify his view stating that he does not claim to be giving convincing arguments, rather they should be described as "recitations tending to produce belief". What is important for our purposes, however, is that the Turing test in no way depends upon the assumption that the brain is a machine. My claim is that if the test was passed in the sense discussed above, then one should conclude that both men and machines can think. One is not forced to assume or conclude from this that brains are machines (or machines are brains) any more than one would assume or conclude that a human who printed very well must be a typewriter.

I do not doubt that "machines" might be construed broadly enough to include brains, but the Turing test is far more interesting if "machines" is taken in a more ordinary and narrow sense which would include digital computers, even if made of another generation of electronic parts, but which would exclude brains. For if brains were machines, then the question "Can machines think?" seems to be answered very easily in the affirmative.

3.3   The Objection Concerning Internal Operation

If a digital computer could pass the Turing test, then there would surely be a natural curiosity and legitimate interest in how the computer could accomplish this feat. It is sometimes argued that if the computer was to accomplish this feat by using very unorthodox methods, then there would be grounds for believing that the computer did not think, and therefore, the Turing test is inadequate.

In general, I believe there is something valuable in this criticism. It does seem possible that a computer might accomplish its behavioral repertoire on a much different basis than a human being; and there would indeed be benefit, as Gunderson points out, in making comparisons between the cognitive processes of human beings and computers and between the operations of the human nervous system and the computer's circuitry. What is not clear is how this is a criticism of the Turing test. The underlying danger is that two very similar claims may be confused:

(i) Evidence about the internal operation of a computer *might alter* a justified inductive inference that the computer can think on the level of a normal, living, adult human being.

(ii) Evidence about the internal operation of a computer *is necessary to make* a justified inductive inference that the computer can think on the level of a normal, living, adult human being.

I believe that (i) is true. For example, an extreme case is that of Baron von Kempelen's very successful chess-playing machine in which a man was so cleverly hidden that although people were allowed to examine all of the interior of the machine at different times, the man inside escaped detection by moving around (Nievergelt and Farrar 1973). In this case it is clear that information about the internal operation of the chess-playing machine would influence one to reconsider his judgments about the machine's actual abilities. In less extreme cases it may be a question of comparing different physical processes which perform similar informational functions. Just how different such physical processes can be and still be regarded as the same information process is an open and interesting question. Although even if the information processes of computers were considered different from information processes of human, it is not clear whether one would conclude that computers did not think or just that they thought by a different means from humans.

But, the essential point is that to grant (i) is only to admit that further evidence might alter inductive inferences and this is certainly no criticism of the Turing test. In order for critics to use the objection concerning internal operation as a criticism against the Turing test they must show that (ii) is true. Not only do the critics fail to show that (ii) is true, but I believe for the reasons given in Section 2 that (ii) must be false. Beyond what we infer about cognitive processes from the behavioral level, we know very little about the relevant internal operations of human beings. Yet, people have legitimately inferred on the basis of behavior that others could think at least since Aristotle who, of course, believed that the brain was a cooling agent for the blood.

3.4   The Objection Concerning the Scope of the Test

If one agrees that it is the behavioral evidence which is most crucial in assessing the thinking capabilities of a computer, it can still be objected that the Turing test is inadequate because it is only one test of behavior. Gunderson (1971) compares the situation to a vacuum cleaner salesman who claims that his vacuum cleaner is all-purpose but only demonstrates that the vacuum cleaner can pick up bits of dust. Gunderson's point is that one expects other activities from a computer which is claimed to think than merely the ability to play one game. Jerry Fodor (1968) argues further, "Turing would presumably have been dissatisfied with a device that could answer questions about how to boil water if it routinely put the kettle in the icebox when told to brew the tea."

Again it is important to distinguish two very similar claims:

(iii) Behavioral evidence which cannot be directly obtained in the Turing test *might alter* a justified inductive inference that a computer can think on the level of a normal, living, adult human being.

(iv) Behavioral evidence which cannot be directly obtained in the Turing test *is necessary* to make a justified inductive inference that a computer can think on the level of a normal, living, adult human being.

I believe that (iii) is true. I do not wish to deny that further testing beyond the Turing test would be valuable and that the results of such further testing might make one revise inferences based on the results of the Turing test alone. It is interesting to note, however, that if the disconfirmation was not too severe, e.g., a situation in which the computer passed the Turing test, had reasonably good nonverbal behavior, but routinely put the kettle in the icebox when told to brew the tea, then one might attribute the problem to whimsy or to difficulties in the computer's motor apparatus rather than reject the hypothesis that the computer was capable of thinking.

Again the essential point is that to grant (iii) is only to admit a well known fact about inductive inferences. In order to attack the Turing test the critic must show that (iv) is true. And again, not only do the critics fail to show that (iv) is true, but I believe for the reasons given in Section 2 that (iv) must be false. It is simply a misleading numbers game to suggest that the Turing test is only one test. The Turing test provides a format for directly or indirectly examining any of a wide variety of activities which would count as evidence for thinking.

4   Conclusion

In this paper I have argued that the Turing test is best not treated as the basis for an operational definition, and in any event acceptance of the Turing test does not allow us to avoid the question of how knowledge of computer thinking is possible. Nonetheless, the Turing test is a significant test for computer thought if it is interpreted inductively. Under such an interpretation the standard criticisms of the Turing test demonstrate not that the test is defective but only that it is subject to the canons of good scientific methodology.

There are however, important limitations of the Turing test. As a practical matter the test is of little value in guiding research and investigators have quite rightly proposed much more limited modifications of the Turing test or alternatives to it. Another drawback of the Turing test is that it places so much emphasis upon the computer's ability to act and deceive that the computer's grasp of the world qua computer is not very well tested.[2] I believe it is likely that if thinking is attributed to computers, the attribution will be a gradual process as computers acquire more and more skills (in much the same way that attribution of thinking is gradually given to a child as he develops). Thus, ironically if a computer was eventually developed which could pass the Turing test, then it would probably be unnecessary to run the test since the inductive evidence for the computer's thinking capacity would have already been gathered during the computer's development.

Finally, it is important to distinguish between Turing's imitation game, a possible empirical test which can be defended conceptually, and Turing's prophecy that "in about fifty years' time it will be possible to programme computers with a storage capacity of about 10^9, to make them play the imitation game so well that an average interrogator will not have more than 70 percent chance of making the right identification after five minutes of questioning." (Turing 1950, *chapter 4*) Since computer science is a young field, one can understand researchers' high hopes pinned to visions of the development of better computers with bigger memories, more parallel processing, and improved heuristic programming. In the long run researchers must have significant results as well as high hopes if Turing's promissory note is to maintain its currency. But, if the vision behind Turing's prophecy should become a reality, then attributing thought to computers might be less a matter of regressing to anthropomorphism than escaping from egocentricity.

Bibliography

Apter, Michael J. 1971. *The computer simulation of behavior*. Harper & Row.

Fodor, Jerry. 1968. *Psychological explanation*. New York, NY: Random House.

---

2 For example, it might turn out that the computer played the imitation game so well because it believed that it really was human! In such a case the computer would likely be regarded as a thinker but as somewhat psychotic (Turing 1950, 442, *chapter 4*).

Gunderson, Keith. 1964. The imitation game. *Mind* 73(290):234–245. *Reprinted in chapter 9.*

———. 1971. The imitation game. In *Mentality and machines,* chap. 2, 39–59. Garden City, NY: Doubleday & Company. Reprint of Gunderson (1964b, *chapter 9*).

Millar, P. H. 1973. On the point of the imitation game. *Mind* LXXXII(328): 595–597. *Reprinted in chapter 12.*

Nievergelt, Jurg, and J. Craig Farrar. 1973. What machines can and cannot do. *American Scientist* 61:309.

Turing, Alan M. 1950. Computing machinery and intelligence. *Mind* LIX(236): 433–460. *Reprinted in chapter 4.*

18

Why Machines Can't Think: A Reply to James Moor

Douglas F. Stalker

In "An Analysis of the Turing Test" (Moor 1976), James Moor claims that all too many have simply misunderstood how Turing's test figures in arguments about the mentality of machines. The test is a familiar one: an interrogator enters Turing's question/answer setup with the aim of finding out which respondent is another person, which a computer. According to Moor, this sort of test can be "interpreted inductively" (304). That is, one can perfectly well view Turing's test as providing "behavioral evidence" (301). Indeed, Moor thinks it can provide enough evidence to secure the point at issue. He takes the test results, when passing, as evidence of an ability to think. Passing, in Moor's sense, comes to this: many different interrogators are allowed as many chances to question as they like, and yet in the end an average interrogator can only spot the machine about 50% of the time (297). Moor thinks this would be "very adequate grounds for inductively inferring that the computer could think" (300). Would it be?

Though Moor calls his interpretation an inductive one, it is really more accurate to call it an explanatory one. This becomes clear when he discusses why we should take a computer's behavior as telling evidence of cognition. Moor first turns to one's own situation with respect to other people. He wants us to pay attention to something most believe: that other people can and do think. Why do we believe this? Moor finds his answer by appealing to a theory:

I believe that another human being thinks because his ability to think is part of a theory I have to explain his actions. The theory postulates a number of inner information processes, but the evidence for the theory comes from the outward behavior of the person. On the basis of his behavior I can confirm, disconfirm, and modify my theory. (299)

On this approach, one's beliefs about the mentality of others are part of an explanatory theory. In order to explain the behavior of others, we invoke a theory that involves the notion of thinking. But this isn't, so far, the full story. It doesn't tell us why we should take a person's behavior as telling evidence of a certain mental life. Going on this explanatory approach, the behavior counts as evidence because it is connected with a going theory. How does it count as telling evidence? To be that, it needs to be connected with the best of the going theories. When it comes to everydayish efforts at explaining the behavior of other people, one is hard put to find anything better than the current mentalistic scheme. That scheme involves, of course, one's common notion of thinking. And it's presumably the scheme that Moor relies on here.

When Moor turns to computers, he urges a parity. He claims that our situation with respect to other people is the same as ours with respect to computers. We need to explain the computer's behavior, and so we invoke a theory. As Moor puts it:

Furthermore, there is no reason why knowledge of computer thinking can not arise in the same way. I can use the computer's behavior as evidence in assessing my theory about its information processing. (299)

Moreover, the computer's behavior is the same kind of behavior we take as evidence that other people can think: "the Turing test permits direct or indirect testing of virtually all of the activities one would count as evidence for thinking" (300). For example, it provides a direct way to check on a computer's verbal behavior. With its question/answer format, Turing's test "permits (even demands) evaluation of linguistic behavior which is central to our inductive inferences about how others think" (300). It also provides an indirect way to check on nonverbal behavior. An interrogator can ask for descriptions of how the respondent would do something that takes some thinking (300). As Moor sees it, what counts as telling evidence for people also counts as that for computers. Thus he invokes a theory that involves the notion of thinking, and this supposedly explains the behavior of a computer that can pass Turing's test.

Let's grant that an explanatory approach is a viable one for questions of computer cogitation. Even so, Moor arrives at his conclusion all too quickly. He glosses over a step that one simply can't pass by. To put the point another way, Moor leaves an essential step unargued and assumed: viz., that his theory for explaining a computer's behavior is better than others about. Without that step, Moor's argument is really no argument at all. For example, Moor takes a computer's linguistic behavior as evidence in the way that a person's linguistic behavior is evidence. He counts both bits of behavior as decided evidence of some thinking on the part of each. It is, Moor claims, just what "one would count as evidence for thinking" (300). But just who and why? In the case of people, such behavior counts because it figures in a theory that serves to explain that and other behavior. And not just any old theory. Evidential weight, as noted above, comes from connections with a theory that is better than alternative ones. To cite a simple example, the verbal behavior of either a person or computer could connect up with any number of incompatible theories purporting to explain. To the winning theory goes the word on what's sensibly evidence of what. Moor just doesn't make this step of theory competition explicit. In fact, he never mentions it. He needs to. It is the vital step in any defense of Turing's test along explanatory lines. How, then, does it go?

Moor has picked a theory to explain a computer's behavior here, its winning ways at the imitation game. That prowess is certainly something that needs to be explained. Moor aims to explain it, of course, with a theory that makes use of the notion of thinking. But is that the best theory around? I don't think so. There is what looks to be a clearly preferable alternative. In dealing with such a computer, I take it that we're dealing with one similar in structure, composition, and size to ones about nowadays. We're dealing, that is, with a machine, a mechanism, not an organism of any sort. With that fixed, there are three factors we can appeal to in order to fashion an explanation of why a computer is doing what it's doing. They are: the computer's physical structure, its program, and physical features of its environment. In short, an explanation can be framed solely in such mechanical terms. To escalate to a full theory, these factors fall under the principles of contemporary mechanics. That theory readily covers this case. With the mechanical information and this theoretic framework available, one can give a perfectly fine description of the behavior of a computer. Of course such a description won't mention a single thought, let alone appeal to any mental notions. That, in short compass, indicates an alternative explanation. And is it preferable to Moor's theory? I think so, and, moreover, think there's no real competition between the two. The usual theoretic virtues (coherence, completeness, simplicity, precision and so forth) are prominent in an explanation that is couched in contemporary mechanics. A theory making reference to thinking pales in comparison, seems a homespun alternative when applied to computers. To be sure, it serves well enough for us ordinary types in our dealings with other people. One doesn't have to pause over picking a better theory for us. We don't have, for example, anything like a program for a person available. With ready access to a computer's program, we have access to a partial explanation of why the machine is doing what it is. Neurophysiology, psychophysics, and the various brands of psychology haven't supplied us with anything like that yet. Indeed, if one adopts an explanatory approach, the interesting question becomes whether we might find someday that we don't need a notion of thinking for other people, and do need it for some type of machine. This comes as no surprise to those who have adopted such an approach. It merely reflects how responsive such an approach need be to shifting and supplanting explanations. In fact, this question will most likely resolve into one about the character and change of explanations themselves. But at present, Turing's test, properly understood along explanatory lines, poses no problem. If a computer could pass Turing's test, one wouldn't need to explain this feat by resorting to the notion of thinking. The currently better theory doesn't involve that sort of explanatory device.

Bibliography

Moor, James H. 1976. An analysis of the Turing test. *Philosophical Studies* 30: 249–257. *Reprinted in chapter 17.*

19

Explaining Computer Behavior

James H. Moor

How would we explain it if a computer's behavior had the range and sophistication of intelligent human behavior? I have argued that if a computer did behave in this way, perhaps in the context of a Turing test, then we would have adequate evidence for making an inductive inference that the computer thinks (Moor 1976, *chapter 17*). Of course, in light of contrary evidence (e.g., we discover a human is hidden inside the machine and doing all the work) we might well revise our judgment; but my claim is that in the absence of contrary evidence we would have sufficient grounds for developing a theory of mind for machines (i.e., a theory which would make reference to thinking, believing, knowing, remembering, etc.) to explain the computer's behavior.

Douglas Stalker (1978, *chapter 18*) objects that we must consider alternative explanations. Stalker maintains that assuming the computer is a machine and not an organism the principles of contemporary mechanics along with information about the computer's physical structure, its program, and the physical features of the environment could be used to fashion an explanation of the computer's behavior which is preferable to an explanation of the computer's behavior involving mental notions.

I agree that one must take into account competing explanations, but different explanations are not necessarily competitors and the kind of explanation which is preferable depends in part upon what kind of explanation yields the most understanding and what kind of event is being explained. In order to illustrate these points consider first a situation of explaining computer behavior in which there is no issue of minds and machines at all. Suppose that an ordinary digital computer is printing a series of payroll checks and we seek an explanation of the activity. Mr. Program explains the event to us by making reference to a series of computer instructions for handling files and manipulating data. Although he has never seen the inside of the computer, Mr. Program assures us that these instructions are part of the internal operation of the machine. Mr. Physics objects that there is a much more preferable explanation in terms of physics. Mr. Physics points out that his inspection of the computer has revealed only mechanical and electronic components; and therefore, he can explain the activity of the computer in terms of a theory of physics which has all of the important theoretic virtues (coherence, completeness, simplicity, etc.) but which makes no reference to programs or instructions of any kind.

Three points are important. First, the dispute between Mr. Physics and Mr. Program may or may not have substance. Not enough information has been given to establish that the two theories are competitors. When the details of the theories are given, it may turn out that they generate incompatible predictions in which case they are competitors. On the other hand, it may develop, once the details of the theories are given, that the two theories can be unified, i.e., for the given subject matter the states and processes of one theory can be understood in terms of the other. The result is that the theories are not real competitors but give two different kinds of description for the same phenomena. Indeed, the explanation of computer behavior might well take place on any number of descriptive levels: physics, electronic circuitry, logical nets, programs, etc. Such explanations would be different but not necessarily rivals.

Second, as a practical matter many explanations of computer behavior are given in terms of programs because such explanations are most understandable. Whatever the theoretic virtues basic physics has, nobody would seriously try to construct an explanation of a computer's behavior on an atom by atom basis. Even on the level of electronic circuitry the explanation of computer behavior would be incomprehensible for an average size computer. As the phenomenon becomes more complex, we cast our explanations in more inclusive descriptions.

Third, explaining the printing of payroll checks in terms of computer programs which have instructions for printing is rather straightforward. On the other hand, explaining the event in terms of physics requires some significant interpretation of the event in terms of the theory since the printing of payroll checks is not an event of basic physics at least under that description.

Now consider the situation in which the computer exhibits a wide range of intelligent behavior—say good enough to pass the Turing test. In this situation is a theory of mind to explain the phenomena a competitor with a theory of physics or a theory involving programs? Again the answer has to be "maybe". One must know the details of the theories in order to make such an assessment. If the theories generate conflicting predictions, then indeed they are competitors. One of the theories must then be modified or rejected. On the other hand, it may turn out that the theories do not conflict, and for the given situation the states and processes of one can be understood in terms of the states and processes of the other. Such a unification would make all of the theories candidates for explanation of the computer's behavior. Since the events to be explained are already understood at a fairly high level of description, e.g., intelligent behavior, it seems natural and probably most understandable to couch the explanation in terms of a theory of mind. If one has the patience, the explanation could also be given at lower levels of description, e.g., involving perhaps thousands of computer instructions or millions of changes in circuit states.

Of course, it can be held that in principle a theory of mind must have an ontological commitment which makes its extension from humans to machines or its unification with a physical theory impossible. One could hold a similar position about extending Mendel's laws from plants to animals or unifying them with a biochemical theory. But what is the advantage of such positions? If a theory can be extended to new areas and unified with other theories thereby significantly increasing our ability to understand and predict, prior ontological preconceptions should be no object.

Bibliography

Moor, James H. 1976. An analysis of the Turing test. *Philosophical Studies* 30: 249–257. *Reprinted in chapter 17.*

Stalker, Douglas F. 1978. Why machines can't think: A reply to James Moor. *Philosophical Studies* 34:317–320. *Reprinted in chapter 18.*

Dumping the Big Question

Dennett (1985, *chapter 16*) speaks for many at a certain frustration with all the discussion of the Big Question.

It is a sad irony that Turing's proposal has had exactly the opposite effect on the discussion of that which he intended. Turing didn't design the test as a useful tool in scientific psychology, a method of confirming or disconfirming scientific theories or evaluating particular models of mental function; he designed it to be nothing more than a philosophical conversation stopper. He proposed—in the spirit of "Put up or shut up!"—a simple test for thinking that was *surely* strong enough to satisfy the sternest skeptic (or so he thought). He was saying, in effect, "Instead of arguing interminably about the ultimate nature and essence of thinking, why don't we all agree that whatever that nature is, anything that could pass the test would surely have it; then we could turn to asking how or whether some machine could be designed and built that might pass the test fair and square." Alas, philosophers—amateur and professional—have instead taken Turing's proposal as the pretext for just the sort of definitional haggling and interminable arguing about imaginary counterexamples he was hoping to squelch.

In sympathy with this sentiment, Noam Chomsky (*chapter 20*) exhorts us in the following article to return to Turing's own view of the Test. Much of the philosophical exegesis concerns itself with "idle questions" in Chomsky's view, in particular, the question "Can machines think?" itself. Rather, a return to the two goals that Chomsky imputes to Turing—"constructing better machines, gaining insight into human intelligence"—is called for. To Chomsky, The Big Question is really a small question after all.

20

Turing on the "Imitation Game"

Noam Chomsky

In his justly famous 1950 paper "Computing Machinery and Intelligence", A. M. Turing (1950, *chapter 4*) formulated what he called "the 'imitation game' ", later known as "the Turing test", a "new form of the question" whether machines can think, designed to focus attention on "the intellectual capacities of a man." This "new question [is] a worthy one to investigate," Turing urged, offering several "conjectures" on machine potential that should "suggest useful lines of research." Human intellectual capacities might be illuminated by pursuit of the task he outlined, which also might advance the welcome prospect "that machines will eventually compete with men in all purely intellectual fields."

The dual significance of the enterprise—constructing better machines, gaining insight into human intelligence—should no longer be in doubt, if it ever was. There are, however, questions about just where its significance lies, about its antecedents, and about the specific research strategy that Turing proposes.

On the matter of significance, Turing expressed his views lucidly and concisely. He begins by proposing "to consider the question, 'Can machines think?' ", but went on to explain that he would not address this question because he believed it "to be too meaningless to deserve discussion," though "at the end of the century," he believed, "the use of words and general educated opinion will have altered so much that one will be able to speak of machines thinking without expecting to be contradicted." He explained further that for his purposes at least, it would be "absurd" to resolve the issue by determining how the words *machine* and *think* "are commonly used" (a project he conceives much too narrowly, though that is not relevant here).

Turing said nothing more about why he considered the question he posed at the outset—"Can machines think?"—"to be too meaningless to deserve discussion," or why he felt that it would be "absurd" to settle it in terms of "common usage." Perhaps he agreed with Wittgenstein that "We can only say of a human being and what is like one that it thinks"; that is the way the tools are used, and further clarification of their use will not advance the dual purposes of Turing's enterprise. One can choose to use different tools, as Turing suggested might happen in fifty years, but no empirical or conceptual issues arise. It is as if we were to debate whether space shuttles fly or submarines swim. These are idle questions. Similarly, it is idle to ask whether legs take walks or brains plan vacations; or whether robots can murder, act honorably, or worry about the future. Our modes of thought and expression attribute such actions and states to persons, or what we might regard as similar enough to persons. And *person,* as Locke observed, is not a term of natural science but "a forensic term ... appropriating actions and their merit; and so belongs only to intelligent agents, capable of a law, and happiness, and misery," as well as accountability for actions, and much else (Locke 1690, Book 2, Chapter 27, Section 26). It would be a confusion to seek "empirical evidence" for or against the conclusion that brains or machines understand English or play chess; say, by resort to some performance criterion. That seems a fair rendition of Turing's view.

Of the two "useful lines of research" that Turing contemplated, one—improvement of the capacities of machines—is uncontroversial, and if his imitation game stimulates such research, well and good. The second line of research—investigating "the intellectual capacities of a man"—is a more complex affair, though of a kind that is familiar in the sciences, which commonly use simulation as a guide to understanding. From this point of view, a machine is a kind of theory, to be evaluated by the standard (and obscure) criteria to determine whether the computational procedure provides insight into the topic under investigation: the way humans understand English or play chess, for example. Imitation of some range of phenomena may contribute to this end, or may be beside the point, as in any other domain.

For the reasons that Turing seemed to have in mind, we also learn nothing about whether Jones's brain uses computational procedures for vision, understanding English, solving arithmetic problems, organizing motor action, etc., by observing that, in accord with our ordinary modes of thought and expression, we would not say that a machine carries out the activities, imitating people. Or, for that matter, by observing that we would not say that Jones himself is performing these actions if he follows instructions that mean nothing to him with input-output relations interpreted by an experimenter as matching human performance of the actions; say, in an "arithmetic room" of the style suggested by John Searle (1980, *chapter 14*), in which Jones implements an algorithm for long division, perhaps modelled on the algorithm he consciously employs; or a "writing room" in which Jones mechanically carries out instructions that map coded sound inputs to outputs interpreted as letters in sequence, instructions that might be a close counterpart to an algorithm implemented by Jones's sensorimotor and linguistic systems when he writes down what he hears. No meaningful question is posed as to whether the complex including Jones is doing long division or writing, so there are no answers, whether or not the procedure articulates in an instructive way what the brain is actually doing.

Questions about computational-representational properties of the brain are interesting and it seems important, and simulation might advance theoretical understanding. But success in the imitation game in itself tells us nothing about these matters. Perhaps, as Turing believed, the imitation game would provide a stimulus for pursuit of the two "useful lines of research" he advocated; he said little about why this research strategy is preferable to other ways to improve machine capacity and study human intelligence, and it does not seem obvious, apart from some cultural peculiarities that an outside observer might assess with a critical eye.

Turning to antecedents, Turing's imitation game is reminiscent of ideas that were discussed and pursued during what we might call "the first cognitive revolution" of the seventeenth century, within the context of "the mechanical philosophy," which was based on the conception of matter as inert and governed by principles of contact mechanics. Descartes and his followers attempted to show that the natural world could be incorporated within this framework, including a good part of human perception and action but not workings of the human mind, notably "free will," which "is itself the noblest thing we can have," (Descartes 1647) Descartes held, and is manifested most strikingly in the ordinary use of language.

The conception raised questions about the existence of other minds: How do we decide whether some creature is a complex mechanism, or is endowed with a mind as well (as we are, we discover in other ways)? To answer this question, experimental tests were proposed to determine whether the creature exhibits properties (mainly language-related) that transcend the limits of mechanism. If it passes the hardest experiments I can devise to test whether it expresses and interprets new thoughts coherently and appropriately as I would, the Cartesians argued, it would be "unreasonable" to doubt that the creature has a mind like mine.

Though similar in some ways to Turing's imitation game, the Cartesian tests for other minds are posed within an entirely different framework. These tests are ordinary science, designed to determine whether some object has a particular property, rather like a litmus test for acidity. The project collapsed when Newton undermined the mechanical world view, so that the mind/body problem could not even be formulated in Cartesian terms; or any others, so it appears, at least until some new concept of "physical" or "material" is formulated. The natural conclusion, spelled out in the years that followed, is that thinking is a property of organized matter, alongside of other mysterious properties like attraction and repulsion. Thought in humans "is a property of the *nervous system,* or rather of the *brain,*" as much "the necessary result of a particular organization [as] sound is the necessary result of a particular concussion of the air" (Priestley 1777, 27–28) . More cautiously, we may say that people think, not their brains, though their brains provide the mechanisms of thought. As noted, it is a great leap, which often gives rise to pointless questions, to pass from common sense intentional attributions to people, to such attributions to parts of people, and then to other objects.

Throughout the same period, the project of machine simulation was actively pursued, understood as a way to find out something about the world. The great artisan Jacques de Vaucanson did not seek to fool his audience into believing that his mechanical duck was digesting food, but rather to learn something about living things by construction of models, as is standard in the sciences. Turing's intentions seem similar in this regard.

Turing's two "useful lines of research" have proven to be eminently worth pursuing, however one evaluates the research strategy he proposed. Turing's sensible admonitions should also be borne in mind, more seriously than they sometimes have been, in my opinion.

Bibliography

Descartes, René. 1647. Letter to Christine of Sweden, 20 November. Reprinted in Descartes 1985, volume III.

———. 1985. *The philosophical writings of René Descartes.* Cambridge, England: Cambridge University Press. Translated by John Cottingham, Robert Stoothoff, and Dugald Murdoch.

Locke, John. 1690. *An essay concerning human understanding.*

Priestley, Joseph. 1777. *Disquisitions relating to matter and spirit.* London, England: J. Johnson.

Searle, John R. 1980. Minds, brains, and programs. *Behavioral and Brain Sciences* 3:417–457. *Reprinted in chapter 14.*

Turing, Alan M. 1950. Computing machinery and intelligence. *Mind* LIX(236): 433–460. *Reprinted in chapter 4.*

Conclusion

Verbal indistinguishability has a powerful basis as an intelligence criterion. It is, after all, the method people use on other people to assess the same condition. This observation, at least, is centuries old. The computational theory of mind raises the stakes. If minds can be supervenient on any old (sufficiently powerful) computer, then how are we to assess whether a computer has a mind? Verbal indistinguishability from a person is a ready candidate to take up the burden.

But as we have seen, Turing himself would not necessarily have given his "imitation game" that burden, and many think the Turing Test's importance is in other venues, even those, like Dennett, who think it is plenty strong enough to serve. Further, strong arguments against any kind of deduction from Turing-Test passing to ascription of intelligence have been put forward.

Perhaps it is in other sorts of reasoning methods—in- or abrather than deduction—where we can find the grounding of the Turing Test as intelligence criterion that it intuitively provides. Perhaps the question is "too meaningless to deserve discussion." Perhaps like all philosophical quandaries, its role is not as part of an answer but as part of the continual search for one.

Acknowledgments

The editor would like to express his sincere appreciation to the following people: To the authors of the compiled works for their kind permissions to reprint their work; to Ivan Sag and the Center for the Study of Language and Information, Stanford, California, and to Oliviero Stock and the Centro per la Ricerca Scientifica e Tecnologica, Trento, Italy, for space and support to finalize the text during spring term of 2002; to Kevin Guthrie and the JSTOR Project for aid in obtaining digital copies of several of the works; to Barbara Grosz, David Israel, and Cassia Wyner for comments on drafts of the book that have improved it immeasurably, and most importantly to Ned Block, Mark Gawron, Barbara Grosz, Jerry Hobbs, David Israel, Geoffey Nunberg, Fabio Pianesi, members of the Harvard Artificial Intelligence Research Group, and other students at Harvard University, for many conversations on topics discussed in the book, which have so improved my understanding and clarified my thinking on the issues involved.

Sources

Epigraph, page vii. William Gibson, *Neuromancer*, copyright © 1984 by William Gibson. Used by permission of Berkley Publishing Group, a division of Penguin Group (USA) Inc.

1. René Descartes, Discourse on the Method, Part V, in *The Philosophical Writings of Descartes*, translated by John Cottingham, Robert Stoothoff, and Dugald Murdoch, volume 1, pages 131–141, 1985. Reprinted by permission of Cambridge University Press.

2. René Descartes, To the Marquess of Newcastle, 23 November 1646, in *The Philosophical Writings of Descartes*, translated by John Cottingham, Robert Stoothoff, Dugald Murdoch, and Anthony Kenny, volume 3, pages 302–304, 1991. Reprinted by permission of Cambridge University Press.

3. Julien Offray de la Mettrie, Machine Man, in *Machine Man and Other Writings*, translated and edited by Ann Thomson, 1996. Reprinted by permission of Cambridge University Press.

4. Alan M. Turing, "Computing machinery and intelligence", *Mind*, volume LIX, number 236, pages 433–460, 1950. Reprinted by permission of Oxford University Press.

5. Alan M. Turing, "Intelligent machinery, a heretical theory", unpublished manuscript of a lecture given to "51 Society" at Manchester, England c. 1951. Turing Archives reference number B.4. Reprinted by permission of Robin Gandy.

6. Alan M. Turing, "Can digital computers think?", typescript of talk broadcast in BBC Third Programme, 15 May 1951. Turing Archives reference number B.5. Reprinted by permission of Robin Gandy.

7. M. H. A. Newman, Alan M. Turing, Sir Geoffrey Jefferson, and R. B. Braithwaite, "Can automatic calculating machines be said to think?", radio interview, recorded 10 January 1952 and broadcast 14 and

23 January 1952. Turing Archives reference number B.6. Reprinted by permission of Robin Gandy.

8. Leonard Pinsky, "Do machines think about machines thinking", *Mind,* volume LX, number 239, pages 397–398, 1951. Reprinted by permission of Oxford University Press.

9. Keith Gunderson, "The imitation game", *Mind,* volume LXXIII, number 290, pages 234–245, 1964. Reprinted by permission of Oxford University Press.

10. Richard L. Purtill, "Beating the imitation game", *Mind,* volume LXXX, number 318, pages 290–294, 1971. Reprinted by permission of Oxford University Press.

11. Geoffrey Sampson, "In defence of Turing", *Mind,* volume LXXXII, number 328, pages 592–594, 1973. Reprinted by permission of Oxford University Press.

12. P. H. Millar, "On the point of the imitation game", *Mind,* volume LXXXII, number 328, pages 595–597, 1973. Reprinted by permission of Oxford University Press.

13. Robert French, "Subcognition and the limits of the Turing test", *Mind,* volume 99, number 393, pages 53–65. Reprinted by permission of Oxford University Press.

14. John Searle, "Minds, brains, and programs", *Behavioral and Brain Sciences,* volume 3, pages 417–457, 1980. Reprinted with the permission of Cambridge University Press.

15. Ned Block, "Psychologism and behaviorism", *The Philosophical Review,* volume XC, number 1, pages 5–43, 1981. Copyright 1981 Cornell University. Reprinted by permission of the publisher and the author.

16. Daniel Dennett, "Can machines think?", in *How We Know,* ed. Michael Shafto, pages 121–145, San Francisco, CA: Harper & Row, 1985. Reprinted by permission of HarperCollins Publishers, Inc.

17. James H. Moor, "An analysis of the Turing test", *Philosophical Studies,* volume 30, pages 249–257, 1976. Reprinted by permission of Kluwer Academic Publishers.

18. Douglas F. Stalker, "Why machines can't think: A reply to James Moor", *Philosophical Studies,* volume 34, pages 317–320, 1978. Reprinted by permission of Kluwer Academic Publishers.

19. James H. Moor, "Explaining computer behavior", *Philosophical Studies,* volume 34, pages 325–327, 1978. Reprinted by permission of Kluwer Academic Publishers.

Bibliography

von Ahn, Luis, Manuel Blum, and John Langford. 2004. Telling Humans and Computers Apart Automatically—How Lazy Cryptographers Do AI. *Communications of the Association for Computing Machinery*, vol. 47(2):57–60, February.

Anderson, J. R. 1983. *The architecture of cognition*, chap. 3, 86–125. Cambridge, MA: Harvard University Press.

Apter, Michael J. 1971. *The computer simulation of behavior*. Harper & Row.

Baillie, G. H. 1929. *Watchmakers and clockmakers of the world*. London, England: Methuen and Co. Ltd.

Bar Hillel, Yehoshua. 1964. *Language and information*. Reading, MA: Addison-Wesley.

de Bergerac, Cyrano. 1657. *Voyage dans la lune (Voyage to the moon)*.

Black, Max. 1949. *Language and philosophy*. Ithaca, NY: Cornell Press.

Block, Ned. 1978a. Reductionism. In *Encyclopedia of bioethics*. New York, NY: Macmillan.

———. 1978b. Troubles with functionalism. In *Perception and cognition: Issues in the foundations of psychology*, ed. C. W. Savage, vol. 9 of *Minnesota Studies in the Philosophy of Science*. Minneapolis, MN: University of Minnesota Press.

———. 1980. Are absent qualia impossible? *Philosophical Review* LXXXIX.

———. 1981. Psychologism and behaviorism. *Philosophical Review* XC(1):5–43. *Reprinted in chapter 15*.

———. 1990. The computer model of the mind. In *An introduction to cognitive science III: Thinking*, ed. Daniel N. Osherson and Edward E. Smith, chap. 3, 147–289. Cambridge, MA: MIT Press.

Boden, M. 1977. *Artificial intelligence*. New York, NY: Basic Books.

Bradford, Phillip G., and Michael Wollowski. 1995. A formalization of the Turing Test. *SIGART Bulletin* 6(4):3–10.

Bringsjord, Selmer. 1996. The inverted Turing test is provably redundant. *Psycoloquy* 7(29).

Brooks, Rodney. 2002. *Flesh and machines: How robots will change us.* New York, NY: Pantheon Books.

Butler, Samuel. 1872. *Erewhon, or over the range.* London, England: Trübner.

Chisholm, Roderick. 1957. *Perceiving,* chap. 11. Ithaca, NY: Cornell University Press.

Church, Alonzo. 1936. An unsolvable problem of elementary number theory. *American Journal of Mathematics* 58(2):345–363.

Coates, Allison L., Henry S. Baird, and Richard J. Fateman. 2001. Pessimal print: A reverse Turing Test. In *Proceedings of the IAPR International Conference on Document Analysis and Recognition.* Seattle, WA.

Colby, Kenneth. 1981. Modeling a paranoid mind. *Behavioral and Brain Sciences* 4(4):515–560.

Copeland, B. Jack. 1999. A lecture and two radio broadcasts on machine intelligence by Alan Turing. In *Machine intelligence,* ed. K. Furukawa, D. Michie, and S. Muggleton, vol. 15, 445–475. Oxford University Press.

———. 2000. The Turing test. *Minds and Machines* 10(4):519–39.

de Cordemoy, Gèraud. 1668. A philosophicall discourse concerning speech, conformable to the Cartesian principles. "In the Savoy, Printed for John Martin, Printer to the Royal Society", reprinted in de Cordemoy 1972.

———. 1972. *A philosophicall discourse concerning speech (1668) and a discourse written to a learned friar (1670).* Delmar, NY: Scholars' Facsimiles and Reprints, Inc.

Crawshay-Williams, Rupert. 1951. Letter to Alan Turing dated 19 April 1951. Turing Archives reference number D.5.

Davidson, Donald. 1990. Turing's test. In *Modelling the mind,* ed. K. A. Mohyeldin Said, W. H. Newton-Smith, R. Viale, and K. V. Wilkes, chap. 1, 1–11. Oxford, England: Clarendon Press.

Dennett, Daniel. 1978a. *Brainstorms.* Cambridge, MA: MIT Press.

———. 1978b. Where am I? In *Brainstorms,* chap. 17, 310–323. Cambridge, MA: MIT Press.

———. 1980. The milk of human intentionality. *Behavioral and Brain Sciences* 3:428–430.

———. 1984. *Elbow room: The varieties of free will worth wanting.* New York, NY: Oxford University Press.

———. 1985. Can machines think? In *How we know,* ed. Michael Shafto, 121–145. San Francisco, CA: Harper & Row. *Reprinted in chapter 16.*

———. 1987a. Fast thinking. In *The intentional stance,* chap. 9, 323–337. Cambridge, MA: MIT Press.

———. 1987b. *The intentional stance.* Cambridge, MA: MIT Press.

Descartes, René. 1637. *Discourse on the Method,* Part Five. Reprinted in Descartes 1985, volume I. *Reprinted in chapter 1.*

————. 1960 [1637]. *Discourse on method and meditations.* New York, NY: Macmillan Publishing Company. Translated with an introduction by Laurence J. Lafleur. See also (Descartes 1637, *chapter 1*).

————. 1646. Letter to the Marquess of Newcastle, 23 november. Reprinted in Descartes 1985, volume III. *Reprinted in chapter 2.*

————. 1647. Letter to Christine of Sweden, 20 November. Reprinted in Descartes 1985, volume III.

————. 1985. *The philosophical writings of René Descartes.* Cambridge, England: Cambridge University Press. Translated by John Cottingham, Robert Stoothoff, and Dugald Murdoch.

Donne, John. 1633. Why hath the common opinion afforded women soules? In *Paradoxes and problems.* Oxford, England: Clarendon Press. Edited with an introduction and commentary by Helen Peters.

Dowe, D. L., and A. R. Hajek. 1998. A non-behavioural, computational extension to the Turing test. In *Proceedings of International Conference on Computational Intelligence and Multimedia Applications,* 101–6.

Dreyfus, Hubert. 1979. *What computers can't do: A critique of artificial reason.* Revised ed. New York, NY: Harper & Row.

Dummett, Michael. 1976. What is a theory of meaning (II). In *Truth and meaning,* ed. G. Evans and J. McDowell. London, England: Oxford University Press.

Farrell, Brian A. 1946. An appraisal of therapeutic positivism. *Mind* LV:217–218.

Feldman, J., and F. Ballard. 1982. Connectionist models and their properties. *Cognitive Science* 205–254.

Fodor, Jerry. 1968. *Psychological explanation.* New York, NY: Random House.

————. 1980. Methodological solipsism. *Behavior and Brain Sciences* 3(1).

French, Robert. 1990. Subcognition and the limits of the Turing test. *Mind* 99(393):53–65. *Reprinted in chapter 13.*

————. 1995. Refocusing the debate on the Turing test: A reply to Jacquette. *Behavior and Philosophy* 23(1):61–62.

————. 1996. The inverted Turing test: A simple (mindless) program that could pass it. *Psycoloquy* 7(39).

Gelernter, David. 1994. *The muse in the machine: Computerizing the poetry of human thought.* New York, NY: Free Press.

Genova, Judith. 1994. Turing's sexual guessing game. *Social Epistemology* 8(4): 313–326.

Gibson, William. 1984. *Neuromancer.* New York, NY: Berkley Publishing Group.

Ginsberg, Matt. 1993. *Essentials of artificial intelligence.* San Mateo, CA: Morgan Kaufmann.

Gödel, Kurt. 1931. Über formal unentscheidbare Sätze der Principia Mathematica und verwandter Systeme I. *Monatshefte für Mathematik und Physik* 38: 173–198.

Good, Irving John. 1962. The mind-body problem, or could an android feel pain? In *Theories of the mind,* ed. Jordan M. Scher, 490–518. New York, NY: The Free Press.

Griffin, Donald R. 1978. Cognition and consciousness in nonhuman species. *Behavioral and Brain Sciences* 1(4):555–629.

Gunderson, Keith. 1964a. Descartes, La Mettrie, language, and machines. *Philosophy* XXXIX(149):193–222.

———. 1964b. The imitation game. *Mind* 73(290):234–245. *Reprinted in chapter 9.*

———. 1971. The imitation game. In *Mentality and machines,* chap. 2, 39–59. Garden City, NY: Doubleday & Company. Reprint of Gunderson (1964b, *chapter 9*).

Harnad, Stevan. 2000. Minds, machines and Turing. *Journal of Logic, Language and Information* 9(4):425–45.

Hartree, Douglas R. 1950. *Calculating instruments and machines.* Cambridge, England: Cambridge University Press.

Haugeland, John. 1981. *Mind design.* Cambridge, MA: MIT Press.

Hayes, Patrick, and Kenneth Ford. 1995. Turing test considered harmful. In *Proceedings of the 1995 International Joint Conference on Artificial Intelligence (IJCAI 95),* vol. 1, 972. Montreal, Quebec, Canada.

Hediger, Heini. 1980. Do you speak Yerkish? The newest colloquial language with chimpanzees. In *Speaking of apes: A critical anthology of two-way communication with man,* ed. Thomas A. Sebeok and Jean Umiker-Sebeok, 441–447. Topics in Contemporary Semiotics, New York, NY: Plenum Press.

Heiser, Jon F., Kenneth Mark Colby, William S. Faught, and Roger C. Parkison. 1980. Can psychiatrists distinguish a computer simulation of paranoia from the real thing? The limitations of Turing-like tests as measures of the adequacy of simulations. *Journal of Psychiatric Research* 15(3):149–162.

Hernandez-Orallo, J. 2000. Beyond the Turing test. *Journal of Logic, Language and Information* 9(4):447–66.

Hodges, Andrew. 1983. *Alan Turing: The enigma.* New York, NY: Simon and Schuster.

Hofstadter, Douglas R. 1981. Reflections [on Searle]. In *The mind's I: Fantasies and reflections on self and soul,* ed. Douglas R. Hofstadter and Daniel C. Dennett, 373–382. New York, NY: Basic Books.

———. 1985. On the seeming paradox of mechanizing creativity. In *Metamagical themas,* 526–46. New York, NY: Basic Books, Inc.

Hofstadter, Douglas R., Melanie Mitchell, and Robert M. French. 1987. Fluid concepts and creative analogies: A theory and its computer implementation. CSMIL Technical Report 10, University of Michigan.

Jacquette, Dale. 1993. Who's afraid of the Turing test? *Behavior and Philosophy* 20(2):63–75.

Jefferson, Geoffrey. 1949. The mind of mechanical man. *British Medical Journal* I, 1949:1105–1110. The Lister Oration delivered at the Royal College of Surgeons of England, June 9, 1949.

Kleene, Stephen C. 1935a. A theory of positive integers in formal logic—part I. *American Journal of Mathematics* 57(1):153–173.

———. 1935b. A theory of positive integers in formal logic—part II. *American Journal of Mathematics* 57(1):219–244.

Klima, Edward S., and Ursula Bellugi. 1979. *The signs of language*. Cambridge, MA: Harvard University Press.

Kolodner, Janet L. 1983a. Maintaining organization in a dynamic long-term memory. *Cognitive Science* 7(4):243–280.

———. 1983b. Reconstructive memory: A computer model. *Cognitive Science* 7(4):281–328.

———. 1984. *Retrieval and organization strategies in conceptual memory: A computer model*. Hillsdale, NJ: Lawrence Erlbaum Associates.

Kripke, Saul. 1972. Naming and neccesity. In *Semantics and natural language*. Dordrecht, Holland: Reidel.

Kurzweil, Raymond. 1999. *The age of spiritual machines: When computers exceed human intelligence*. New York, NY: Viking Press.

Kurzweil, Raymond, and Mitchell Kapor. 2002. A wager on the Turing Test: The rules. Available at http://www.kurzweilai.net/meme/frame.html? main=/articles/art0373.html.

de La Mettrie, Julien Offray. 1748. *L'homme machine*. Leyde: E. Luzac fils. Translation from *Machine Man and Other Writings*, translated and edited by Ann Thomson, Cambridge, England: Cambridge University Press, 1996. *Reprinted in chapter 3*.

Lakoff, George. 1987. *Women, fire and dangerous things*. Chicago, IL: The University of Chicago Press.

Landes, David S. 1983. *Revolution in time: Clocks and the making of the modern world*. Cambridge, MA: Belknap Press of Harvard University Press.

Letson, Russell. 1982. Portraits of machine consciousness. In *The mechanical god: Machines in science fiction*, ed. Thomas P. Dunn and Richard D. Erlich, vol. 1 of *Contributions to the Study of Science Fiction and Fantasy*, 101–108. Westport, CT: Greenwood Press.

Locke, John. 1690. *An essay concerning human understanding*.

Lovelace, Countess of. 1842. Translator's notes to an article on Babbage's analytical engine. Scientific Memoirs, ed. R. Taylor.

Lucas, John. 1961. Minds, machines, and Gödel. *Philosophy* XXXVI:112–127.

Lycan, William. 1979. New lilliputian argument against machine functionalism. *Philosophical Studies* 35.

———. 1981. Form, function, and feel. *Journal of Philosophy* LXXVIII:24–50.

McCarthy, John. 1979. Ascribing mental qualities to machines. In *Philosophical perspectives in artificial intelligence*, ed. M. Ringle. Atlantic Highlands, NJ: Humanities Press.

Meltzer, Bernard. 1971. Bury the old war-horse! *Bulletin of the AISB group of the British Computer Society* 12.

Meyer, D. E., and R. W. Schvaneveldt. 1971. Facilitation in recognizing pairs of words: Evidence of a dependence between retrieval operations. *Journal of Experimental Psychology* 227–234.

Millar, P. H. 1971. On defining the intelligence of behaviour and machines. Paper to the Second Joint Conference on Artificial Intelligence. London, England.

———. 1973. On the point of the imitation game. *Mind* LXXXII(328):595–597. *Reprinted in chapter 12.*

Miller, George, Eugene Galanter, and Karl H. Pribram. 1960. *Plans and the structure of behavior.* New York, NY: Holt, Rinehart, and Winston.

de Montaigne, Michel. 1987b [1576]. *An apology for Raymond Sebond.* New York, NY: Viking Penguin. Translated and edited with an introduction and notes by M. A. Screech.

Moor, James H. 1976. An analysis of the Turing test. *Philosophical Studies* 30: 249–257. *Reprinted in chapter 17.*

———. 1978. Explaining computer behavior. *Philosophical Studies* 34:325–327. *Reprinted in chapter 19.*

———. 2001. The status and future of the Turing test. *Minds and Machines* 11(1): 77–93.

Moravec, Hans. 1999. *Robot: Mere machine to transcendent mind.* New York, NY: Oxford University Press.

Naor, Moni. 1996. Verification of a human in the loop or identification via the Turing Test. Draft. Department of Applied Mathematics and Computer Science, Weizmann Institute of Science. Available at http://www.wisdom. weizmann.ac.il/~naor/PAPERS/human_abs.html.

Naur, Peter. 1986. Thinking and Turing's test. *BIT* 26:175–187.

Newell, Alan. 1979. Physical symbol systems. Lecture at the La Jolla Conference on Cognitive Science.

Newell, Alan, and Herbert Simon. 1979. Computer science as empirical inquiry: Symbols and search. *Communications of the Association for Computing Machinery* 19.

Newell, Alan, and Herbert A. Simon. 1963. GPS: A program that simulates human thought. In *Computers and thought*, ed. A. Feigenbaum and V. Feldman, 279–93. New York, NY: McGraw Hill.

Newman, M. H. A., Alan M. Turing, Sir Geoffrey Jefferson, and R. B. Braithwaite. 1952. Can automatic calculating machines be said to think? Radio interview, recorded 10 January 1952 and broadcast 14 and 23 January 1952. Turing Archives reference number B.6. *Reprinted in chapter 7.*

Nievergelt, Jurg, and J. Craig Farrar. 1973. What machines can and cannot do. *American Scientist* 61:309.

Nunberg, Geoffrey. 1984. Individuation in context. In *Proceedings of the West Coast Conference on Formal Linguistics,* ed. Mark Cobler, Susannah MacKaye, and Michael T. Wescoat, vol. 3, 203–217. Stanford, CA: The Stanford Linguistics Association.

Papadimitriou, Christos H. 2003. *Turing: A novel about computation.* Cambridge, MA: The MIT Press.

Penrose, Roger. 1989. *The emperor's new mind: Concerning computers, minds, and the laws of physics.* New York, NY: Oxford University Press.

Piccinini, G. 2000. Turing's rules for the imitation game. *Minds and Machines* 10(4):573–82.

Pinsky, Leonard. 1951. Do machines think about machines thinking. *Mind* LX(239):397–398. *Reprinted in chapter 8.*

Priestley, Joseph. 1777. *Disquisitions relating to matter and spirit.* London, England: J. Johnson.

Purtill, Richard L. 1969. Doing logic by computer. *Notre Dame Journal of Formal Logic* X(2).

———. 1971. Beating the imitation game. *Mind* LXXX(318):290–294. *Reprinted in chapter 10.*

Putnam, Hilary. 1975a. The meaning of "meaning". In *Language, mind, and knowledge,* ed. Keith Gunderson, vol. 7 of *Minnesota Studies in the Philosophy of Science.* Minneapolis, MN: University of Minnesota Press.

———. 1975b. *Mind, language, and reality.* Cambridge, England: Cambridge University Press.

Pylyshyn, Z. W. 1980. Computation and cognition: Issues in the foundations of cognitive science. *Behavioral and Brain Sciences* 3(1).

Robertson, D. S. 1999. Algorithmic information theory, free will, and the Turing test. *Complexity* 4(3):25–34.

Ronald, E. M. A., and M. Sipper. 2001. Intelligence is not enough: On the socialization of talking machines. *Minds and Machines* 11(4):567–76.

Rorty, Amélie, ed. 1976. *The identities of persons.* Berkeley, CA: University of California Press.

Rorty, Amélie. 1979. *Philosophy and the mirror of nature.* Princeton, NJ: Princeton University Press.

Rumelhart, David, and James McClelland, eds. 1986. *Parallel distributed processing.* Cambridge, MA: MIT Press.

Russell, Bertrand. 1929. *Our knowledge of the external world.* W.W. Norton.

———. 1940. *History of western philosophy.* New York, NY: Simon and Schuster.

Ryle, Gilbert. 1949. *The concept of mind.* London, England: Hutchinson.

Sampson, Geoffrey. 1973. In defence of Turing. *Mind* LXXXII(328):592–594. *Reprinted in chapter 11.*

Schank, Roger C., and Robert P. Abelson. 1977. *Scripts, plans, goals, and understanding: An inquiry into human knowledge structures.* Hillsdale, NJ: Lawrence Erlbaum Press.

Scott, Ridley (director). 1982. Blade runner. Beverly Hills, CA: The Ladd Company.

Scriven, Michael. 1953. The mechanical concept of mind. *Mind* LXII(246): 230–240.

———. 1961. The compleat robot: A prolegomena to androidology. In *Dimensions of mind,* ed. Sidney Hook. New York, NY: New York University Press.

Searle, John R. 1979. What is an intentional state? *Mind* 88:74–92.

———. 1980. Minds, brains, and programs. *Behavioral and Brain Sciences* 3: 417–457. *Reprinted in chapter 14.*

Shannon, Claude E., and John McCarthy, eds. 1956. *Automata studies.* Princeton, NJ: Princeton University Press.

Shaw, George Bernard. 1921. As far as thought can reach. In *Back to Methuselah: A metabiological pentateuch,* part V. New York, NY: Brentano's.

Shieber, Stuart M. 1994. Lessons from a restricted Turing test. *Communications of the Association for Computing Machinery* 37(6):70–78.

———. 2004. The Turing test as interactive proof. In submission.

Shoemaker, Sydney. 1975. Functionalism and qualia. *Philosophical Studies* 27.

———. 1981. Absent qualia are impossible—a reply to Block. *The Philosophical Review* 90(4):581–599.

Stalker, Douglas F. 1978. Why machines can't think: A reply to James Moor. *Philosophical Studies* 34:317–320. *Reprinted in chapter 18.*

Stewart, Potter. 1964. Jacobellis v. Ohio, 378 U.S. 184 (1964). Appeal from the Supreme Court of Ohio.

Thijssen, W. Th. M. 1977. Some new data concerning the publication of "L'Homme Machine" and "L'Homme Plus Que Machine". *Janus* LXIV:159–177.

Traiger, S. 2000. Making the right identification in the Turing test. *Minds and Machines* 10(4):561–72.

Turing, Alan M. 1936. On computable numbers, with an application to the Entscheidungsproblem. In *Proceedings of the London Mathematical Society,* vol. 42 of 2, 230–265.

———. 1950. Computing machinery and intelligence. *Mind* LIX(236):433–460. *Reprinted in chapter 4.*

———. 1951a. Can digital computers think? Typescript of talk broadcast in BBC Third Programme, 15 May 1951. Turing Archives reference number B.5. *Reprinted in chapter 6.*

————. 1951b. Intelligent machinery, a heretical theory. Unpublished manuscript of a lecture given to "51 Society" at Manchester, England c. 1951. Turing Archives reference number B.4. *Reprinted in chapter 5.*

————. 1969 [1947]. Intelligent machinery. In *Machine intelligence*, ed. Bernard Meltzer and Donald Michie, vol. 5, 3–23. New York, NY: American Elsevier.

de Vaucanson, Jacques. 1979 [1742]. *An account of the mechanism of an automaton.* Buren (GLD), The Netherlands: Frits Knuf. Translated out of the French Original, by J. T. Desaguliers, L.L.D. F.R.S. Chaplain to his Royal Highness the Prince of Wales.

Watt, Stuart. 1996. Naive psychology and the inverted Turing test. *Psycoloquy* 7(14).

Weizenbaum, Joseph. 1966. Eliza—A computer program for the study of natural language communication between man and machine. *Communications of the Association for Computing Machinery* 9(1):36–45.

Weizenbaum, Joseph. 1974. Automating psychotherapy. *Communications of the Association for Computing Machinery* 17(7):425.

————. 1976. *Computer power and human reason.* San Francisco, CA: W. H. Freeman and Co.

Whitby, Blair. 1996. The Turing test: AI's biggest blind alley? In *Machines and thought*, ed. Peter Millican and Andy Clark, vol. 1 of *The Legacy of Alan Turing*, chap. 3. Oxford, England: Clarendon.

Wiener, Norbert. 1948. *Cybernetics: Or control and communication in the animal and the machine.* Cambridge, MA: MIT Press.

Winograd, Terry. 1972. *Understanding natural language.* New York, NY: Academic Press.

————. 1973. A procedural model of language understanding. In *Computer models of thought and language*, ed. Roger Schank and Kenneth Colby. San Francisco, CA: W. H. Freeman and Co.

Wittgenstein, Ludwig. 1958. *Philosophical investigations.* New York, NY: Macmillan Publishing Co.

Wooldridge, Dean E. 1963. *The machinery of the brain.* New York, NY: McGraw-Hill.

Ziff, Paul. 1959. The feelings of robots. *Analysis* 66–67.

Index

In addition to this printed index, an online interactive index is available at http://www.theturingtest.com/.